TABLE OF CONTENTS

FOREWORD

This book is an effort to put some logic into a natural bidding system.
Hopefully this book will answer many of the questions you have about bidding. Is this or that bid forcing? What is a reverse? When should I
open the "Short Club"? How do I show a void after Blackwood? When is
four no trump Blackwood? And a host of other similar questions.

Second, bidding is vital. It hasn't remained static these past ten years.
There have been many new and wonderful ideas advanced on bidding and some
of the antiquated bids and concepts are on their way out - finally.

I am referring specifically to The Strong Two Bid, The Forcing Jump Raise,
The Super Strong Responder Jump Shift, The Free Raise and others.

These have been replaced by bids that come up with greater frequency and
can be used far more logically. The substitutes have been described at
length.

Third, an effort has been made to show you the futility of simply counting
points and expecting to know what to bid. You can't! Nobody can! There's
more to it than just points. If that was all there was everyone would be
an expert bidder. But the opposite is true. Hardly anyone is. Why?

Well, to be an expert or even an adequate bidder you must learn to evaluate
your hand AS THE BIDDING PROGRESSES. Your hand does not keep a fixed count
throughout. The count fluctuates, sometimes wildly, particularly with distributional hands.

Furthermore, you must learn to think about and visualize YOUR PARTNER'S
HAND. You are not only trying to bid your own thirteen cards but also to
put your partner's bidding in context with your hand.

Frequently you should have a reasonably good idea of partner's distribution
which is equally important as his point count. Also, you should know who
is the "captain" of the hand or, to put it another way, who makes the final
decision as to the eventual contract.

Alas, about one third of this book is written with the idea that you have a steady partner. You cannot expect to get a good result from a beautiful bid if your partner doesn't know what it means!

All conventional agreements outside of Stayman and Blackwood, which most everyone uses, require partnership discussion and agreement. If you are lucky enough to have a favorite partner go over some of these things together. See if you think alike.

And finally there are rules. Every book has rules but you don't have to memorize them to be a good bidder. Remember those in school who memorized everything for the exam and blanked out completely when the exam was over? We have a parallel at the bridge table. Some try to master bidding by memorizing the rules on a tablecloth! If they only knew that one gram of common sense was worth 50 tablecloths!

What we are trying for here is a little understanding of the most pleasurable and challenging of all card games. Sure it takes an effort but it's worth it. Ask any bridge player.

EDWIN KANTAR

LOS ANGELES, CALIFORNIA

1. THE OPENING BID OF ONE OF A SUIT

Most bidding sequences commence with an opening bid of one of a suit. The rules for opening the bidding are so simple that a child can learn them in ten minutes. Most bidding problems rear their ugly heads later in the auction when you must reevaluate your hand on the basis of all the bidding that you have heard. This requires judgment. Judgment is a combination of experience and common sense. The aim here is to teach a little common sense.

The Original Count

The original count is very simple. Merely add your high card points to your LONG suit points.

High Card Points		Long Suit Points	
Ace	= 4	Five card suit	= 1
King	= 3	Six card suit	= 2
Queen	= 2	Seven card suit	= 3
Jack	= 1		

When you add your high card points to your long suit points you get your total point count.

There are two good reasons for counting points for long suits rather than short suits when originally evaluating a hand or bidding one of your own suits:

(1) It gives you a better conception of the game when you realize that long suits are what determine a hand's value.

(2) It is slightly more accurate.

Example hands:
S. AKQ2
H. 432
D. 432
C. 432

Those who count for long suits and those who count for short suits both evaluate this hand at nine points, because there is no long or short suit.

S. AKQ32
H. 32
D. 432
C. 432

Players who count one point extra for a long suit count this hand at ten points and players who count one extra for a doubleton also count it at ten points. Same count. But which do you think is more valuable, the fifth spade or the doubleton heart?

S. AKQ432 Long suit counters count this hand at eleven,
H. 2   awarding two points for the six card suit,
D. 432   while short suit counters arrive at eleven
C. 432   points, counting two for the singleton.
           Again the count is the same, but the concep-
           tion of the hand should be the appreciation
           of the spade length, not the heart shortness.

Now for some examples when the count is slightly different:

(1) S. AKQ2   Long suit counters count this one at eleven, but short
    H. 5432   suit counters count it at thirteen, giving two for the
    D. 2   singleton. Before deciding who is right, look at two
    C. Q432   similar hands.

(2) S. AKQ32 Long suit counters count this hand at twelve (it's ob-
    H. 5432   viously a better hand than the previous example), but
    D. 2   short suit counters still count the hand at thirteen.
    C. Q32

(3) S. AKQ432 Both long and short suit counters count this hand at
    H. 432   thirteen. Anyone who has played any bridge can see at
    D. 2   a glance that (3) is the best hand of the bunch and that
    C. Q32   (2) is better than (1). Yet the short suit counters count
              each and every one for thirteen, while the long suit
              counters give more points to the better hand.

In this book when bidding one's own suit one will count long suit points and add them to high card points to arrive at the total point count of the hand.

2

Opening the Bid

In order to open the bidding with one of a suit the hand must contain thirteen points, at least ten of which are high card points.

As we will soon see, even this rule has exceptions (they all do) as there are many twelve point hands that qualify as opening bids.

Opening bids can best be understood by discussing hand patterns, the distribution of your cards. After all, the two main ideas of good bidding are to tell your partner your point count and hand pattern.

The 4-3-3-3 Hand Pattern

The completely symmetrical distribution has the least offensive potential and requires the full thirteen count to open.

In third or fourth seat when no rebid need be considered, a _strong_ four card suit and twelve points will do.

| | (1) | S. 543
H. AKJ9
D. Q43
C. Q85 | (2) | S. J54
H. AQJ10
D. K65
C. J85 |

(1)   S. 543
      H. AKJ9
      D. Q43
      C. Q85

(2)   S. J54
      H. AQJ10
      D. K65
      C. J85

Open either of these hands 1H in third position as a lead director but pass in any other seat. It is seldom, if ever, a bridge crime to pass a twelve point 4-3-3-3 hand.

The 4-4-3-2 Hand Pattern

This, the most common of all hand patterns, requires but twelve points to open, with but one stipulation. With only twelve the doubleton suit must not be Jx, Qx or QJ. If it is, pass.

(1)   S. Q4
      H. A87
      D. K984
      C. K864

(2)   S. AQ106
      H. 65
      D. KQ95
      C. J105

Hand (1) is not an opening bid, but hand (2) should be opened 1D.

The 4-4-4-1 Hand Pattern

This hand pattern is very promising as partner need fit but one of the four card suits. For this reason hands with this pattern can be opened with as little as 11 H.C.P. if the strength is concentrated in two suits. If the strength is divided fairly evenly among the three suits a twelve count is needed to open.

(1)	S. AK87		(2)	S. A875
	H. 4			H. 4
	D. A1098			D. KJ87
	C. 8765			C. QJ65

Hand (1) opens 1D but (2) is better advised to pass and perhaps enter the bidding later with a takeout double if the opponents bid hearts.

Incidentally, with this hand pattern if the singleton is either the jack or queen eleven points must be held outside of the singleton suit to open. Singleton jacks and queens tend to be valueless too often.

The 5-3-3-2 Hand Pattern

This, the second most common of all distributions, requires twelve points to open if the five card suit is strong and there is a concentration of strength in two suits. If not, wait for thirteen.

(1)	S. AK1094		(2)	S. A8765
	H. A76			H. A65
	D. 86			D. Q87
	C. 865			C. J9

Hand (1) is definitely a 1S opening bid and hand (2) is definitely not! Hopefully you are beginning to appreciate the value of intermediate cards (nines and tens), as well as the plus factor of concentrated strength as opposed to divided strength.

The 5-4-2-2 Hand Pattern

This is similar to the 5-3-3-2. Thirteen points are needed to open, but twelve will do with a concentration of strength in the long suits.

(1)	S. AK876	(2)	S. K8765
	H. 65		H. AJ
	D. A1065		D. Q765
	C. 65		C. J4

Hand (1) opens 1S and hand (2) passes. It is almost always a plus factor to have the high cards in your long suits rather than in your short ones.

The 5-4-3-1 Hand Pattern

Same as the 5-3-3-2 and the 5-4-2-2. Thirteen to open, but twelve is fine if the high cards are in the long suits.

(1)	S. AQ1087	(2)	S. J9876
	H. 5		H. 2
	D. AJ97		D. KQ87
	C. 654		C. AJ5

Open (1) with 1S but pass (2). This is a fun distribution loaded with potential, but one must always consider the possible problem of partner responding in your singleton suit. In (1) the opener can rebid his spades without too much trouble. But in (2) a spade rebid on five to the jack would be misleading and rebidding the diamonds at the three level would guarantee extra values. However, if the opener can handle a response in the singleton suit with this distribution twelve will do even if the high cards are not all in the long suits.

(1)	S. J9876	(2)	S. KQ87
	H. AJ5		H. 2
	D. KQ87		D. J9876
	C. 2		C. AJ5

Either of these hands have easy rebids if partner responds in the singleton suit. With (1) 2D can be rebid over 2C and with (2) 1S over 1H. Either of these hands can be opened.

The Rest

The remaining hand patterns, of less frequency, are:

$$5-4-4-0, \quad 5-5-3-0, \quad 5-5-2-1$$

$$6-3-2-2, \quad 6-3-3-1, \quad 6-4-2-1$$

These distributions all require thirteen points to open but again twelve will do just fine if the high cards are in the long suit(s).

Some Tips When It Comes To Opening

1. Do not count singleton jacks. Singleton queens are temporarily worth one point and singleton kings two points. Do not stretch to open a hand that has a singleton jack, queen or king.

2. Honor cards in long suits are more valuable than in short suits. This is why some hands can be opened with as little as twelve points.

3. Honor cards in combination are better than honor cards divided. For example, AKx in one suit is better than Axx and Kxx in two suits.

4. In close situations intermediate cards (nines and tens) should be weighed. Obviously AQ1095 is a better suit than AQ654, but they are both counted the same (by inexperienced players, that is!).

5. Another factor which influences passing or opening is the rank of the long suit. Tend to be more aggressive when holding the major suits.

6. All opening bids of one must contain at least 10 H.C.P.; however, over 90% will contain eleven or more high card points.

Which Suit To Open

Here we have a few rules with the usual number of exceptions. Keep in mind that a four card major may be opened contrary to some systems that require five. However, as you will see, a major suit opening will normally have five cards and the responder always assumes five.

1. Bid the longest suit first, not the strongest.

    (1) S. AKQJ
        H. A4
        D. 98765
        C. 54

    Open 1D, not 1S

But if the two suits are next to each other in rank and the four card suit is the HIGHER ranking suit, then open the four card suit if the suit is strong and the hand is minimum. (Less than 17 points.)

```
    (1)   S. AKQJ            (2)   S. 65             (3)   S. 65
          H. 98765                 H. AK98                 H. AK98
          D. A4                    D. KQ765                D. KQ987
          C. 76                    C. 54                   C. A5
```

With (1) open 1S and rebid the hearts.

With (2) open 1H and rebid the diamonds.

With (3) open 1D and rebid the hearts. (Seventeen or more.)

REMEMBER, THIS RULE OF OPENING THE FOUR CARD SUIT BEFORE THE FIVE
CARD SUIT IS DONE ONLY IF THE TWO SUITS ARE ADJACENT (TOUCHING) IN
RANK, THE FOUR CARD SUIT IS STRONG, AND THE HAND IS MINIMUM. (Six-
teen or less.)   IN ALL OTHER CASES LONGER SUITS ARE BID FIRST.

2. With two five card suits bid the higher ranking suit first.

```
    (1)   S. 76              (2)   S. K8765
          H. AJ987                 H. 2
          D. 4                     D. AKQ98
          C. AK987                 C. 54

          Open 1H                  Open 1S
```

But if the two five card suits are specifically clubs and spades,
open 1C if the hand has 13-15 or 19-20 and 1S with 16-18.

```
    (1)   S. KJ876           (2)   S. AKJ87           (3)   S. AQJ98
          H. 54                    H. 43                    H. K4
          D. 2                     D. 2                     D. 2
          C. AK876                 C. AKQ87                 C. AJ1076

    (13) Open 1C             (19) Open 1C             (17) Open 1S
```

3. With two four card suits that are touching bid the higher ranking suit
    first.

```
    (1)   S. AK98            (2)   S. 65              (3)   S. 76
          H. KQ76                  H. AJ108                 H. A54
          D. Q43                   D. AK98                  D. KQ87
          C. 54                    C. 654                   C. KQ76

          Open 1S                  Open 1H                  Open 1D
```

In the case of clubs and diamonds it is optional which suit to open.
If the hand is dead minimum open 1C to avoid the embarrassment of a
2C response to a 1D opening bid. (You don't really want to carry the
bidding to the three level with a dead minimum and that's what happens
if you raise your partner's 2C response to 3C.)

If the major suit is not biddable (Q109x or better) open the other four card suit.

    (1)   S. J765   (2)   S. 65
            H. AK108   H. Q765
            D. A65   D. AKJ9
            C. Q4   C. A65

            Open 1H   Open 1D

This can lead to some rebid problems, but in the long run it works out best.

If the two four card suits are not touching open the lower ranking suit first.

    (1)   S. AQ87   (2)   S. AK76   (3)   S. 65
            H. 54   H. 54   H. AJ98
            D. AJ87   D. A87   D. 543
            C. Q43   C. Q765   C. AQJ9

            Open 1D   Open 1C   Open 1C

The one outstanding exception here is in third or fourth seat with a minimum hand, a good four card major and poor four card minor. As you need not worry about a rebid after partner has passed, open the major.

    (1)   S. AKJ8   (2)   S. 654
            H. 654   H. AKJ9
            D. A765   D. 54
            C. 54   C. KJ76

            Open 1S   Open 1H
            in third   in third
            or fourth   or fourth
            seat.   seat.

4.   With three four card suits open the suit beneath the singleton. If the singleton is in clubs, open 1S.

    (1)   S. AJ87   (2)   S. 4   (3)   S. AQ98
            H. 2   H. AJ98   H. KQ76
            D. K1087   D. AJ76   D. KJ76
            C. AQ65   C. A984   C. 2

            Open 1D   Open 1H   Open 1S

If the suit beneath the singleton is a major and it is not biddable (Q109x or better) open the suit beneath.

```
(1)  S. J765          (2)  S. 7
     H. AK87               H. 10987
     D. AJ87               D. AK87
     C. 2                  C. AQ98

     Open 1H              Open 1D
     instead             instead
     of 1S               of 1H
```

No Trump Opening Bids With Balanced Hands

No trump bidding is a section unto itself. No trump opening bids are made
only with balanced hand patterns. These are: 4-3-3-3; 4-4-3-2; 5-3-3-2.
Any other hand pattern would be an exception.

When discussing these balanced hand patterns we refer to high card points
only. True, we make adjustments for strong five card suits, but extra
points are not added for long suits. The counts mentioned are all high
card points.

The schedule for opening balanced hands goes like this:

Open 1NT   15 and a good five card suit to 18 without a five card suit.

Open 2NT   20, 21 or 22. (22 with 4-3-3-3 only.)

Open 3NT   25-26

Open 2C and   22-23-24
rebid 2NT

Open 2C and   27-28
rebid 3NT

Exception: With a strong five card major and a small doubleton open the

           major.

           With a weak five card major open 1NT.

```
     (1)  S. AJ1098        (2)  S. J9865
          H. 32                 H. AK7
          D. AJ9                D. A10
          C. KQJ                C. AJ6

          Open 1S              Open 1NT
```

Open ALL balanced hands in the 15/16-18 range with 1NT unless you have 18
and a five card suit or a strong five card major and a small doubleton.
It is permissible to open 1NT or 2NT with a small doubleton.

Opening Bid Quiz

Assume you are the dealer. What action would you take with each of the following hands?

A. S. AJ1087
    H. KQ76
    D. 2
    C. J108

B. S. Q
    H. A7654
    D. QJ3
    C. K865

C. S. AQ87
    H. 2
    D. Q876
    C. AK76

D. S. 6
    H. J876
    D. AK87
    C. KQ98

E. S. AJ876
    H. 43
    D. 4
    C. AK876

F. S. AK876
    H. K3
    D. 4
    C. AJ987

G. S. 65
    H. AJ98
    D. KQ105
    C. K54

H. S. AJ87
    H. 65
    D. AQ76
    C. K76

I. S. J10876
    H. 4
    D. AK876
    C. A4

J. S. 105
    H. AQ9
    D. KJ87
    C. AQ98

K. S. KJ4
    H. A3
    D. KQ876
    C. AJ4

L. S. Q4
    H. AJ108
    D. A54
    C. K765

M. S. KQ1076
    H. 87
    D. AK2
    C. A76

N. S. AQ
    H. Q8765
    D. KJ8
    C. A109

O. S. J5
    H. KQ7
    D. AJ8
    C. AQ452

P. S. AK87
    H. A876
    D. KQ76
    C. 2

Q. S. 5
    H. AK98
    D. QJ876
    C. A76

R. S. AJ5
    H. K87
    D. J1087
    C. AJ7

S. S. 2
    H. A87
    D. AKJ9
    C. J9876

T. S. Q7
    H. KJ87
    D. A76
    C. Q765

U. S. AJ10876
    H. KQ10
    D. 765
    C. 5

V. S. AQ76
    H. 2
    D. K876
    C. Q987

W. S. KQJ4
    H. AKJ87
    D. A4
    C. 54

X. S. AKJ10
    H. ---
    D. 87654
    C. AJ98

Y. S. AK87
    H. 43
    D. AJ9
    C. J432

Z. S. K76
    H. J976
    D. A108
    C. KJ2

Solutions

A. 1S   Only 12 points, but concentrated in the long suits.

B. Pass   A singleton queen is worth only one point. This hand also comes to 12 points, but the strength is not concentrated.

C. 1D   Suit beneath singleton.

D. 1D   Heart suit is not biddable.

E. 1C   With five clubs and five spades the normal opening is 1C unless the hand counts to 16-18 points, in which case open 1S.

F. 1S   17 points. See explanation above.

G. 1H   Open the higher ranking of two four card touching suits.

H. 1D   Open the lower ranking of two four card non-touching suits.

I. 1S   With two five card suits open the higher ranking.

J. 1NT   Even with the small doubleton.

K. 1D   With 18 points plus a five card suit you are too strong for 1NT.

L. 1C   With two four card non-touching suits open the lower ranking.

M. 1S   Not 1NT with a strong five card major and a small doubleton.

N. 1NT   Open 1NT with a weak five card major and 16-17 points.

O. 1NT   In spite of the spade weakness.

P. 1S   Suit beneath singleton.

Q. 1H   With two touching suits, the higher ranking four cards and the lower ranking five cards, open the higher ranking if the four card suit is strong and the hand has 16 or fewer points.

R. 1D   Any four card minor suit is biddable.

S. 1D   See answer to "Q".

T. Pass This distribution can be opened with as little as 12 points, but not with Jx, Qx, or QJ in the doubleton suit.

U. 1S   Only twelve points, but concentrated in the long suits.

V. Pass This distribution can open with as little as 11 points, but they must be concentrated in two suits. If not, 12 is the minimum.

W. 1H   This hand is strong enough to bid both suits in the proper order. (If opener mentions two adjacent suits by first bidding the lower and then the higher, he must have at least 17 points and greater length in the first suit. This is known as a "reverse".)

X. 1D   Longest suit first, not strongest.

Y. 1C   With four clubs and four spades, 1C is the opening bid.

Z. Pass This distribution requires 13 points in first or second seat.

The Short Club

Because of the importance of this topic an entire chapter is devoted to the short club. For a blow by blow account of the short club, read Chapter 15 "The Short Club Obsession".

Opening Bids of Two

Traditionally an opening two bid has been the strongest opening bid in bridge. It is unconditionally forcing to game and requires very little from partner in the right places to make slam. This is known as "The Strong Two". In expert circles the strong two has been replaced by "The Weak Two".

Today any bridge player must be prepared to play either strong or weak two bids, depending upon his own and partner's preference. Both will be discussed.

Strong Two Bids are not opened with balanced hands. These hands fall into the no trump family and are normally opened either 2NT or 3NT. Therefore there hardly exists a Strong Two Bid on a four card suit and in practice it is somewhat rare with a five card suit! Remember with 5-3-3-2 distribution the hand is treated as balanced and opened in no trump. However there are hands that have five card suits which are sufficiently unbalanced to open a strong two. Distributions such as 5-4-3-1, 5-4-2-2 and 5-5-2-1, for example, qualify if the hand is strong enough.

Using the count discussed on page one a Strong Two Bid might have as little as 20 points with excellent controls, but typically it will add up to at least 21 or 22.

In addition, if you use this slightly reduced count for your Strong Two Bids your partner will not live in terror of passing your opening bids of one when he holds four or five points. He will no longer fear that you have 20 or 21 H.C.P. and an unbalanced hand.

Quiz on Strong Two Bids

You deal and hold the following hands: What is your count and what is your
opening bid?

A.	S. AK4	B.	S. AK10	C.	S. AKJ9		
	H. AKJ1098		H. KQ87		H. AQ10876		
	D. 4		D. AK4		D. A76		
	C. 543		C. AQ5		C. ---		

D.	S. KQJ98	E.	S. AJ985	F.	S. AJ108765		
	H. A3		H. K4		H. KQ4		
	D. AKJ765		D. AK5		D. A4		
	C. ---		C. KQJ		C. 3		

Solution To Quiz On Strong Two Bids

A. 1H (17) Hand not strong enough to open with a game demand two bid.
Substitute the ace of clubs for a small one and the hand
would qualify for a 2H opening.

B. 3NT (25) Balanced hands do not open two of a suit.

C. 2H (20) Notice the four first round controls. In all borderline
situations let the number of _first_ round controls (aces
and voids) determine your actions. With only one or two
bid conservatively; with three or four, aggressively.

D. 2D (21) Even though the hand has only 18 H.C.P. it has fantastic
potential and of course there are those three first round
controls.

E. 2NT (21) Balanced hands do not open two of a suit - and when bidding
no trump count only high card points.

F. 1S (17) The hand is not strong enough to make a game forcing opening.

The Weak Two Bid

As mentioned previously the Weak Two bid has supplanted the Strong Two bid in expert play. It offers many advantages that the Strong Two does not, and as a matter of self-protection the convention should be understood.

Requirements for a Weak Two Bid

1. A six card suit headed by three of the top five honors, or two honors and a nine-eight combination.

2. Between 7-10 H.C.P., but never a hand that qualifies for an opening one bid. The weaker the point count (7-8), the more strength in the bid suit. A Weak Two opening can be likened to a three opening except the Weak Two promises a six rather than a seven card suit.

3. The most common distributions are 6-3-2-2, 6-3-3-1 and 6-4-2-1. A Weak Two should not be opened with a side five card suit and rarely a void.

4. The Weak Two is very similar to a two level overcall with regard to the trick taking potential of the hand. A Weak Two bid promises between five and six taking tricks. Closer to six vulnerable.

5. A standard Weak Two bid will have 1-1/2 to 2 defensive tricks.

6. A third seat Weak Two bid may be made on a strong five card suit for lead directing purposes. The Weak Two in third seat negates the need for light third hand openings of one of a suit with strong five or six card suits and 9-11 points.

Examples of Weak Two Bids

S. AKJ1087
H. 43
D. 654
C. 87

8 H.C.P.
Almost six taking tricks.
Open 2S.

S. K7
H. 85
D. KJ10954
C. Q109

9 H.C.P.
Approximately five taking tricks.
Open 2D.

S. 75
H. AQJ974
D. Q52
C. 82

9 H.C.P.
Between 5 and 6 taking tricks.
Open 2H.

S. K65
H. 54
D. 87
C. AJ10987

8 H.C.P.
About five taking tricks.
Pass.
Sorry, no Weak Two bids in clubs.

What do you open with each of the following hands?

(1)   S. 54   (2)   S. ---   (3)   S. A42   (4)   S. KQ4
        H. AQJ9876   H. KQ9865   H. KQJ987   H. J98754
        D. Q43   D. K7   D. 4   D. K10
        C. 5   C. J10876   C. Q98   C. 54

(1)   3H.   Weak Two bids are not made with seven card suits. It's a no-no.

(2)   Pass.   Two suited hands are not suitable for a Weak Two bid. Another

           no-no.

(3)   1H.   Too strong for a Weak Two bid.

(4)   Pass.   This heart suit needs a transfusion.

Advantages of the Weak Two Bid

1. It allows early entry into the auction, forcing the opponents to ex- change information at a higher level with a greater degree of risk.

2. It uncovers excellent sacrifices.

3. It eliminates the temptation to open the bidding with one of a suit on hands that have a strong suit, but insufficient point count.

4. It shows partner your entire hand in one bid and helps direct the lead in case the opponents buy the hand.

Showing Strong Balanced Hands When Using the Weak Two Bid

Many strong balanced hands and all suited game going hands are opened 2C when playing Weak Two bids. The 2C opening is completely artificial and opener describes his hand on the rebid.

As balanced hands are easiest to describe this is the scale:

         20-21-22   Open 2NT

         22-23-24   Open 2C and rebid 2NT

         25-26   Open 3NT

         27-28   Open 2C and rebid 3NT

         22 point hands are optional. If the dis-

         tribution is 4-3-3-3 they can be opened

         2NT. Otherwise open 2C and rebid 2NT.

Opening 2NT with 20 and 21 points has great advantages. First, the hand is played from the strong side of the table, the high cards being concealed from the defenders. When not using 20 or 21 point 2NT openings the hand is opened one of a suit. If partner responds 1NT the big hand raises to 3NT and the strong hand comes down on the table, making life all too easy for the defense.

Also, responder, holding four or five points, is apt to pass an opening bid of one of a suit. But, with those same four or five points he will be able to bid over an opening bid of 2NT and a more reasonable contract can be reached.

Strong Unbalanced Hands

If the 2C bidder has an unbalanced hand he simply bids his suit at his first opportunity. For example:

Opener	Responder
2C	2H
2S	

Opener has shown a strong two bid in spades and already knows his partner has a reasonable hand from the positive response of 2H.

A Jump Rebid by the Two Club Opener

If the opening 2C bidder jumps at his first opportunity he is promising a completely solid suit and requesting partner to show aces and kings.

Opener	Responder
2C	2H
3S	4D

Opener shows a solid spade suit and responder shows the ace of diamonds after having made a positive response in hearts.

If the responder has no aces, but either a king or a side singleton with at least three trumps, he bids 3NT and then shows his second round controls at his next opportunity. If he has no aces, no kings and no singletons, he raises opener's suit to game.

16

Opener	Responder	Opener	Responder
S. AK	S. 10752	2C (1)	2D (2)
H. AKQJ987	H. 63	3H (3)	3NT (4)
D. AQ32	D. KJ4	4C (5)	4D (6)
C. ---	C. Q632	7H (7)	Pass

(1) I have a big hand.

(2) I have a little one.

(3) I have a solid heart suit.

(4) I have at least one second round control.

(5) What is it?

(6) The king of diamonds or a singleton diamond with at least three hearts.

(7) I like this system.

Responding to a Strong Two Club Opening

Experts know that there is no entirely satisfactory method of responding to any strong bid which is opened at the two level. The loss of bidding space makes it difficult to find out enough about the responding hand beneath the game level.

Systems that show strong hands by means of an artificial 1C opening work out best. However these systems have other problems, particularly with hands having a club suit.

We will concern ourselves here with the best method of responding to an artificial two club opening.

Currently there are three popular methods of responding to a two club opening. The first is artificially by controls.

1. Responding by Controls: Ace = two controls

King = one control

When using this method responder's first bid is completely artificial, simply announcing the number of controls he has. After the initial

control showing response, all responses are natural. That is, the
responder shows his suit or suits.

Opener	Responder	Meaning
2C	2D	One control or less.
2C	2H	Two controls. Either one ace or two kings.
2C	2S	Three controls. One ace and one king.
2C	2NT	Three controls. Three kings.
2C	3C	Four or more controls.
2C	3D,3H,3S	One loser, six or seven card suits.

Opener	Responder	Opener	Responder
S. AKJxxx	S. xx	2C	2D (One king or less)
H. AKQ10	H. xxxx	2S	2NT
D. KQ	D. xxx	3H	4H
C. x	C. K10xx	Pass	

Opener knows immediately from the first response that the opponents
have the other two aces so does not try for a slam.

Opener	Responder	Opener	Responder
S. KQxx	S. Axx	2C	2H (One ace or two kings)
H. AKx	H. xxx	2NT	3NT
D. KQx	D. Jxx	Pass	
C. AQx	C. J10xx		

Opener's rebid shows twenty-two to twenty-four points and responder
raises to game. Had responder rebid 3C over 2NT that would be Stayman.

A second method that many experts like, but can be dangerous for the average player, is "Two Diamonds Automatic".

2. Two Diamonds Automatic
    Using this method, the responder almost always responds 2D which has
    no meaning whatsoever. It simply allows the opener to clarify his
    artificial opening at the lowest level possible. The responder de-
    scribes his strength on the rebid. Many experts use a second nega-
    tive of 2NT to mean that the original 2D response was made on a
    terrible hand. Any other second response shows positive values.

It should be mentioned that when using this convention it is not abso-lutely mandatory to respond 2D to an opening 2C bid. If the responder holds a strong five or six card suit he can mention it directly, but with a weak five or six card suit (even holding a good hand) the first response is 2D followed by a rebid showing the suit.

Opener	Responder	Opener	Responder
S. AKQ10xx	S. x	2C	2H (Strong suit)
H. Axx	H. KQJxx	2S	3D
D. x	D. QJ10xx	3H	4H
C. AKx	C. xx	4NT	5C
		6H	Pass

Once the opener knows that responder has a strong heart suit (usually two of the top three honors) it is easy to visualize the slam.

Opener	Responder	Opener	Responder
S. AKJ10x	S. xxx	2C	2D (Meaningless)
H. AKQxx	H. xx	2S	2NT (Very weak hand)
D. AQ	D. Jxxxx	3H	3S
C. x	C. J10x	4H	4S
		Pass	

Opener knows responder is terribly weak (usually less than four or five points) and simply shows partner his distribution so partner can put him into the right suit. The second negative of 2NT should be enough to turn the opener off, even with his actual powerhouse.

Finally we come to the method that I think is probably best. For want of a better title let's call it "Two Diamonds Negative".

3. Two Diamonds Negative

Using this method an initial response of 2D warns the opener that the responder has a weak hand. Usually less than 6 H.C.P.

Therefore, any other response is positive and the response of 2NT is used frequently to show balanced hands in the 7-9 range. A response in a suit does not absolutely guarantee a powerful suit, but rather a reasonable hand with a reasonably strong five or six card suit.

As a general rule, with four card suits and a reasonable hand, the responder makes his initial response in no trump.

With a strong diamond suit the responder jumps to 3D at his first opportunity. Remember that a response of 2D shows a weak hand and has nothing to do with diamonds.

Opener	Responder	Opener	Responder
S. AKxxxx	S. x	2C	3D
H. AKx	H. QJx	7D!	Pass
D. AQxx	D. KJ109xx		
C. ---	C. Qxx		

Opener doesn't have to waste much time with this one. Where can a trick possibly be lost?

Opener	Responder	Opener	Responder
S. AQx	S. J10xx	2C	2D (Weak)
H. KQxx	H. J109x	2NT (22-24)	3C (Stayman)
D. AKx	D. x	3H	4H
C. AQx	C. Jxxx	Pass	

Responding to a Weak Two Bid

The responder to the Weak Two bid is in a fairly comfortable position since he knows so much about his partner's hand. He has various alternatives, depending upon his strength and his degree of fit with partner's suit.

Responding to a Weak Two in the Majors with Fitting Hands

With at least three cards in partner's suit responder will normally:

(1) Pass

(2) Raise to three preemptively. Opener must pass.

(3) Raise to game, either preemptively or to make. Let the opponents worry whether you have a strong hand or are just trying to make life more miserable for them.

Paradoxically, the pass with three card support is usually made with 10-12 points and the raise to three with less! The reason is that with 10-12 or even 13 "bad points" the opponents won't have enough strength to compete and you can probably buy the hand for two. Remember, it generally takes 15 or 16 points to make game opposite a weak two.

Weaker hands (6-10) with a side doubleton or singleton should raise immediately in order to make it harder for the opponents to find their fit.

After a 2H opening by partner and a pass to your right consider the following responding hands and the tactics recommended:

(1)	S. A5	(2)	S. AJ8	(3)	S. AJ7	(4)	S. 5	(5)	S. 76
	H. K87		H. 654		H. K106		H. Q76		H. KJ9
	D. J876		D. QJ108		D. AK765		D. A87654		D. KQ1087
	C. 10876		C. K98		C. 65		C. 876		C. J87

(1) Raise to 3H and then let them go where they wish. Not vulnerable against vulnerable a raise to four is possible. If you do raise to four do so with a strong voice. Never let them know that you are taking an "advance sacrifice" by either perspiring or losing your voice.

(2) Pass. Not enough to make game and too much to worry about the opponents competing.

(3) Raise to four with the intention of making your bid. A raise to four with a fit is made with hands worth 15 points and up.

(4) Raise to four preemptively. If you don't have enough nerve to do this, at least raise to three.

(5) Raise to 3H. The better you fit hearts, the better the opponents fit another suit - probably spades.

Keep in mind your preemptive raises will work much better if your right hand opponent passes. If he doubles or bids the cat is out of the bag. Your sneaky raise will be read for exactly what it is by your left hand opponent and consequently will not be as effective. Also, when raising preemptively, keep an eye on the vulnerability. Vulnerable against not, restrain yourself a bit.

Responding to a Weak Two Bid in the Majors with Non-Fitting Hands

A non-fitting hand is one which has a singleton or void in partner's suit. A doubleton is considered reasonable support because partner is known to have a good six card suit. Indeed it is possible to raise partner directly to game with a doubleton and compensating outside values.

As aggressive as we are with a fit in partner's suit, we are equally conservative with a non-fitting hand.

In order to even entertain the thought of bidding with a non-fitting hand responder should have more than an opening bid!

Assuming your partner opens with 2S and the next hand passes, what would you respond with each of the following hands?:

(1) S. 5
     H. A876
     D. KQ76
     C. KJ87

(2) S. 5
     H. AK87
     D. AQ87
     C. Q1087

(3) S. K4
     H. A8765
     D. AK54
     C. 54

(4) S. 76
     H. KQ8
     D. AK98
     C. A1087

(5) S. 5
     H. K5
     D. AKQ9876
     C. K54

(6) S. 5
     H. K5
     D. A98765
     C. KJ87

(7) S. ---
     H. A9875
     D. KJ876
     C. Q108

(8) S. 5
     H. AK987
     D. AQJ98
     C. Q4

Solutions

(1) Pass If you can't see yourself passing with hands like this do
           yourself a favor and don't play Weak Two bids. Remember
           your partner has an average of about 9 H.C.P.

(2) 2NT   And even this is a stretch. A good case could be made for
           a pass.

(3) 4S   Should make easily. The hand is well suited to a spade con-
           tract with all those aces and kings.

(4) 2NT   Gives partner a choice of either 4S or 3NT.

(5) 3NT   To play and partner is not allowed to return to his suit.

(6) Pass No likely game here. Why look for trouble? Remember that
           a 3D response is forcing.

(7) Pass Same as above only more so.

(8) 3H   Maybe partner can support hearts. If he rebids 3S, more
           problems!

Opener	Responder	Meaning
2S	3S	Preemptive. Opener must pass.
2S	4S	Either a preemptive bid or a strong hand. Responder is captain.
2S	2NT	Forcing. Looking for more information. With a misfit responder should have 16 H.C.P. or more.
2S	3C,3D,3H	Forcing. Looking for support.
2S	3NT	Opener must pass.

The same meaning is attached to responses to a Weak Two in diamonds or hearts.

Defense to Weak Two Bids

When the player to your right opens with a Weak Two bid don't panic. Treat it as if it were a one bid and bid accordingly. You may:

(1) Double.   Shows an opening bid or better with support for each of the unbid suits, particularly the unbid major or majors.

(2) Overcall 2NT.   Shows the strength of an opening 1NT bid. Partner raises to game with eight or more points or cue bids the opponent's suit which is treated as Stayman.

East	South	West	North
2D	2NT	Pass	3D
Pass	?		

North's 3D bid is Stayman. If South has a four card major he bids it; if not he rebids 3NT.

If North mentions a major in response to the 2NT overcall the response is treated as forcing. If North bids a minor at the three level the response is not forcing.

East	South	West	North
2S	2NT	Pass	3H (Forcing)
2S	2NT	Pass	3C (Not Forcing)

(3) Overcall with a strong suit of your own. Normally this shows an opening bid with a reasonable six card suit.

(4) Jump to 3NT. This shows 19-21 points, a balanced hand, and typically two stoppers in the opponent's suit. With one stopper double and then jump to 3NT.

Do not allow the fact that opener has a relatively weak hand goad you into thinking you have a good one. Bid your hand, not his! It is no disgrace to pass when your right hand opponent opens a Weak Two. Your partner still has a chance to speak and he is allowed to compete with slightly less in the "dead seat". (If he passes the bidding will be dead.)

Assume you are South, and East, to your right, opens 2H. What do you bid with each of the following hands?:

(1)   S. AJ87
      H. 43
      D. K876
      C. Q107

(2)   S. AK87
      H. 43
      D. AQ87
      C. 1087

(3)   S. Q4
      H. AJ9
      D. KQ87
      C. A1087

(4)   S. AK8
      H. K4
      D. AK87
      C. Q876

(5)   S. AJ8
      H. AQ9
      D. KQ8
      C. KJ76

(6)   S. Q10876
      H. 54
      D. AJ8
      C. Q98

(7)   S. AK1092
      H. 54
      D. AJ7
      C. 765

(8)   S. K87
      H. K76
      D. A8765
      C. K4

(9)   S. AQJ1087
      H. A4
      D. KQ7
      C. 54

(1)   Pass   Not enough to double in the direct* position. Enough to double in the dead position. (10 or more with proper distribution.)

(2)   Dbl.   Same as if the hand is opened 1H to your right.

(3)   2NT   16-18.

(4)   Dbl.   To be followed by 3NT.

(5)   3NT   19-21 and two stoppers in the opponents suit.

(6)   Pass   Not enough for a two level overcall.

(7)   2S   What else?

(8)   Pass   A three level overcall shows a much better suit and this hand is too light to bid 2NT.

(9)   3S   Invitational to game.

Wasted Bid

As any new suit response to a Weak Two is forcing, a response of 4C is, for practical purposes, unnecessary. My suggestion is that a direct response of 4C be an ace-asking bid. The response keeps the hand at a lower and safer level particularly if the partnership is missing two aces.

Opener	Responder	Opener	Responder
S. KJ10765	S. AQ8	2S	4C (aces?)
H. 2	H. AK10	4D (none)	4S
D. 75	D. KQJ862	Pass	
C. KQ95	C. 2		

Without this convention responder might eventually bid 4NT and play the hand at 5S, risking a possible ruff.

* See page 151.

A New Convention

A new idea which has merit is a response of 2NT to a Weak Two which asks
opener for a singleton. For example:

Opener	Responder
2S	2NT
3C	

Opener shows a singleton club. The 2NT response is forcing to game and
responder is in charge. If responder rebids 3NT opener must pass. He has
already shown his singleton.

If opener does not have a singleton he rebids his suit with a minimum and
raises to 3NT with a maximum. The beauty of this convention is that your
partner does not have to use his judgment (always dangerous) when you respond 2NT. He either has a singleton or he doesn't.

Opener	Responder		Opener	Responder
S. AJ10765	S. KQ4		2S	2NT
H. 2	H. A8765		3H	4NT
D. QJ7	D. AK109		5D	6S
C. 1098	C. 2			

Responder bids 2NT to request distributional information. Opener shows a
singleton heart and responder visualizes a slam. Responder bids Blackwood
and puts the hand in six which is a laydown.

Preemptive Opening Bids

When it comes to preempting, the average player thinks in terms of opening
three of a suit....period. An opening four bid is unheard of and preempting after partner has opened is virtually non-existent.

Let's take these cases separately. What is the difference between an opening bid of three and four? Tricks. Nothing more than tricks.

An opening three bid has between six and seven tricks and a four bid between seven and eight tricks. If you know how to count tricks you know
how to preempt. You will also have a head start on knowing when to overcall.

```
(1)  S. QJ108642      (2)  S. KQJ10753      (3)  S. AQJ10432
     H. 2                  H. 2                  H. ---
     D. 3                  D. 3                  D. K5
     C. A765              C. A765              C. 8765
```

When counting tricks first look to your long suit. This is the suit that you wish to make the trump suit. Assuming a normal division of the remaining cards around the table, how many tricks can you take in your long suit?

Hand (1)   Can take five tricks in spades assuming the loss of the ace and the king. What about the rest of the hand? Aces, of course, are worth one trick; kings are worth a half of a trick, and most important ANY FOUR CARD SIDE SUIT IS WORTH A FULL TRICK. Therefore count one additional trick in clubs to bring your grand total to seven tricks. Seven tricks makes for a borderline situation. An opening three bid shows 6-7 tricks and a four bid 7-8 tricks. Normally three is opened with seven tricks unless not vulnerable against vulnerable in which case four is a possibility. Open 3S.

Hand (2)   This hand can take six spade tricks and the club suit is worth two more tricks bringing the grand total to eight. Open 4S.

Hand (3)   This hand can take six and a half spade tricks (sometimes the finesse works; sometimes it doesn't), a half a trick in diamonds, and one trick in clubs for the four card suit. The grand total is eight tricks. Open 4S.

What about point count? Point count is of secondary importance when pre-empting, but there are a few no-nos. An opening three bid should never have more than 10 H.C.P. (typically it will have 6-9) and should not have as many as two defensive tricks. In other words it should not contain two aces or a solid suit. All of these - too many points, too many defensive tricks, a solid suit - make the hand too strong for a three bid. Oh yes, most important of all, the three bidder should have a good seven card suit.

A four bid has a little more leeway. You are allowed to have more than 10 H.C.P. for a four bid particularly after partner has passed and slam is remote. A four bid typically has a range of 7-12 H.C.P. It should not contain more than two defensive tricks along with a seven or eight card suit.

The reason, of course, for stressing preempts is the paralyzing effect they have upon the opposition - even expert opposition. If they risk entering the auction at the three or four level they run the risk of encountering a costly penalty double by the partner of the preemptive bidder who might have a very good hand. If they play scared and don't bid at all they might find that they could have made a game or even a slam had they not been so cowardly. How much easier for them had you not preempted and allowed them to bid at the lower levels with less risk.

Up to now we have been discussing preempting basically in a major suit. There is a slight problem in the minors. If you open four of a minor you can never again play the hand in 3NT. Therefore, opening bids of four of a minor are less common and tend to be made after partner has passed, making game remote, or with hands that simply do not look suitable for no trump under any circumstances.

(4)	S. 32		(5)	S. 7
	H. 3			H. 5
	D. AQJ10876			D. QJ109653
	C. Q54			C. AQ65

Employing the idea that first or second seat minor preempts invite 3NT, open 3D with (4) and 4D with (5). Trashy first or second seat minor three bids are out. The suit must have either the ace or the hand must have a possible outside entry (an ace or a king), so that partner can establish the suit at no trump.

After Partner Has Passed

After partner has passed and you are considering a preempt in the third seat, your tactics change. Partner can't be terribly strong so the requirements can be relaxed. You might even preempt with a six card suit - not vulnerable.

```
     (6)  S. Q42          (7)  S. 864          (8)  S. 865
          H. 2                 H. 3                 H. 4
          D. 43                D. AKJ9864           D. Q104
          C. KJ109765          C. 32                C. KQJ1032
```

Hand (6)   Opens 3C in the third seat, but passes in first or second. Remember that opening three bids in first or second seat are invitational to 3NT. In third seat partner is not allowed to convert to 3NT after passing originally.

Hand (7)   Opens 3D in any position.

Hand (8)   Passes in first or second seat, but opens 3C in third seat. This is done simply to harass the opponents and direct partner's lead. Partners must be taught that opening three bids in the third seat are not to be tampered with!

What about preempting after partner has opened the bidding? Sure, why not? When used properly preemptive bids are very descriptive and usually lead to the best contract.

```
Opener     Responder

  1C          3H          What type of hand does responder have?
```

Responder has a hand very similar to an opening 3H bid. Presumably a seven card heart suit and a hand that can take between six and seven tricks. Opener takes a look at his "quick tricks" and decides whether to raise or pass. Of course opener can bid another suit or even 3NT, but in real life he usually raises or passes.

Let's assume opener has each of these hands on the same sequence:

```
     (9)  S. AK76        (10)  S. KJ76         (11)  S. A76
          H. 2                 H. 32                 H. 2
          D. A76               D. K65                D. K4
          C. KQ765             C. KQ76               C. AKQ8765
```

With (9)   Opener raises to 4H. Opener has four tricks for partner and
           the singleton is no deterrent when partner is known to have a
           reasonable seven card suit.

With (10) Opener passes - fast! If you even thought of bidding 3NT you
           are what is called "a very dangerous partner". To make 3NT, it
           takes more than a stopper here and there when the total point
           count between the two hands is about twenty and there is no run-
           ning suit. Remember partner's hearts are not solid when he
           makes a preemptive bid at the three level.

With (11) Opener bids 3NT not on the basis of partner's hearts, but rather
           his own club suit. Responder passes as he has already told his
           whole story with his preempt. If nothing else, this book will
           emphasize the importance of allowing partner to make the final
           decision if you have already spoken your piece.

What about a direct response of four of a major to an opening bid? Similar
to a four opening with one caution. Partner has opened, and, if you have
too good a hand, you may miss a slam. There are other ways of showing
partner a long suit.

For example, partner opens 1D and you hold:

(12)	S. AQJ9874	(13)	S. AKJ10985	(14)	S. KJ1097652
	H. 43		H. A43		H. K43
	D. 2		D. 2		D. ---
	C. KJ5		C. K5		C. 65

With (12) The proper response is 1S. On the rebid responder jumps to 4S,
           telling partner he has a wonderful suit as well as an opening
           bid.

With (13) Responder makes an immediate jump shift to 2S. This tells the
           opener that responder has slam on his mind.

With (14) Responder does bid 4S immediately. Notice that responder does
           not have enough to open the bidding with 1S as he did in the
           other examples. A direct jump to four of a major over an open-
           ing bid is always made on less than opening bid strength. It is
           a hand that promises about 7-8 tricks with a seven or an eight
           card suit. Typically it has 7-9 H.C.P.

Defense to an Opening Three Bid

Let it be known that there is really no good defense to an enemy preemptive opening. The bid has already taken away too many levels from you and your partner for there to be any super accurate bidding. But life goes on.

Standard procedure with an opening bid or better is to double for takeout with support for each of the unbid suits and overcall with a good six or seven card suit.

Another possibility is to bid 3NT. This suggests one of two types of hands. Either a balanced hand with 16-20 points, hopefully with two stoppers in the opponent's suit, or a gambling-type bid with a long running minor suit and one stopper in the opponent's suit.

Try this little quiz to see how well you can handle one of these preemptive bids.

Neither side vulnerable:

	East	South
	3H	?

South holds:

(1)	(2)	(3)
S. AJxx	S. AJ10xxx	S. Ax
H. x	H. xx	H. KQ10xx
D. KQxx	D. AQx	D. xxx
C. Kxxx	C. xx	C. Qxx

(4)	(5)
S. Kx	S. Axx
H. Kx	H. xx
D. AKQJxx	D. Kxxx
C. Jxx	C. AQxx

Solutions

(1) Dbl.   South has excellent support for the unbid suits plus four card support for the unbid major, which is very important.

(2) 3S   An overcall of a preemptive bid typically shows a six card suit and approximately an opening bid.

(3) Pass   No matter how loudly you double, a double is still for takeout in this position, and you cannot double without support for the unbid suits.

31

(4) 3NT   With a solid minor suit and one stopper in the opponent's suit
           a gamble must be taken. Do not take the coward's way out and
           bid 4D.

(5) Pass Close to a double, but with a hand just barely worth an opening
           bid it is important to have four card support for the unbid
           major.

Defense to an Opening Four Bid

If you thought defending against an opening three bid was tough, just wait!
Combatting an opening four bid is even tougher.

The best way to handle these four bids is to divide them up into three categories:

I. Opening bids of four of a minor suit.

East	South
4C	Dbl.

The most common defense is the double. It is made with either one
of two types of hands:

    (1) S. AK5   (2) S. AQ985
         H. AQ76   H. AKJ6
         D. KJ8   D. Q43
         C. 654   C. 2

A hand that is strong enough to open 1NT (1) or one that has a good
sound opening bid with shortness in the opponent's suit (2). Partner usually passes unless he has a long major suit.

II. Opening bids of 4H.

    Again the best defense is the double and it shows either a strong
    no trump hand or a hand that has good support for spades.

    (1) S. AJ10   (2) S. KQ98
         H. K105   H. 54
         D. AQ98   D. AKJ87
         C. KJ8   C. K4

Either of these hands doubles an opening bid of 4H. Partner normally
passes, but is allowed to bid a long spade suit. If partner bids a

minor suit at the five level he is strictly on his own and should
have some good excuses ready if the roof falls in.

III. Opening bids of 4S.

The most common defense again is the double. This is strictly
a penalty double. If partner bids any suit at the five level he
must have a freak hand with a very long suit.

So far the only defense we have covered is the double. Of course it is possible to overcall with a long suit of your own, but it is dangerous at this
level. Nevertheless, with a good six or more likely seven card suit it generally pays to make your presence felt by bidding your suit.

The Takeout Bid of Four No Trump

There is still another possibility when the opponents open four of a major.
A direct overcall of 4NT is used by agreement to show one of two types of
hands.

Assume your right hand opponent opens 4S and you hold:

```
S. ---
H. AKJx
D. KQJx
C. AKJxx
```

You could use the 4NT overcall to show this hand - a gigantic three suited
hand, usually with a void in the opponent's suit and a strong desire to
play in slam. It is a beautiful bid and if it comes up once in your lifetime consider yourself lucky.

The other possibility is to use the overcall of 4NT over four of either
major to show a hand like this:

```
S. x
H. x
D. AKxxxx
C. KQ10xx
```

This type of takeout is strictly for the minors, and although it may not
come up too often it is not out of Disneyland as the other. Be smart. Use
the 4NT overcall to show a strong minor two-suiter.

2. RESPONDING TO AN OPENING BID

To make accurate responses to partner's opening bid the responding hand
must keep in mind:

1. Basically there are two types of responses - limited and unlimited.
   A limited response describes a hand within a range of 2-3 points.
   An unlimited response announces a minimum count, but no maximum.
   All raises and no trump responses are limited. All new suit re-
   sponses unlimited.

2. Weak responding hands try to make limited responses as quickly as
   possible.

3. Stronger responding hands have more latitude and usually show their
   strength and distribution by making unlimited responses.

4. The partnership is searching for an eight card or longer major suit
   fit. If this does not exist the possibility of a no trump contract
   is next in order of importance. Finally, one plays in a minor suit
   contract if all else fails.

5. A balanced hand facing a balanced hand plays best in no trump.

Limited Responses

All no trump responses are limited. (All counts refer to H.C.P. only.)
   A response of 1NT shows 6-9 points.
   A response of 2NT shows 13-15 points.
   A response of 3NT shows 16-17 Points.

All raises are limited. (All counts refer to support points. Support
                         points = H.C.P. plus short suit points.)
   The raise from 1 to 2 shows 7-10 points.
   The raise from 1 to 3 shows 10-12 points.*
   The raise from 1 to 4 shows 9-12 points.**

 *Limit Raise (See page 41).

**Less than ten points in high cards, typically five or six card trump sup-
  port with a side singleton or void.

34

Whenever either player makes a limit bid his partner becomes the captain and generally places the final contract.

Unlimited Responses

Any new suit by the responding hand is unlimited and forcing. If responder mentions a new suit at the one level the range is six or more H.C.P.; at the two level ten or more H.C.P.

	Opener	Responder	
a)	1D	1H	Responder has six or more H.C.P.
b)	1D	2C	Responder has ten or more H.C.P.

These are the two basic responses from which most unlimited sequences stem. You must have a firm understanding at the ground level or you will flounder on the upper floors.

No Trump Responses

The 1NT Response

The most common of all no trump responses is 1NT. It is most likely to occur in response to a major suit opening. The reason for this is that after a minor suit opening there is more bidding space for responder to show his longest suit at the one level.

You hold: S. xx H. Kxxxx D. Axx C. xxx   Partner opens 1S.
You have no alternative but to limit yourself with a 1NT response. Your hand is clearly not strong enough to venture to the two level and bid 2H. That response would require 10 H.C.P.

On the other hand if partner opens 1C or 1D you should make the unlimited response of 1H rather than the limited response of 1NT. Why?

In general it does not pay to by-pass a good four card major suit let alone a five card major suit at the level of one to respond 1NT. When partner opens with a minor suit show your major and then limit yourself at your next opportunity. By-passing a four card major in order to respond 1NT frequently leads to the loss of a 4-4 major suit fit.

The assumption is that if responder bids 1NT in response to a minor suit opening he probably does not have a four card major or if he does it is so emaciated looking that he has purposely decided not to bid it.

For example, over a 1C opening it is certainly not unreasonable to respond 1NT with the following hand: S. AJx   H. xxxx   D. KJx   C. xxx.

It is also dangerous to respond 1S to a 1H opening with four bad spades and a weak hand. Opener will frequently raise to 2S with three card support and you will be stuck in an awkward contract.

Holding: S. Jxxx   H. Kx   D. Q10x   C. Jxxx   it is wiser to respond 1NT to a 1H opening rather than 1S.

A similar problem exists when responding specifically to a 1D opening bid with four weak hearts and a bad hand. Opener is very unlikely to hold four hearts because with four hearts and four diamonds or four good hearts and five diamonds the proper opening bid is 1H.

Therefore the responder need not go out of his way to respond 1H to a 1D opening bid. Better to respond 1NT with a weak hand.

Over a 1C opening bid the range of the 1NT response is 8-10 points. The reason is that over 1C it is very easy for the responder to find some bid at the one level. Therefore if he does respond 1NT it is because he has a no trump hand.

Avoid responding 1NT with 10 H.C.P. to any other suit. If partner has fif-teen points he will pass and you will miss too many game contracts. If you must, be sure to have a singleton in your partner's major suit, no tens and no five card suit!

Holding: S. x   H. Kxxx   D. Qxxx   C. AJxx   you might respond 1NT to a 1S opening but 2C is certainly not incorrect.

The 1NT response to a major suit does not promise a balanced hand. For example if partner opens 1S and you hold: S.--- H. Jxxx D. Kxxxxx C. QJx your best response is 1NT and this is not exactly what one would call a balanced hand.

However, a 1NT response to 1C and usually 1D does show a balanced-type hand.

The 2NT Response

A direct response of 2NT absolutely promises a balanced hand and 13-15 H.C.P. If you fancy your dummy play you can try bidding 2NT with 12 H.C.P. and a reasonable five card suit, perhaps with some tens to bolster up your hand.

This response is limited and forcing to game. Do not make the common error of responding 2NT "to show the points". You must have a balanced hand with at least one stopper in each of the unbid suits. There is no such animal as a 2NT response with a singleton or void.

The big problem is deciding whether to make the limited response of 2NT over a minor suit opening or to show a four card major suit first and then, perhaps, jump in no trump later.

In general, respond 2NT if the four card major is weak, but show the major first if it is fairly strong (QJxx or better).

Of course any five card major is always shown in preference to an original 2NT response.

Assume you hold each of the following hands and your partner opens 1C:

	(1)		(2)		(3)
	S. AJx		S. Ax		S. Kx
	H. Jxxx		H. KQ10x		H. QJxxx
	D. KQx		D. Jxxx		D. Kxx
	C. Kxx		C. Axx		C. Axx

What is your response?

Respond 2NT with the first hand, but 1H with the other two. Of course if your partner doesn't support hearts with the last two hands you will make a no trump rebid. BALANCED HANDS THAT DO NOT RESPOND IMMEDIATELY IN NO TRUMP MAKE AN EFFORT TO REBID NO TRUMP AT THE NEXT OPPORTUNITY.

2NT Over Two Level Interference

Assume the bidding has proceeded:

North	East	South	West
1H	2D	2NT	

A non-jump response of 2NT, even a two level overcall, is limited to 10-12 H.C.P. and is not forcing. If responder has a normal 2NT response he must jump to 3NT after a two level overcall.

The 3NT Response

This response crowds the auction, and although it gives partner a good picture of your hand (16-17 H.C.P. plus a balanced hand), it makes life difficult for the opener with an unbalanced hand.

If opener has a balanced hand though, it is easy for him to evaluate the total potential of the two hands quickly and accurately.

Although many experts make a rule never to respond 3NT there is no satisfactory alternative. Therefore I suggest that you do respond 3NT if you have the proper distribution and point count and let your partner take charge from there.

Balanced hands that have eighteen or nineteen H. C. P. are covered in the chapter on the jump shift by the responder.

Raising Partner's Suit

The Single Raise of a Major

Earlier we said when originally evaluating a hand we should count H. C. P. and then add them to LONG SUIT POINTS. However, when it comes to supporting or raising partner we count H. C. P. and add them to SHORT SUIT POINTS.

Under no circumstances do you count both long and short suit points at the same time unless you have a strong death wish.

When bidding your own suit or suits use the Long Suit Method. When supporting partner use the Short Suit Method.

Later, as the bidding develops, it might be obvious that the hand is a misfit. In this case a wise player will count for neither long nor short suit points. Misfitted hands are not given extra points for anything!

Support Point Scale

When supporting partner with three or more cards:

1. Count 1 extra point for each doubleton.
2. Count 3 extra points for each singleton.
3. Count 5 extra points for a void.
4. Deduct 1 point when raising with three trumps holding a singleton or void.

Assume you pick up this hand and partner opens 1H:

```
S. AQ10x
H. x
D. 10xxx
C. xxxx
```

You should count your hand at six points, giving yourself nothing for your singleton heart because it is in your partner's suit! The proper response is 1S with your strong four card suit.

Now assume you hold the same hand and your partner opens 1S. Your hand has now increased three points in value and is worth nine points in support of spades. YOUR SINGLETON IS WORKING FOR YOU, NOT AGAINST YOU. Your proper response is 2S.

The single raise shows 7-10 support points. Ten point single raises are the exception. Under no circumstances should a single raise be given with more.

The single raise in a major can be made with either three or four card support. The raise does NOT promise an honor in partner's suit.

When confronted with a choice of giving partner a single major raise or responding 1NT it is usually better to raise, particularly with a side doubleton or singleton.

The real problem hands are those with 4-3-3-3 distribution. These hands can go either way. Assume your partner opens 1S and you hold:

    (1) S. Jxx   (2) S. Axx
         H. Kxx   H. KJx
         D. 10xxx   D. xxxx
         C. QJx   C. xxx

Expert opinion is to respond 1NT with 6 or 7 H.C.P. and 4-3-3-3 distribution to slow partner down. (The 1NT response sounds more discouraging to the ear.) With 9 or 10 points raise the major and holding exactly 8 use your wonderful judgment, leaning towards the raise.

If your hand contains a side singleton or doubleton along with three card major support simply raise the major and don't worry about it.

Raise 1S to 2S with either of the following hands:

    (1) S. 765   (2) S. 432
         H. 4   H. 43
         D. A7654   D. AK87
         C. Q987   C. 8765

With 10 H.C.P. and a doubleton or a side five card suit do not raise immediately even with the three card support. Bid your suit first. You are too strong for a single raise.

    (1) S. A87   (2) S. K76
         H. 54   H. 54
         D. KQJ87   D. 5432
         C. 543   C. AK65

To a 1S opening, respond 2D on (1) and 2C on (2).

And finally the impossible hand! You hold: S. 5
                                             H. A94
                                             D. AJ76
                                             C. 108765

Your partner opens 1H and the next player passes.

You have eleven points in support of hearts (9 H.C.P. plus 2 for the singleton because you have only three card support) which makes your hand too strong for a raise to 2H. Under no circumstances do you raise your partner from one to two with more than ten support points.

On the other hand to go into the two level to bid a new suit you are supposed to have at least 10 H.C.P. As a response of 1NT is complete lunacy we must select between 2H and 2C.

The proper response is 2C. IT IS PERMISSIBLE TO GO INTO THE TWO LEVEL WITH LESS THAN 10 H.C.P. IF YOU HAVE MORE THAN TEN POINTS IN SUPPORT OF PARTNER'S SUIT.

However, if partner opens 1S and you have the same hand the proper response is 1NT. You are counting nothing for your singleton spade.

The Single Raise of a Minor

As every effort is made to respond in a major to a minor suit opening it stands to reason that a single raise in a minor shows at least four card support. The range is the same (7-10) and the responder should not fear supporting clubs. (See "The Short Club Obsession".)

However, raise 1D to 2D with three card support and this type hand:

```
S. KJ2
H. 3
D. K109
C. 765432
```

The Forcing Double Raise - Goodbye

The Limit Raise - Hello

One hates to tamper with old stand-bys like motherhood, marriage and forcing double raises. But the time has come.

The double raise as a forcing to game response showing 13-16 support points is on its last legs. It has been replaced, and rightly so, by the limit raise, an immediate jump from one to three, which describes a hand with four or more trump and exactly 10-12 points in support of partner's suit.

Partner can pass this raise with a minimum opening bid. In practice he
will pass about one out of four times.

Use of the limit raise (which is already standard in most systems) eliminates one of the problem areas of the game, namely the temporizing response
in another suit when holding excellent major suit support and 10-12 support points.

Hands like this were always unbiddable using forcing double raises. Assume
partner opens 1S and you hold:

(1) S. A8765   (2) S. KQ87
      H. AJ10   H. A4
      D. 54   D. 5432
      C. J76   C. J109

What were you supposed to do with these hands which were too strong for
even a loud 2S raise? There was no acceptable response and all the double
talk in the world could not prove there was. Now there is a perfectly
reasonable way of describing this type of hand.

The proper response is 3S, showing a hand a little stronger than a raise
to 2S. A limit raise can be likened to a jump raise by a passed hand:

Opener	Responder
	Pass
1S	3S

Using limit raises, responder is showing exactly the same strength whether
he has passed or not. A limit raise is a limit raise....period.

Limit raises are so simple that hardly any explanation is required other
than the fact that four or more trumps are required. Limit raises are used
in the minor suits as well as in competition. Limit raises always show the
same strength.

Responding with 13-16 Support Points
and Four Card Major Support

Throughout the rest of this book it will be assumed that limit raises are
being used. Therefore we must have a way to show the hand that was former-
ly a jump from one to three.

Currently there are a number of ways to do this, but I shall limit this discussion to two methods. The first is the simplest and unless you have a steady partnership will surely be the best.

Opener	Responder	Opener	Responder
S. AQ873	S. KJ92	1S	2C
H. A4	H. K3	2D	4S
D. K765	D. 832	Pass	
C. 65	C. AK42		

The simple way is to bid your four, five or six card side suit and then jump to four of partner's major at your next opportunity. This "delayed game raise" promises four trumps and 13-16 support points. It is not a sign off.

The second method, which I use, is slightly more complicated, but it does differentiate between a number of responding hands that have four card support.

(1) Balanced hands that have four card support jump to 2NT and then four of partner's major on the rebid.

Opener	Responder	Opener	Responder
S. AQ873	S. KJ92	1S	2NT
H. A4	H. K3	3D	4S
D. K765	D. 832	Pass	
C. 65	C. AK42		

When responder jumps to 2NT opener assumes a balanced hand with 13-15 points and definitely not four card support for his major. However, if responder's next bid is <u>game</u> in the major responder is showing four card support.

Opener	Responder	Opener	Responder
S. AK743	S. QJ92	1S	2NT
H. 54	H. 83	3NT	4S
D. AQ3	D. KJ102	Pass	
C. 654	C. AQ9		

(2) Hands that have five or six card side suits bid the suit and then jump to four of partner's major.

Opener	Responder	Opener	Responder
S. 76	S. 108	1H	2C
H. AQ876	H. K1095	2D	4H
D. KQ87	D. A4	Pass	
C. Q7	C. AJ1032		

Opener now pictures an unbalanced hand and realizes that less high card count is required for a slam.

(3) Hands that have a singleton with no side five or six card suit jump to the four level of the singleton suit over a 1S opening and to 3S over 1H if the singleton is spades!

This one is pretty wild and is called Singleton Swiss. It is a beautiful convention if nobody forgets. Heaven help you though if someone does!

Opener	Responder	Opener	Responder
S. AK765	S. QJ104	1S	4D!
H. AK5	H. Q1083	4NT	5D
D. 6543	D. 2	6S	Pass
C. 4	C. AQ76		

Responder shows 13-16 support points for spades, plus a singleton diamond and no long side suit. Opener now realizes that his diamond holding is not so bad after all and tries for a slam. When partner shows an ace he bids one.

I won't feel hurt if you don't use my method for showing four card major support, but I will feel terrible if you don't use limit raises. They are clearly superior.

The Triple Raise from One to Four

This is primarily used in the majors, although a raise from one to four in the minors shows the same type hand.

The triple raise, as ever, shows a hand with five or six card support, a singleton or void somewhere, and about 9-12 support points. Its distinquishing feature is the absence of high cards. A triple raise must have less than 10 H.C.P.

Typical triple raises from 1H to 4H look like this:

(1)	S. 3	(2)	S. 10876	(3)	S. 5
	H. AJ876		H. K8765		H. A1087
	D. K7654		D. ---		D. 54
	C. 54		C. QJ109		C. QJ8765

Now let's see how much of this you have digested. Assume partner opens 1H and you hold the following responding hands playing limit raises and the method I like best for responding with four trumps and a good hand:

Quiz on Supporting Partner

(1)	S. 54	(2)	S. A876	(3)	S. AJ76
	H. K76		H. KQJ9		H. KQ87
	D. A7654		D. 43		D. 2
	C. 1087		C. 653		C. QJ76

(4)	S. 65	(5)	S. KQ876	(6)	S. Q76
	H. AK87		H. J10876		H. A65
	D. K54		D. ---		D. 43
	C. QJ76		C. 654		C. KQ654

(7)	S. A5	(8)	S. J87	(9)	S. J765
	H. QJ87		H. 1087		H. 432
	D. KJ8765		D. KJ7		D. A10876
	C. 2		C. J1076		C. 5

Solutions to Quiz on Supporting Partner

(1) 2H   No second choice.

(2) 3H   Limit Raise.

(3) 4D   Singleton Swiss.

(4) 2NT Planning on bidding 4H at your next turn regardless of partner's next bid.

(5) 4H   No discussion.

(6) 2C   A limit raise should not be given with three trumps. Even using five card majors it is a doubtful practice.

(7) 2D   Intending to bid 4H at the next opportunity.

(8) 1NT Trying to slow the old chap down a bit.

(9) 2H   Don't worry about the three little trumps. You don't have to play the hand, partner does.

Unlimited Responses   (One Over One)

Any new suit by the responder is unlimited and forcing. At the level of one it promises a minimum of 6 H.C.P. with no maximum although in practice responder will seldom have more than 15 H.C.P. (See Chapter on Jump Shift).

The important points to remember about a one over one response are:

(1)   It is possible to respond one over one with only 5 H.C.P. when hold-ing a very strong four or five card suit (usually a major).

    S. 654   Respond 1H to an opening bid of either minor.
    H. KQ1087
    D. 543
    C. 63

(2)   With two five card suits respond in the higher ranking suit first, regardless of the relative strength of the suits.

    S. 97654   Respond 1S to either a 1H or a 1C opening bid.
    H. A3
    D. KQ1076
    C. 5

(3)   With two four card suits respond in the suit that is closest in rank to partner's suit.

    S. KJ98   Respond 1H to an opening bid of either 1C or 1D.
    H. AQ76
    D. 654
    C. 75

    S. AQ87   Respond 1D to an opening bid of 1C.
    H. 54
    D. KQ107   Respond 1S to an opening bid of 1H.
    C. 765

An exception is made to this rule when holding a relatively weak responding hand (6-10 H.C.P.), a strong four card major and a weak four or even five card minor.

    S. 76   Respond 1H to an opening bid of 1C. Even if there
    H. AKJ9
    D. 8765   were a fifth small diamond it would be correct to
    C. 1087
                 respond 1H with this hand. However, with a good

                 hand responder should bid suits in the normal order.

                 (Longer first or the one closest to partner's with

                 two or three four card suits.)

With three four card suits bid the one closest in rank to partner's
suit.

```
S. KJ87        Respond 1D to an opening bid of 1C.
H. A1087
D. QJ87        Respond 1H to an opening bid of 1D.
C. 5
               But respond 4C to an opening bid of either major.

               (Singleton Swiss.)  If not using this toy simply

               respond 1S to 1H or 2D to 1S and then jump to four

               of partner's major on your rebid.
```

Unlimited Responses   (Two Over One)

The major difference between a two over one and a one over one response is
that responder needs a minimum of 10 H.C.P. rather than six.

Because of this rather inhibiting rule the responder cannot always show his
suit over a major suit opening.

```
S. 65          If partner opens 1S the response is, perforce, 1NT.
H. 976
D. AQ987       The hand is not strong enough to enter the two level
C. J108
               in a new suit.  Of course, if partner opens 1H the

               proper response is 2H.
```

There are two major exceptions to the 10 H.C.P. rule:

(1)   When responder has a powerful five card heart suit, 9 H.C.P. and at

      least a doubleton in opener's suit.

```
S. 65          Respond 2H to an opening bid of 1S and pass if
H. AKQ102
D. 876         partner rebids 2S.
C. 876
```

(2)   When responder has a powerful six card suit with 8 H.C.P. (all in

      the suit).

```
S. 5           Respond 2C to an opening 1S bid and rebid the clubs.
H. 543
D. 543
C. AKJ1098
```

In all other cases responder will have at least 10 H.C.P. and usually more.
After a two over one response the hand plays in game more often than not.

A two over one response is similar to a one over one when it comes to suit selection. Again the higher ranking of five card suits and the one closest to partner's with four card suits.

    S. 5   Respond 2H to an opening bid of 1S and 1H to an
    H. J10876
    D. AK987   opening bid of 1C.
    C. K5

    S. AJ   Respond 2C to an opening bid of 1S but 1H to an
    H. KJ98
    D. 543   opening bid of 1D.
    C. Q1087

Merely because a hand contains 10 or more H.C.P. does not mean the first response must be at the two level. Indeed, many one over one responses temporarily conceal hands with much more than 10 H.C.P.

However, if the responder does venture into the two level on his original response his partner will count on him for at least 10 H.C.P.

Quiz on Unlimited Responses

On each of the following hands assume partner has opened with one of each suit and respond accordingly. Therefore, each problem will have four separate answers.

(1) S. KQ76   (2) S. 87   (3) S. KQ876
     H. 87   H. A8765   H. Q10765
     D. AJ87   D. 876   D. 54
     C. 543   C. Q106   C. 4

(4) S. 6   (5) S. J1087   (6) S. KJ8
     H. J76   H. KJ87   H. 97
     D. Q9876   D. K765   D. A1043
     C. KJ76   C. 4   C. KQ76

(7) S. AQ108   (8) S. KQJ9   (9) S. 875
     H. 76   H. 86   H. K108
     D. AJ765   D. 108765   D. 76
     C. 76   C. J6   C. AQJ108

Solutions to Quiz on Unlimited Responses

(1)	1C-1D	1D-1S	1H-1S	1S-3S
(2)	1C-1H	1D-1H	1H-2H	1S-1NT
(3)	1C-1S	1D-1S	1H-4H	1S-4S
(4)	*1C-2C	1D-2D	1H-2H	1S-1NT
(5)	1C-1D	**1D-1H	1H-3H	1S-3S
(6)	1C-1D	1D-2C	1H-2NT	1S-2C
(7)	1C-1D	1D-1S	1H-2D	1S-2D
(8)	1C-1S	1D-1S or 2D	1H-1S	1S-2S
(9)	1C-3C	1D-2C	1H-2C	1S-2C

*With a weak responding hand and no major to show, it is better to raise immediately and limit the hand.

**Showing the major first and then planning to support diamonds because the hand is strong enough to make two bids.

Chart of All Common Responses with
Their Meanings and Ranges

Opener	Responder	Meaning	Range
1H	2H	Limited	7-10 Support Points
1H	3H	"	10-12 " "
1H	4H	"	9-12 " "
1H	1NT	Limited	6-9 H.C.P.
1H	2NT	"	13-15 "
1H	3NT	"	16-17 "
1H	1S	Unlimited	6 or more H.C.P.
1H	2C	"	10 " " "

3. REBID BY THE OPENER

As we begin to build our sequences inevitably we encounter the term "captaincy". Is this a part-score, game, or slam hand? Who makes the final decision?

WITH FEW EXCEPTIONS THE PARTNER OF THE PLAYER WHO HAS MADE THE FIRST LIMIT BID (TOLD HIS STORY) IS CAPTAIN OF THE HAND AND PLACES THE FINAL CONTRACT.

Sometimes opener is captain and sometimes responder. If the opening bid is a limit bid, such as 1NT or 2NT, then responder assumes captaincy. However, if the opening bid is one of a suit (considered unlimited) and responder limits his hand by either raising or bidding no trump, opener assumes captaincy.

Keep in mind that the partner of the player who has made the first limit bid can add up the resources of the two hands and is therefore in a better position to place the contract.

It stands to reason that the quicker someone limits his hand, the easier it is to arrive at the proper final contract. However, as we have seen, responder cannot always limit his hand immediately and frequently responds one over one (six or more) or two over one (ten or more).

Now let's swing back to the opener. If responder makes an unlimited response it is up to the opener to try to limit his hand on the rebid. Then the responder can assume captaincy. Sometimes the opener will not be able to limit himself on the rebid. Then the responder will try to limit himself on his rebid. IN MOST SEQUENCES EITHER THE OPENER OR THE RESPONDER WILL LIMIT HIS HAND WITH HIS FIRST OR SECOND BID.

The most confusing sequences take place when neither opener nor responder limits himself immediately. Sometimes it is unavoidable but the theme here will be to try to limit oneself as quickly as possible.

For practical purposes we can say that an opening bid of one of a suit will generally range from 11 H.C.P. to 19 H.C.P. but we subdivide opening

bids by using our total evaluation count: high card points added to long
suit points.

12-15 Minimum

16-18 Intermediate

19-20 Powerful or Powerhouse

Rebidding Hands in the 12-15 Range

Minimum hands make minimum rebids.

The most common rebids are:

(1) Raising partner's suit one level.

(2) Rebidding 1NT.

(3) Rebidding the original suit.

(4) Bidding a second suit.

(1) Raising partner's suit.

A single raise, usually from one to two of a major, promises a minimum of three card support plus a side singleton or doubleton. It is
rare to raise with 4-3-3-3 distribution.

```
S. AJ5      Open 1D and raise 1S to 2S.
H. 54
D. AQ876
C. Q107

S. AJ87     Open 1D and raise 1S to 2S.
H. 43
D. AK87
C. 1087
```

(2) Rebidding 1NT.

A rebid of 1NT shows a balanced minimum hand - no singletons (unless
it be a singleton honor in partner's suit).

```
S. AJ5      Open 1C and rebid 1NT over any one level response.
H. K108
D. Q65      Hands with 4-3-3-3 distribution rebid 1NT rather
C. A765
            than support partner.  But with AKx xxx xxx AQJx

            open 1C and raise 1S to 2S.

S. A6       Open 1C and rebid 1NT over a 1D or a 1S response
H. KQ4
D. Q87      but raise 1H to 2H.
C. K8765
```

51

Notice that a raise takes priority over a 1NT rebid (with a side doubleton) and that both a raise and a rebid of 1NT take priority over the rebid of the original five card suit.

(3) Rebidding the original suit.

In general one avoids rebidding five card minor suits. Five card major suits should not be rebid unless there is no reasonable alternative or the suit has three or four honor cards and can play opposite a small doubleton.

S. AJ   Open 1H and rebid 2D over 1S, 2D over 2C, and 3D
H. A8765
D. KQ76   over 2D. Notice the five card major is not rebid.
C. 105

S. A7   Open 1D and raise 1H to 2H, rebid 1NT over 1S. But
H. KQ7
D. KJ987   rebid 2D over 2C. A 2NT rebid after a <u>two</u> level re-
C. 1087
           sponse shows 15-17 points and is forcing for one round.

S. KJ9   Open 1H and raise 1S to 2S, raise 2C to 3C and rebid
H. KQ876
D. 2   2H over 2D. (No alternative.)
C. KJ87

The direct rebid of a minor suit shows six cards about 85% of the time. The direct rebid of a major suit shows a six card suit about 70% of the time.

S. AJ9876   Open 1S and rebid 2S over any response.
H. K4
D. 654
C. A4

S. KQ4   Open 1C and rebid 2C over 1D but raise 1H to 2H or
H. A87
D. 2   1S to 2S. The direct raise of a major takes priority
C. K108765
           over rebidding a six card minor if the supporting
           trumps are strong and the six card suit relatively
           weak.

Conversely, if the minor is strong and the support minimal rebid the six card minor. With 10xx Ax xx AKJ9xx open 1C and rebid 2C over any one level response.

(4) Whenever opener rebids a new suit at the one level or a <u>lower</u> rank-
     ing new suit at the two level he may have either a minimum (12-15)
     or an intermediate (16-18) type hand. This makes life difficult
     for the responder because opener is still unlimited.

     Sequences such as these:

Opener	Responder		Opener	Responder
1H	1S		1D	1H
2C			1S	

     can show either minimum or intermediate type hands. Presumably,
     if it is an intermediate type hand, it is unbalanced; otherwise
     the opening bid would have been 1NT.

S. 5	S. 52	S. Q4
H. AK876	H. AKJ87	H. AKJ87
D. 543	D. 54	D. 54
C. A1097	C. AK76	C. AK76
(12)	(16)	(18)

     These hands ranging in point count from 12-18 open 1H and rebid
     2C over a 1S response.

S. AK87	S. AK87	S. A876
H. 2	H. 4	H. A
D. A8765	D. A876	D. AK876
C. 765	C. A765	C. Q32
(12)	(15)	(18)

     These hands open 1D and rebid 1S over a 1H response. As you can
     see, responder must be wary when opener bids a new suit at the
     one level or a lower ranking new suit at the two level. Opener
     is unlimited and with 10 or more points responder should find a
     second bid.

Intermediate Hands   (16-18)

Hands in the 16-18 point range are considered intermediate.

If the hand is balanced it is opened 1NT to avoid rebidding problems.

If the hand is unbalanced the longest suit is opened and opener tries to
show his additional strength on his rebid.

He may: (1) Jump to 2NT or even 3NT.

             (2) Jump raise partner's suit.

             (3) Jump in his own suit.

             (4) Bid a new suit.

The Jump to 2NT After a One Level Response

Opener	Responder
1C	1D or 1H or 1S
2NT	

The jump rebid of 2NT shows a balanced hand with 18-19 H.C.P. and stoppers in the unbid suits. It is not forcing but responder must have exactly six points to pass.

The reason opener may have as little as 18 H.C.P. is that hands with that count and five card suits are too strong to open 1NT.

          S. AJ
          H. KQx
          D. AJx
          C. K10xxx

This hand opens 1C, not 1NT, and jumps to 2NT over any one level response.

It would be remiss not to mention that experts have a habit of using this jump rebid to show hands like this also:

          S. Kx   S. AQ
          H. Kx   H. Qxx
          D. AJx   D. AQ9xxx
          C. AJ10xxx   C. Kx

Each of these hands is opened with the minor suit but the rebid is 2NT after a one level response. Notice that these hands have only 16 and 17 H.C.P. respectively but they have the six card minor to take up the slack.

The Jump to 3NT After a Two Level Response

Opener	Responder
1H	2D
3NT	

Opener shows 18-19 points plus a balanced hand. The jump to 3NT is not a sign off. If responder has thirteen or more points he tries for slam.

The Jump to 3NT After a One Level Response

Opener	Responder
1C	1H
3NT	

Traditionally, this rebid has shown a balanced hand with 20 or 21 H.C.P. No longer. We now open these hands with 2NT. Therefore, the jump to 3NT in this sequence shows a different type hand altogether. It promises a long solid or near-solid minor suit, at least one stopper in each of the unbid suits, and no interest in responder's major at all. Indeed, the opener may have a singleton or void in partner's suit! Opener usually has 16 or 17 H.C.P.

Opener	Responder	Opener	Responder
S. ---	S. KQxxxx	1C	1S
H. KQx	H. xxx	3NT	Pass
D. K10x	D. Qx		
C. AKQxxxx	C. xx		

Opener warns responder of a very long club suit and no interest in spades. Responder gets the message!

The Jump Raise

The jump raise promises four card support and 16-18 support points. Hands in this category often begin as minimum hands, but are happily converted to intermediate hands because of a newly found fit.

(1)	S. AK76	(2)	S. KJ87	(3)	S. A1076
	H. 2		H. 4		H. ---
	D. AQ1098		D. AK76		D. KQ765
	C. 543		C. K654		C. K432

All of these hands are minimum opening bids of 1D. If partner responds 1H they remain minimum openings and rebid 1S.

However, if the response is 1S reevaluation takes place. Hand (1) is now worth 16 points in support of spades (13 H.C.P. plus three for the singleton). Hand (2) is worth 17 points and Hand (3) 17 also (five for the void). The rebid in each case is 3S. This is not forcing and responder can pass with a total count of seven or less.

The Jump Rebid

A jump rebid promises a six or seven card suit and a <u>total hand evaluation of 16-18 points</u>.

<pre>
     (1) S. 5   (2) S. 54   (3) S. AQJ10742
          H. A65   H. A4   H. K3
          D. AKJ1076   D. AK6   D. K92
          C. K65   C. KQ10976   C. 2
             (17)   (18)   (16)
</pre>

Hand (1)   Opens 1D and jumps to 3D over any response.

Hand (2)   Opens 1C and jumps to 3C over any response except possibly 1S in which case the alternate jump rebid of 2NT is slightly preferable with both unbid suits stopped.

Hand (3)   Opens 1S and jumps to 3S over any response.

Bidding a New Suit

Earlier, when discussing minimum hands in the 12-15 point range, we mentioned there was an overlap with the 16-18 point hands when opener bids a new suit at the one level or a lower ranking suit at the two level. However, if opener bids a new suit at the three level or a new <u>higher</u> ranking suit at the two level, there is a different type of overlap. <u>No longer can opener be minimum</u>. He must have either an intermediate or powerful-type opening bid. The ear must be in tune to these sequences.

Opener	Responder
1H	2D
3C	

Opener is either intermediate or powerful.

Opener	Responder
1H	2C
2S	

Same as above.

Opener	Responder
1H	2C
2D	

Opener is either minimum or intermediate.

These rules force the opener to do some calculating before mentioning the
second suit. For example:

```
S. AK765
H. 43
D. AJ87
C. 54
```

Open 1S and over 2C rebid 2D but over 2H rebid 2S.

Notice that opener can show his diamond suit at the two level (a lower
ranking suit at the two level does not promise extra strength) but cannot
show a new suit at the three level without promising at least an intermediate type hand. Therefore, opener must reconcile himself to not always being able to show his second suit.

This is the most typical case:

```
S. A4
H. KQJ7
D. A6543
C. 43
```

With a 1D opening bid and a 1S or 2C response opener must not mention his
heart suit (a new higher ranking suit at the two level shows at least an
intermediate type hand). He is, therefore, compelled to rebid either his
anemic diamond suit or 1NT over 1S with a slight deficit in the club de-
partment.

The alternate method of handling touching two-suited hands that are not
strong enough to show the higher ranking suit at the two level is to open
1H and rebid 2D over a black suit response. This has the advantage of bidding both suits but the disadvantage of having partner think the hearts are
longer.

Authorities have argued for years over which is the better opening. Here
is a vote for 1H if the suit is strong.

```
Another typical case:    Opener   S. 5
                                  H. AJ876
                                  D. K4
                                  C. KJ876
```

Opener begins with 1H and over a 1S or a 1NT response has an easy rebid of 2C. However, if responder says 2D, opener dare not show clubs for fear of telling responder he has an intermediate hand. He must simply rebid 2H, hoping to get another chance to show clubs. If, for example, responder rebids 2NT, opener bids 3C secure that responder cannot place him with a big hand because opener has previously limited himself with his 2H rebid.

Rebidding the Powerhouse Hand   (19-21)

Hands in this category insist upon game if partner even whispers a response. They either:

- (1) Jump to game in partner's suit.
- (2) Jump shift.
- (3) Bid a new suit after a two level response, without jumping, to obtain more information at a lower level.
- (4) Jump to game in the original suit (usually a major).
- (5) Jump to 3NT.

Jump to Game in Partner's Suit

When your hand reevaluates to 19-21 points in support of partner's suit you may take him directly from one to four. This is not a shutout but slam invitational.

Open 1D and raise a 1S response to four with each of the following hands:

(1)	(2)	(3)	(4)
S. AK76	S. KQ76	S. AKJ8	S. KJ98
H. K4	H. 2	H. 32	H. 2
D. AKQ76	D. AK7654	D. AKJ7	D. AQ54
C. 54	C. KJ	C. K87	C. AQ54

The Jump Shift and the Simple Change of Suit
by Opener with 19-20 H.C.P.

The jump shift is simply a jump in a new suit to force the bidding to game. If opener has a 19-20 point unbalanced hand he is forced to make a jump shift after a <u>one level</u> response if he wants to be sure and hear his partner's sweet voice again.

After a two level response a jump shift is optional <u>as any new suit is</u> <u>forcing</u>.

	(1)	S. AK76	(2)	S. AKJ87	(3)	S. A4
		H. AK		H. AK87		H. AK87
		D. 54		D. A4		D. AKJ87
		C. AQ765		C. 54		C. 54

Hand (1)   Opens 1C and over a one level response in a red suit jump shifts to 2S.

Hand (2)   Opens 1S and over 1NT jumps to 3H. Over a two level response opener may elect not to "show the points" but alternately try to find out more about partner's hand by simply rebidding a <u>forcing</u> 2H.

Hand (3)   Opens 1D and over a 1S or a 2C response rebids 2H. A new suit by opener is forcing over a two level response and a new higher ranking suit at the two level by opener is forcing after a one level response (See Chapter on Reverse Bidding). Remember that the idea is to keep the bidding as low as possible until a fit is found. Jumping is simply done to insure that partner will not pass. If he cannot pass it is usually wiser not to jump.

The Jump to Game in the Original Suit

This type of rebid generally shows an excellent six card or more often a seven card suit and 19-20 points. In other words, a hand just shy of a forcing two opening bid. It is not a shutout.

	(1)	S. Q4	(2)	S. AKJ8763
		H. AKJ10876		H. A
		D. 2		D. Q108
		C. AQ2		C. K4

Hand (1)   Open 1H and rebid 4H over any response.

Hand (2)   Open 1S and rebid 4S over any response.

Quiz on Opener's Rebid

I. Assume you open 1C on each of the following five hands. What is your rebid over 1D, 1H, 1S or 1NT from partner?

(1) S. A2
     H. AJ4
     D. 765
     C. KQ765

(2) S. AJ7
     H. Q2
     D. 65
     C. KQ9876

(3) S. AK87
     H. 65
     D. AK
     C. AJ876

(4) S. KQ76
     H. 76
     D. A6
     C. AJ1076

(5) S. 4
     H. Q987
     D. A87
     C. AKJ87

II. Assume you open 1D on each of the following five hands. What is your rebid over 1H, 1S, 1NT or 2C?

(1) S. 54
     H. AKJ6
     D. AKQ76
     C. J10

(2) S. AJ7
     H. 65
     D. AJ1076
     C. KQ4

(3) S. AJ8
     H. 54
     D. AKJ987
     C. K5

(4) S. 2
     H. AJ98
     D. AKQ1087
     C. K4

(5) S. 76
     H. K4
     D. AKQJ8
     C. AQJ6

III. Assume you open 1H with each of the following five hands. What is your rebid over 1S, 1NT, 2C or 2D?

(1) S. 2
     H. AQ10765
     D. K76
     C. K76

(2) S. 76
     H. AKJ1076
     D. AQ10
     C. 65

(3) S. 5
     H. AJ876
     D. AQ87
     C. K76

(4) S. 4
     H. KQ107
     D. A987
     C. A987

(5) S. KQ5
     H. AJ1076
     D. 54
     C. A108

IV. Assume you open the following five hands with 1S. What is your rebid if partner responds 1NT, 2C, 2D or 2H?

(1) S. AK764
     H. 65
     D. A87
     C. KJ8

(2) S. AK876
     H. K6
     D. Q87
     C. K87

(3) S. AKJ9876
     H. 2
     D. KQ4
     C. A3

		S. AKJ87			S. QJ876
(4)		H. 5	(5)		H. 54
		D. 54			D. AKJ76
		C. AKJ76			C. 3

Solutions to Rebid Quiz by Opener (Reading Across)

PART I.	(1)	1C-1D 1NT	1C-1H 2H	1C-1S 1NT	1C-1NT Pass
	(2)	1C-1D 2C	1C-1H 2C	1C-1S 2S	1C-1NT 2C
	(3)	1C-1D 2S	1C-1H 2S	1C-1S 4S	1C-1NT 2S or 3NT
	(4)	1C-1D 1S	1C-1H 1S	1C-1S 3S	1C-1NT Pass
	(5)	1C-1D 1H	1C-1H 3H	1C-1S 2C	1C-1NT 2C

PART II.	(1)	1D-1H 4H	1D-1S 2H	1D-1NT 2H	1D-2C 2H
	(2)	1D-1H 1NT	1D-1S 2S	1D-1NT Pass	1D-2C 3C
	(3)	1D-1H *2NT	1D-1S 3D	1D-1NT 3NT	1D-2C 3D
	(4)	1D-1H 4H	1D-1S 2H	1D-1NT **2H	1D-2C 2H
	(5)	1D-1H 3C	1D-1S 3C	1D-1NT 3C	1D-2C 4C

*Or possibly 3D.

**Show the four card suit before rebidding the six card
suit with intermediate or powerful opening bids. With
minimum hands rebid the six card suit and then show the
four if you have another opportunity.

PART III.	(1)	1H-1S 2H	1H-1NT 2H	1H-2C 2H	1H-2D 2H
	(2)	1H-1S 3H	1H-1NT 3H	1H-2C 3H	1H-2D 3H
	(3)	1H-1S 2D	1H-1NT 2D	1H-2C 2D	1H-2D *3D
	(4)	1H-1S **2C	1H-1NT 2C	1H-2C ***2D	1H-2D ****3C
	(5)	1H-1S 2S	1H-1NT Pass	1H-2C *****3C	1H-2D ******2NT

61

PART III.   *With borderline hands be careful about bypassing 3NT
                 with a jump to 4D over 2D.

                 **With three four card suits opener should bid the next
                 suit up the line if partner responds in the singleton
                 suit.

                 ***Intending to support clubs later and thus show a single-
                 ton spade. A direct raise to 3C is also acceptable.

                 ****Intending to support diamonds and thereby show a single-
                 ton spade. A direct raise is also possible. (For the
                 life of me, I do not know why I construct hands to which
                 I don't know the answers!)

                 *****A rebid of 2H is also acceptable because the heart suit
                 is so strong. Take away the ten of hearts and substi-
                 tute a smaller one and a raise to 3C would clearly be
                 better.

                 ******This bid is supposed to show 15-17 H.C.P., but this
                 hand is equivalent with the ten spots.

PART IV.   (1)   1S-1NT   *1S-2C   *1S-2D   *1S-2H
                        Pass   3C   3D   2NT

            (2)   1S-1NT   *1S-2C   *1S-2D   *1S-2H
                        Pass   2NT   2NT   2NT

            (3)   1S-1NT   1S-2C   1S-2D   1S-2H
                        4S   4S   4S   4S

            (4)   1S-1NT   1S-2C   1S-2D   1S-2H
                      **2-1/2C   4C   3C   3C

            (5)   1S-1NT   1S-2C   1S-2D   ***1S-2H
                        2D   2D   3D   2S

          *If partner has three spades he must show delayed sup-
          port, so there is no worry about missing a spade con-
          tract.

          **Between 2C and 3C. 3C is probably better. (If only
          we could bid in fractions!)

          ***Not strong enough to show the second suit at the three
          level.

62.

Rebid by the Opener After a Limited Response

(Hand Reevaluation)

Whenever responder supports opener's suit or responds no trump he limits his hand. Opener becomes captain. Let's consider each possibility separately.

Responder Bids 1NT

If responder bids either one or two no trump, opener remains in no trump with all balanced hands. The scale goes something like this:

After a 1NT response showing 6-9 H.C.P.:

Opener passes with 15 or less.

Opener raises to 2NT with 17-18.

Opener raises to 3NT with 19-20.

If opener has precisely 16 and has not opened 1NT he must judge whether to pass or raise to 2NT. The deciding factor is the strength of opener's five card suit. If it has good intermediate cards (nines and tens), raise; if not, pass.

If opener has a six card suit he either rebids it, jump rebids it, or in some cases continues on in no trump!

	South	North
	1S	1NT
	?	

(1)	S. AJ10876	(2)	S. KQ10976	(3)	S. AKQ876
	H. K4		H. AK4		H. 107
	D. A54		D. KJ7		D. A7
	C. 54		C. 2		C. Q42

Hand (1)   Rebids 2S.

Hand (2)   Rebids 3S.

Hand (3)   Has a no trump spade suit. (A no trump suit is one which will take the same number of tricks in no trump as in a suit.) As it is easier to take nine tricks than ten, one often gambles on 2NT or even 3NT with hands like this. With a seven trick hand such as this 2NT is probably best. Change the queen of

clubs to the ace and a raise to 3NT is better as the hand

has eight fast taking tricks.

Responder Bids 2NT

This response is forcing to game and shows a balanced hand with 13-15 H.C.P.

If opener has a balanced hand he should not rebid his five card suit.

S. AK765   Open 1S and if partner responds 2NT raise to 3NT.
H. 54
D. K76   Do not rebid the spades!
C. QJ8
             A spade rebid here shows a six card suit.

With balanced hands opener follows this scale:

    With 12-17 raise to 3NT

    With 18-19 raise to 4NT

    With 20-21 raise to 6NT

With unbalanced hands - hands containing either a six card suit, two five

card suits or a 5-4-3-1 hand - opener rebids his six card suit or shows his

second suit before committing the hand to no trump.

S. AJ876   Open 1S and rebid 3D over 2NT.
H. 4
D. AK76   Do not rebid 3S!
C. J87

S. 65   Open 1H. If partner responds 2NT, rebid 3H to show a six card
H. AQ8765
D. K5   suit. Partner can now raise with a doubleton if he wishes.
C. K76

One slight problem creeps up from time to time. If opener has four spades

and four hearts and responder has four hearts a four-four heart fit may be

missed. Therefore, opener can, if he wishes, rebid 3H over 2NT with 4-4 in

the majors. Responder will then raise to 4H with four card support or pre-

fer spades with three card support in which case opener simply retreats to

3NT. Responder is not allowed to insist upon game in spades with only

three card support in this sequence.

Opener	Responder	Opener	Responder
S. KQ76	S. 84	1S	2NT
H. AK87	H. Q1053	3H	4H
D. 54	D. A107	Pass	
C. Q65	C. AK52		

Opener	Responder	Opener	Responder
S. AJ65	S. K42	1S	2NT
H. KQ87	H. A53	3H	3S
D. A76	D. K98	3NT	Pass
C. 43	C. QJ52		

Responder Bids 3NT   (16-17 H.C.P.)

This is by far the most awkward of all the no trump responses. Opener is secure with a balanced hand because the bidding will remain in no trump, opener using the following scale:

　　With 12-15 pass.

　　With 16+ insist upon some sort of slam usually by bidding 6NT.

In this sequence 4NT by opener over 3NT is Blackwood. Otherwise devious methods must be employed to ask for aces.

With weak unbalanced hands opener either rebids a six card suit or shows the second suit. With strong unbalanced hands opener jumps in the six card suit or jumps in the second suit in order to make a forcing bid.

Opener	Responder	Meaning of Opener's Last Bid
1S	3NT	Blackwood - one of the rare cases where 4NT is
4NT		Blackwood when no suit has been agreed on.

Opener	Responder	
1S	3NT	Minimum hand with six card suit.
4S		Responder will normally pass.

Opener	Responder	
1S	3NT	Natural and forcing. Responder cannot as yet tell
4C, 4D		how strong opener is. This is a tough sequence.

Opener	Responder	Meaning of Opener's Last Bid
1S	3NT	Responder can pass this sequence.
4H		

Opener	Responder	
1S	3NT	Forcing to slam.
5H		

Opener	Responder	
1S	3NT	Highly invitational. Shows a powerful spade suit
5S		and little else.

Responder Raises Opener's Suit

There is almost no such animal as a hand that does not improve once partner supports your suit. The question is "how much"?

Once either player can be assured of at least an eight card fit readjustments are made.

Let's take a sample hand:

S. AJ876
H. 4
D. AK76
C. 765

Opener	Responder
1S	2S
?	

Originally opener adds his H.C.P. (12) to his distributional points (1) and arrives at a count of 13 points. This incidentally, is what we call a "good" 13 point hand. Why? Because the honor cards are in the long suits, they are in combination with each other and the distribution is attractive.

Change the jack of spades to the jack of clubs:

S. A8765
H. 4
D. AK76
C. J54

and the hand is weaker.

In any event when partner supports a suit so that you are assured at least an eight card fit this is what you should do:

In addition to your original count (H.C.P. plus long suit points):

Add one point for each doubleton (but don't add anything if
your distribution is 5-3-3-2).

Add two points for each singleton.

Add three points for each void.

Eliminate all unsupported jacks from your counting: Jx, Jxx, Jxxx.

Eliminate unsupported queens from your counting if the opponents
have bid the suit.

Now if the opponents haven't left the table while you were doing all of
this calculating you should have a fairly accurate reevaluation.

Practice time. Assume you have opened each of the following hands with 1H
and partner raises you to 2H, what point count do you have after all of
your Einstein-type calculations?

(1)	S. 4	(2)	S. 76	(3)	S. AJ87	(4)	S. 6
	H. AK7654		H. AK876		H. KQ9874		H. AQ876
	D. A43		D. J4		D. 54		D. Q2
	C. Q87		C. KQ76		C. A		C. AK876

Hand (1)   Originally worth 15 points; after support worth 17 points.
(You have added two points for the singleton.)

Hand (2)   Originally 14 points (doubleton jacks are counted - reluctantly);
after reevaluation 15 points. You have two doubletons but the
jack loses its identity.

Hand (3)   Originally 16 points; after reevaluation 19 points. You are adding one point for the doubleton and two for the singleton.

Hand (4)   Originally 17 points; after reevaluation 20 points. However, if
one or both opponents have bid diamonds do not count the queen.

Now that you have reevaluated your hand after you have been supported, follow this scale:

With 15 or less   Pass.

With 16-17   Make a game try (new suit or three of agreed suit).

With 18 or more   Insist upon game. New suit or game in agreed suit.
(Responder assumes a new suit is a game try. A new
suit is, of course, forcing for one round.)

One last problem when reevaluating a hand that has received support...
hands that have four card suits!

```
S. AK76
H. AQ76
D. K876
C. 2
```

You open 1S and partner responds 2S. You are not assured of an eight card
fit and it is difficult to evaluate the hand. My rule is this:

If you open a four card major suit and receive a single raise do not bid
again unless you have at least 16 H.C.P. In the example hand bid again.
Rebid 3H in case partner has four or five hearts and only three spades.

However, if after a 1S opening your partner responds 3S showing four card
support you can reevaluate your hand as previously discussed because you
are assured of an eight card fit.

Summary: If the bidding has indicated an eight card fit use the 1-2-3
short suit count in addition to your established count to determine the
new value of your hand. This can be done by either opener or responder.

You hold:
```
S. KJ10742
H. 2
D. Q1098
C. 65
```

Partner opens 1NT. You are assured of an eight card spade fit which means
your hand is worth 11 points with spades trump, (originally 6+2) and now 3
extra (one for the doubleton and two for the singleton) once the fit has
been established. Jump to 4S! Now all you have to do is make it.

> BUT: If the bidding indicates that your long suit will not be trump,
> deduct your long suit points completely. Misfitted hands count
> NEITHER FOR LONG NOR SHORT SUITS.

Tips for the Opener on the Rebid

1. Try and limit your hand as quickly as possible if partner makes an unlimited response.
2. Avoid rebidding five card minor suits and weak five card major suits.

3. Supporting partner's suit, rebidding no trump, and showing a second suit all take precedence over rebidding the original five card suit.

4. Understand that when you show two suits at the level of one or a lower ranking suit at the level of two you are not necessarily showing extra values. You could be minimum or you could have as much as 17-18.

5. If you bid a new suit at the three level or a higher ranking second suit at the two level you must have at least 17. This is called a "reverse" and it constitutes a one round force after a one level response and a game force after a two level response.

6. 4-4-4-1 hands open the suit beneath the singleton. If partner responds in the singleton suit bid the next suit up the line. Do not rebid no trump unless you open 1H holding a singleton ace, king or queen of spades. With a singleton club open 1S but rebid 2H rather than 2D if partner responds 1NT or 2C. It is important not to miss the heart fit.

7. If responder makes a limited response you are the captain. You should be able to place the hand in either the part-score, game, or slam zone by adding the two hands together.

8. If your rebid has shown the strength of your hand let your partner carry the ball from there. Too many players constantly bid the same values over and over forgetting that they have already told partner their story.

9. Do not jump raise partner's original suit without four trumps, but tend to raise an original response in a major as quickly as possible with three card support.

10. One of the nastiest of all rebid problems arises when opener has forgotten to open 1NT with a balanced 16-18 or 15 with a strong five card suit. Do not let this happen to you.

4. REBID BY THE RESPONDER

The responder's rebid, if there is one, depends upon the following:

    (1) Did the responder limit himself on his original response or is he still unlimited as far as opener is concerned?

    (2) Did opener limit himself on his rebid or did he bid two suits which, as we have seen, can show a wide variety of strength?

    (3) Is partner's last bid forcing? Is the partnership in the midst of a forcing sequence?

Rebid by the Responder if He Has Previously Limited Himself

The most common limited responses are 1NT, 2NT, 3NT, single raises, double raises and triple raises. Theoretically you have told your entire hand in one bid and partner is captain. Yet partner can transfer the captaincy back to you by inquiring whether your limited response was at the top or bottom of the range.

For example, when you respond 1NT you have limited yourself to 6-9 H.C.P. But partner may want to know whether it is six or seven (minimum for your previous bidding) or eight or nine (maximum for your previous bidding).

Sequences such as this:

Opener	Responder
1S	1NT
2NT	?

Responder bids 3NT with a maximum; passes with a minimum.

Another example:

Opener	Responder
1S	2S
3S	?

With a count of seven or eight responder passes. But with nine or ten, responder bids game.

If you have limited yourself with a double raise opener will either pass or bid game in the major. What if he bids another suit?

Opener	Responder
1S	3S
4D	

Opener cannot want to know whether responder is minimum or maximum because he has already committed the hand to game. Opener is clearly making a slam try. Responder must now evaluate his hand for slam purposes paying particular attention to his diamond holding. For example, the diamond king would be a very valuable card on this bidding whereas the club king may not.

If you have limited yourself with 2NT and partner bids another suit he is also trying to tell you something:

Opener	Responder
1S	2NT
3C	?

Do not plunge automatically into 3NT if you have either three card spade support or a doubtful stopper in either red suit. Give spade preference if you have it, or bid your stronger red suit to avoid a bad no trump contract.

Opener	Responder (1)	Responder (2)	Responder (3)
S. AQ943	S. J76	S. K4	S. K4
H. Q65	H. A932	H. J432	H. AK109
D. 2	D. AJ3	D. AK106	D. J432
C. AK108	C. QJ7	C. Q32	C. Q32

Opener	Responder (1)	
1S	2NT	Responder gives preference.
3C	3S	
4S	Pass	

Opener	Responder (2)	
1S	2NT	Assured of diamond strength opener
3C	3D	plays no trump. Opener has already
3NT	Pass	shown five spades the moment he bid

3C so he need not repeat the suit. (With four clubs and four spades the hand is opened 1C.)

Opener	Responder (3)
1S	2NT
3C	3H
4H	Pass

When responder bids 3H, opener knows responder is strong in hearts and not too hot in diamonds, therefore no trump must be a bad proposition. Responder already knows opener has five spades and four clubs and a cardinal rule of the game is not to repeat something partner already knows. Opener raises to 4H and hopes for the best. (Responder knows opener has only three hearts as he would have rebid 3H over 2NT with a four card suit.)

Rebid by the Responder if He Has
Not Previously Limited Himself

An unlimited responder may have made an original new suit response at either the one or two level. Opener only knows responder's minimum point count so the rebid must clarify if possible.

If the First Unlimited Response
Was Made at the One Level

For the sake of discussion let's assume the bidding has started in either of these two ways:

(1) Opener	Responder		(2) Opener	Responder
1D	1H		1D	1H
2D	?		1S	?

Sequence (1) Opener has limited himself and responder is, temporarily at least, the captain.

Sequence (2) Opener is, for practical purposes, unlimited so responder is going to try to limit his hand first.

72

A one level responder should mentally subdivide his hand into these divisions:

The weak unlimited hand 6-10 points.

The intermediate unlimited hand 11-13 points.

The game going unlimited hand 13-16 points.

The slam invitational unlimited hand 17-19 points.

The certain slam hand 19-21 points.

Each of these categories is going to have overlaps. It is inevitable. The factors involved that are going to influence the rebid aside from the point count are:

(1) Is the hand a fit or a misfit?

(2) Are your high cards in partner's suit or not?

(3) Do you have any wasted honor cards? (Those queens and jacks again and misplaced kings under a bidder.)

(4) The vulnerability.

(5) Is there a part score?

(6) How good are your opponents?

(7) How bad is your partner? The best contract in the world will go down if your partner doesn't know how to play it.

The Unlimited Responding Hand in the 6-10 Range

This type of hand does not necessarily bid again but if it does it must make a weak rebid.

(1) By making a simple rebid in the same suit.

Opener	Responder	Opener	Responder
S. 4	S. KJ10765	1H	1S
H. AK832	H. 54	2C	2S
D. 1084	D. Q76	Pass	
C. AQ73	C. 54		

A simple rebid shows a six card suit (or a very strong five card suit) and a weak hand.

(2) By taking simple preference back to opener's first suit.

Opener	Responder		Opener	Responder
S. J	S. K8765		1D	1S
H. A63	H. 54		2C	2D
D. KQ432	D. 876		Pass	
C. KJ43	C. A65			

(3) By rebidding 1NT if it is still possible.

Opener	Responder		Opener	Responder
S. QJ43	S. A108		1D	1H
H. 52	H. K1076		1S	1NT
D. AK876	D. 43		Pass	
C. K4	C. J976			

The 1NT rebid by the responder generally shows 7-9 H.C.P. There are some 6 or 10 H.C.P. hands that also rebid 1NT but one never assumes an exception. Play your partner for 7-9 H.C.P. on this sequence.

(4) By raising partner's second suit (a major) to the two level.

Opener	Responder		Opener	Responder
S. AQ32	S. K876		1D	1H
H. Q5	H. A1087		1S	2S
D. KJ987	D. 54		Pass	
C. 104	C. J76			

This raise is almost identical in strength to an original raise from 1S to 2S with one gigantic exception. IT GUARANTEES FOUR CARD SUPPORT. A DIRECT RAISE OF ANY SECOND SUIT BY EITHER PLAYER PROMISES FOUR CARD SUPPORT.

(5) By passing. The responder is allowed to pass at his second opportunity if:

    (a) The opener has not made a forcing rebid.

    (b) The responder is minimum and the last bid by the opener leaves the partnership in a reasonable contract (at least seven trumps).

(1) Opener	Responder		Opener	Responder
S. A5	S. K876		1C	1D
H. KQ7	H. 43		1NT	Pass
D. 1076	D. QJ98			
C. KQ432	C. J87			

However if opener's rebid had been 2H, a jump shift forcing to game, responder would have to go on and would rebid 2NT.

(2) Opener	Responder	Opener	Responder
S. 2	S. A10765	1D	1S
H. 1098	H. 765	2C	Pass
D. AK864	D. J7		
C. A943	C. J108		

Reverse the diamonds and clubs and responder would give simple preference to 2D.

The Unlimited Responding Hand in the 10-13 Range

Hands in this range invariably make at least two bids.

If opener's rebid has shown a minimum hand responder invites game. If opener's rebid has shown an intermediate hand responder insists upon game. If opener's rebid has shown a powerful hand a slam is possible if the hand fits.

What are the most common rebids in the 10-13 range?

(1) A jump rebid.

Opener	Responder	Opener	Responder
S. 2	S. AQ10876	1H	1S
H. QJ876	H. K5	2C	3S
D. A32	D. J107	Pass	
C. KQ98	C. 32		

A jump rebid is invitational and can only be passed by an opener who is both minimum and misfitted. It promises a six card suit, possibly seven, never five.

(2) A jump preference.

Opener	Responder	Opener	Responder
S. J2	S. KQ765	1H	1S
H. KQ1043	H. A87	2D	3H
D. AKJ5	D. Q65	4H	Pass
C. 98	C. 32		

A jump preference to the three level in a major suit guarantees three card support. Never four. After a one level response a jump

preference is not forcing. (Except: a jump preference to 3C after a
1D response is considered forcing.)

(3) Two No Trump

Opener	Responder	Opener	Responder
S. Q7	S. KJ8	1D	1H
H. 98	H. A7654	2C	2NT
D. K9732	D. J4	Pass	
C. AK74	C. Q98		

The rebid of 2NT, a common rebid, is not forcing, simply invitational.
It can show as little as 10 H.C.P.

A jump rebid to 2NT shows the same hand:

Opener	Responder
1D	1H
1S	2NT (10-13)

If the responder has only 10 H.C.P. he should have a five card suit.
With a weakish looking 10 point hand responder is better advised to
make the more conservative rebid of 1NT. With 13 responder might
also jump rebid 3NT. However with a singleton in opener's first
suit and a hand weak in intermediate cards, a more conservative
course usually works best.

(4) A jump raise of partner's major suit to the three level or a single
raise of partner's second suit (a minor) to the three level.

(1) Opener	Responder	Opener	Responder
S. KQ76	S. AJ98	1C	1H
H. A2	H. KJ98	1S	3S
D. 75	D. 43	4S	Pass
C. KQ983	C. J107		

The jump to 3S in this sequence normally shows 11-12 or an "ugly"
13 support points. Naturally, it guarantees four trumps. It is
not forcing.

(2) Opener	Responder	Opener	Responder
S. 2	S. AK87	1H	1S
H. QJ1032	H. 54	2C	3C
D. AJ2	D. 654	3NT	Pass
C. AK76	C. QJ85		

This single raise in a minor to the three level is the equivalent
of the double raise to the three level in a major. It shows 10-13

support points and is invitational to 3NT. It goes without saying
that it guarantees four card support.

(5) The bid of a new suit. This is a luxury not afforded the unlimited
responding hand in the weakest category.* However there are some
hands in the 10-13 zone that still cannot limit themselves accurately.
These hands must bid a new suit and wait patiently for opener to
limit himself.

Two suited hands fall into this category and semi-balanced hands without a stopper in the unbid suit often find themselves stranded here.

Opener	Responder	(1) Responder
1C	1S	S. AJ987
2C	2D	H. 54
		D. KQ1076
		C. 2

A new suit by the responder is unlimited and the presumption is at
least a 10 point hand although it is frequently more.

Opener	Responder	(2) Responder
1H	1S	S. AQ765
2C	?	H. Q8
		D. 876
		C. K87

Now with all the ways we have of showing hands in this point range
we still have troubles! What in the world is responder supposed to
do with this hand at this point? A jump rebid in spades shows a
six card suit. A rebid of 2NT promises at least one stopper in diamonds - the unbid suit. A raise in clubs promises four card support.
A jump preference in hearts promises three card support.

*Only one exception here:	Opener	Responder
	1C	1D
	1H	1S

In this one sequence responder may have as little as 8 or 9 points
checking out a possible 4-4 spade fit if opener happens to be 4-4-1-4.
Of course 1NT is an alternative which limits the hand immediately.

What to do?

With this type of hand the expert falls back on good old "fourth suit forcing". He actually rebids 2D! Not because he wants to, mind you, but because he has to! He cannot conveniently limit himself.

Perhaps bids like this should be left to the experts but it can't hurt to know what they do when they actually pick up these hands. In general, bidding the fourth suit holding nothing but two or three small cards should be avoided if there is any reasonable alternative - at least until your partner becomes as expert a bidder as you!

The Unlimited Responding Hand in the 13-16 Range

These hands insist upon game no matter how minimum opener is. The responder has various simple techniques of making sure the hand plays in game. He can:

(1) Bid game in his own major suit if it is self-sufficient - usually a
    seven card suit but conceivably a strong six carder.

Opener	Responder	Opener	Responder
S. 2	S. AJ109764	1D	1S
H. 1098	H. K4	2C	4S
D. AQ862	D. K43	Pass	
C. AK43	C. 2		
S. KQ76	S. 5	1D	1H
H. 102	H. AKQ987	1S	4H
D. KQ987	D. A6		
C. K3	C. 10762		

And there you are - in game. Now all you have to do is make it. (Minor suited hands in this range often try for no trump rather than five of a minor.)

(2) Jump to game in partner's original major suit. This is called
    a "delayed game raise" and is discussed under "limit raises".

Opener	Responder	Opener	Responder
S. 4	S. AK876	1H	1S
H. J10743	H. AQ65	2C	4H
D. A98	D. 43	Pass	
C. AQJ6	C. 54		

The delayed jump to game in a minor is a rarity to say the least.

Opener	Responder
1C	1D
1H	5C

Among other things it prevents opener from using Blackwood. Later, when we discuss jump shifts and forcing sequences we shall see how to avoid this problem in a minor with a good hand.

(3) Jump directly to 3NT.

Opener	Responder		Opener	Responder
S. 2	S. AKJ5		1H	1S
H. A9832	H. 54		2C	3NT
D. KQ	D. AJ98		Pass	
C. KJ843	C. 765			

A second round jump to 3NT shows approximately the same strength as an original jump to 2NT. If responder has two four card suits it is preferable to rebid no trump rather than show the second four card suit. A 2D rebid over 2C would be incorrect.

(4) Bid a new suit.

This is the old stand-by when the hand cannot be accurately limited or the hand has such distributional potential that it would take three bids to describe it accurately.

Opener	Responder	Responder
1H	1S	S. AK765
2C	?	H. A76
		D. K876
		C. 2

Responder rebids 2D and then supports hearts thus showing a singleton club. Hands in this range do lots of distributional bidding because they are strong enough to handle the situation.

Incidentally, responder has no other available rebid anyway. A jump preference to 3H is not forcing and a delayed game raise to 4H guarantees four trumps. Responder must use the indirect approach with this as well as many other good hands that contain a singleton or void.

Opener	Responder	Responder
1H	1S	S. AK765
2D, 2H	3C	H. 5
		D. 54
		C. AQ765

A second suit by the responder might also be the beginning of a power-ful two suiter. If responder bids a new suit at the three level the hand must play in game.

(5) Jump in a new suit.

Opener	Responder	Responder
1D	1S	S. AKJ76
2C, 2D	3H	H. AQJ87
		D. 54
		C. 2

A second round jump from a higher ranking suit to a lower ranking suit beneath 3NT shows a strong five-five hand and is one of the very few times opener can support the second suit directly with only three trumps.

Stronger responding hands are dealt with in the chapter on Jump Shifts.

Rebids by the Unlimited Two Over One Responder

Once the previous section has been absorbed the following should be rela-tively easy. In the preceding examples responder made an unlimited bid at the one level.

If, however, the responder's first unlimited bid is made at the two level there is less to worry about for both parties. Responder is known to have at least 10 H.C.P. so the problem of the weak responding hand is non-existent.

Furthermore most hands in the 16+ category jump shift originally so what we are really dealing with when responder makes an original two over one response are hands in the 10-15 or 10-16 point range.

We subdivide these into only two categories: 10/11-13 and 13-16.

Notice that 13 point hands are borderline. Similarly, 16 point hands are borderline jump shifts.

The Rebid by the Responder Who Has Made an
Unlimited Response at the Two Level with 10-13

Since responder has already shown at least 10 H.C.P., he doesn't have to do too much more aggressive bidding. What does he do?

(1) Rebids his own suit.

This promises a six or seven card suit and is the only time responder is allowed into the two level with less than 10 H.C.P. After a two level response, the rebid of the original suit is the closest bid to a sign off that the responder has at his disposal.

Opener	Responder		Opener	Responder
S. KQ1084	S. 6		1S	2C
H. K4	H. J543		2D	3C
D. AJ76	D. K4		Pass	
C. 32	C. AJ10876			

The range of this particular sequence is 8-9-10 H.C.P.

(2) Takes partner back to his original suit at the cheapest possible level.

Opener	Responder		Opener	Responder
S. KQ742	S. A65		1S	2D
H. QJ32	H. 54		2H	2S
D. 2	D. KQJ76		Pass	
C. KJ7	C. 543			

Simple preference after a two level response normally shows three card support, never four, possibly a doubleton honor, and is not forcing. (With four card support a limit raise is given.) Opener usually continues bidding with 15 or more working points.

(3) Rebids 2NT

Opener	Responder		Opener	Responder
S. J7632	S. A4		1S	2C
H. AKJ9	H. Q76		2H	2NT
D. A2	D. K65		3NT	Pass
C. J5	C. Q10876			

All 2NT rebids by the responder show 10-12 H.C.P. whether the first new suit response was at the one or two level. With an obvious misfit responder might even rebid 2NT with 13 H.C.P. but it would be an exception.

Opener	Responder	Opener	Responder
S. KJ942	S. 5	1S	2C
H. KJ3	H. 10765	2S	2NT
D. J65	D. AK32	Pass	
C. K10	C. AQ54		

This is the time for conservative action. True you have 13 H.C.P. but which suit are you going to develop for tricks? If partner has a touch more than a minimum he will give you 3NT.

(4) Raises partner's first suit to the three level with three card support or raises his second suit to the three level with four card support. Not forcing.

Opener	Responder	Opener	Responder
S. AQJ32	S. K54	1S	2D
H. A76	H. 54	2S	3S
D. 42	D. AK765	4S	Pass
C. K106	C. 543		
S. QJ984	S. 65	1S	2D
H. QJ62	H. A765	2H	3H
D. K5	D. AQ876	Pass	
C. KQ	C. 54		

(5) Bids a new suit if the hand cannot be otherwise limited. Two suiters and good old "fourth suit forcing" enter into the picture here.

Opener	Responder	Responder
1S	2H	S. 2
2S	3D	H. AK1087
		D. AQ1076
		C. 54
1S	2C	S. 76
2D	?	H. 876
		D. A109
		C. AK765

You guessed it. 2H! What else?

(6) Passes.

If responder makes an original two over one response he cannot pass at his next opportunity unless opener rebids his own suit or raises responder's suit to the three level.

Opener	Responder		Opener	Responder
S. AQ9432	S. 65		1S	2D
H. Q2	H. K765		2S	Pass
D. 32	D. KQ765			
C. A72	C. Q4			

Opener	(1) Responder	(2) Responder	Opener	Responder
S. KQ943	S. 5	S. 6	1S	2C
H. 42	H. K765	H. A1065	3C	Pass
D. AK	D. J65	D. QJ106		
C. J1092	C. AQ543	C. K654		

With either of these mangy responding hands pass a single raise. HOWEVER UNDER NO CIRCUMSTANCES MAY A TWO LEVEL RESPONDER PASS IF OPENER CHANGES SUIT OR REBIDS 2NT.

The Unlimited Two Over One Responder with 13-16 Points

This hand, of course, insists on game. The options are:

(1) Jump to game in the first bid suit. (Usually a major.)

Opener	Responder		Opener	Responder
S. AK8632	S. 5		1S	2H
H. 2	H. AQ109765		2S	4H
D. A72	D. K65			
C. 743	C. KJ			

(2) Jump to game in partner's suit

Opener	Responder		Opener	Responder
S. Q109432	S. AJ8		1S	2C
H. A63	H. 54		2S	4S
D. KQ	D. A76			
C. 92	C. KJ876			

or make a jump preference to the three level if partner does not rebid the suit.

Opener	Responder		Opener	Responder
S. KQ932	S. AJ8		1S	2C
H. A2	H. 54		2D	3S
D. KQ104	D. A76		4S	Pass
C. 43	C. KJ876			

A jump preference after a two level response is forcing and shows three card support. With four card support responder jump rebids 4S.

(3) Jump to 3NT.

Opener	Responder
S. Q10762	S. A4
H. A2	H. KQ4
D. AJ109	D. Q76
C. Q3	C. KJ876

Opener	Responder
1S	2C
2D	3NT
Pass	

This is the equivalent of an original 2NT response. It is not a shut out and if opener now bids 4NT it is natural (no suit agreement) showing approximately 17-18 H.C.P.

(4) Bid a new suit.

As ever this shows either a two-suited hand, a three-suited hand or is "fourth suit forcing".

Opener	Responder	Responder
1S	2C	S. A4
2D	2H	H. KQ87
		D. 2
		C. A87654

Responder begins to show the distribution by bidding the hearts intending to rebid clubs on the next round if feasible.

Opener	Responder	Responder
1H	2D	S. 5
2H	3C	H. K5
		D. AJ1087
		C. AQ1087

Opener	Responder	Responder
1S	2C	S. A76
2S	3D	H. 4
		D. KQ65
		C. AQ765

Intending to support spades at the next opportunity to show the single-ton heart.

Opener	Responder	Responder
1S	2C	S. A6
2H	?	H. K76
		D. 432
		C. AQJ87

Here we go again. Responder cannot accurately limit himself so he bids 3D, hoping to hear more about partner's hand.

AFTER FOURTH SUIT FORCING OPENER IS NOT ALLOWED TO BID NO TRUMP WITHOUT A STOPPER IN THE FOURTH SUIT (IN WHICH CASE THE HAND WILL BE PLAYED FROM THE RIGHT SIDE OF THE TABLE) BUT IN AN EMERGENCY THREE SMALL CARDS WILL DO. MERCIFULLY, THE OPPONENTS MAY NOT BE ABLE TO RUN TOO MANY TRICKS IN THAT SUIT AGAINST A NO TRUMP CONTRACT.

Examples of Fourth Suit Forcing Sequences

Opener	Responder	Opener	Responder
S. AQ876	S. K5	1S	2C
H. AJ1076	H. Q53	2H	3D
D. 65	D. 1087	3H	4H
C. 4	C. AKJ43	Pass	

Opener	Responder	Opener	Responder
S. AQ876	S. K3	1S	2C
H. AJ65	H. KQ2	2H	3D
D. K76	D. 532	3NT	Pass
C. 2	C. AJ876		

(5) Jump in a new suit.

This is rare after a two level response as most jump bids would take the hand past 3NT.

Sequences such as this:

Opener	Responder
1S	2C
2S	4H, 4D

have special meanings which are discussed in the chapter on Fragment Bids in another book I have written "Everything You Wanted to Know About Conventions".

Before tackling the next quiz entitled "Rebids by the Responder" here are a few tips to help point you in the right direction.

Tips for the Responder

1. Any new suit by the responder is a one round force unless opener rebids 1NT.

2. With few exceptions responder is duty-bound at some point during the auction to show three card support for partner's major suit opening bid.

3. Responder is expected to distinguish between three and four card major suit support for opener's original suit. With four card support he must either give an immediate raise or a delayed game raise. (Bid a new suit and then jump to game in partner's major on the rebid.)

4. With three cards in each of opener's suits responder must take the opener back to his first suit - even if it means increasing the level.

5. A direct raise of a second suit promises at least four card support.

6. A new suit by the opener is forcing if the first response was in a new suit at the two level. A new suit by the opener is not forcing after a one over one unless it is a reverse which is a one round force.

7. Responder tries to limit himself as quickly as possible, particularly with weak hands. The stronger the hand the less urgent the immediate limitation.

8. With two five card suits respond in the higher ranking suit first.

9. With two or three four card suits respond in the suit nearest in rank to partner's suit.

10. Balanced responding hands try to bid no trump as quickly as possible.

11. If the responding hand has thirteen or more points it is his duty to see the hand plays in game - barring a gigantic misfit.

12. With eleven or twelve points the responder must make at least two bids if his first response was unlimited.

Rebid by Responder Quiz

I. Assume the bidding has proceeded:

Opener	Responder
1D	1H
1S	

What should responder rebid with each of the following hands?

(1) S. AJ76
     H. KQ65
     D. A4
     C. 654

(2) S. 4
     H. AKJ76
     D. 65
     C. AQJ76

(3) S. 87
     H. AQJ10976
     D. J4
     C. A5

(4) S. 76
     H. A10765
     D. 76
     C. QJ87

(5) S. 5
     H. AKJ876
     D. 654
     C. K109

(6) S. K107
     H. AJ976
     D. 54
     C. K108

(7) S. 876
     H. KQ654
     D. 87
     C. J87

(8) S. 8765
     H. Q1087
     D. AQ4
     C. 54

(9) S. 76
     H. AK87
     D. KJ106
     C. 765

(10) S. A76
     H. AJ765
     D. AJ6
     C. 65

II. Assume the bidding has proceeded:

Opener	Responder
1S	2C
2D	?

What should responder rebid with each of the following hands?

(1) S. A105
     H. 76
     D. A98
     C. KQ765

(2) S. AJ76
     H. 76
     D. 87
     C. AKJ87

(3) S. J4
     H. 87
     D. A987
     C. KQ1076

(4) S. 65
     H. K6
     D. 87
     C. KQ109543

(5) S. A76
     H. KQ76
     D. 2
     C. AQ876

(6) S. 105
     H. KQ87
     D. J76
     C. AKJ8

(7) S. 5
     H. K1054
     D. A4
     C. AQJ876

(8) S. 765
     H. AK4
     D. 65
     C. K7654

(9) S. Q4
     H. Q1065
     D. QJ6
     C. A1076

(10) S. 5
     H. AJ6
     D. 54
     C. AKJ10876

Solutions to Rebid by Responder Quiz

Part I. (1) 4S   Promises 13 points and at least four card support.

(2) 3C   2C is acceptable but 3C is better as it describes a strong two suited hand.

(3) 4H

(4) 1NT

(5) 3H   Invitational.

(6) 2NT   Invitational.

(7) Pass Be glad you don't have to play this one.

(8) 2S

(9) 3D   Invitational.

(10) 2C!   Fourth suit forcing. No other bid will limit your hand properly.

Part II. (1) 3S   Jump preference. Forcing to game after a two level response. Promises 3 card support.

(2) 4S   Delayed game raise. Promises four card support.

(3) 3D   Not forcing. Invitational.

(4) 3C   Not forcing. Not even invitational unless opener has extra values including a club fit of sorts.

(5) 2H   Intending to bid spades later to show the singleton diamond. This is known as bidding "around the singleton" and is only done with a very fine responding hand.

(6) 3NT   Not 2H. With a balanced hand bid no trump as quickly as possible.

(7) 2H   3C would be a sign off and there is no rush to bid no trump with such an unbalanced hand.

(8) 2S   No second choice. Your hand is a bit weak for 2NT, the only other possibility.

(9) 2NT   Invitational.

(10) 4C   This was not discussed earlier. A jump to four of responder's original minor is forcing to game as are all jumps that bypass 3NT.

5. DEFENSIVE BIDDING

(THE OVERCALL)

After the opponents have opened the bidding any suit bid by the defending side not in response to a takeout double is termed an overcall. Overcalls like women and their clothing come in all shapes and sizes.

There is the one level overcall, the two level overcall, the intermediate jump overcall (I.J.O.), the weak jump overcall (W.J.O.) and the strong jump overcall (S.J.O.). Help!

Overcalls can be made on four card suits (rarely), five card suits (usually), six card suits, seven card suits and even eight card suits!

Overcalls can be made with as few as 8 H.C.P. and with as many as 15. Can we possibly make sense of all this chaos?

The One Level Overcall

The simple overcall at the one level is the most common method of entering the auction. Because of the more stringent requirements for the takeout double, the overcall is forced into double duty for the defensive side.

A typical one level overcall contains:

    (1) A five card suit.

    (2) A range of 10-15 points.

All of these hands overcall any opening bid with 1S.

S. AK765	S. KQ1087	S. J10876	S. AJ942
H. 43	H. A109	H. AK	H. 43
D. A76	D. 5	D. A652	D. AQ652
C. 543	C. 7653	C. 65	C. 7

The moment we discuss overcalling with six card suits we run into the W.J.O. or I.J.O. problem. For example:

    (1)   S. AJ10876   Assume your right hand opponent opens 1C.
           H. K4
           D. 654
           C. 54

If you are playing W.J.O.'s, which are roughly equivalent to Weak Two Bids, overcall 2S. If, however, you are playing I.J.O.'s, which are roughly equivalent to minimum opening bids (14-16) with good six card suits, over-call 1S.

If you have:

(2) S. AKJ875
    H. AJ5
    D. 54
    C. 63

overcall 2S playing I.J.O.'s as this type of jump overcall promises a strong six card suit and typically 14-16 points. Playing W.J.O.'s, simply overcall 1S and bid spades again later if convenient.

No matter which way you decide to play your jump overcalls you will wish you were playing the other way about half the time. At rubber bridge, I prefer I.J.O.'s; at duplicate, W.J.O.'s - not vulnerable. The superstrong jump overcall is obsolete.

Overcalling at the One Level on a Four Card Suit

Some bridge books will tell you not to overcall on a four card suit... period. Don't believe them. Experts do it repeatedly with wonderful re-sults. The trick is to know when to overcall with a four card suit, when to double and when to pass.

If you do overcall with a four card suit it must be at the one level, the hand must be worth an opening bid, the four card suit should have three of the top five honor cards and the hand must not be suitable for a takeout double or an overcall of 1NT.....AND YOUR PARTNER IS GOING TO ASSUME YOU HAVE A FIVE CARD SUIT.

Assume your right hand opponent opens 1C and you hold each of the following hands:

(1) S. A765	(2) S. KQ108	(3) S. AKJ9	(4) S. AKJ8	(5) S. KQ107
H. A7	H. A765	H. 4	H. K74	H. K4
D. K42	D. KJ7	D. J876	D. Q32	D. A5432
C. Q876	C. 65	C. A765	C. A102	C. 32

Hand (1) Does not have a strong enough four card suit and the hand is not suitable for a takeout doube (too many clubs). Pass.

Hand (2) Doubles rather than overcalls because of the strength of the hand and the fact that support is held for the unbid suits.

Hand (3) Overcalls 1S because the hand is unsuitable for a double with the singleton heart.

Hand (4) Overcalls 1NT to show the strength and distribution.

Hand (5) Overcalls 1S rather than 1D. Hands like this are not strong enough to bid twice so bid your major and hope for a fit.

Overcalling with Two Five Card Suits

The general rule of bidding the higher ranking suit first applies. Over an opening bid of 1D:

	(1)		(2)
	S. K7654		S. 65
	H. AKJ76		H. Q10876
	D. 54		D. 3
	C. 2		C. AKJ87

Bid 1S (see Michael's Cue Bid, page 201) with (1) and 1H with (2).

Responding to a One Level Overcall

Most one level overcalls are, perforce, in major suits and the assumption is that partner has a five card suit. If responder has three card support or longer, a fit has been discovered. Simply raise and tell partner your strength.

(All counts for raising include support points)

Raise from one to two with 7-10 and three or four trumps.

Raise from one to three with 11-14 and four trumps.

Raise from one to four preemptively with four or more trumps, a singleton or void on the side and a hand that would raise an opening bid from one to four.

Cue bid the opponent's suit and raise to three of partner's suit with three trumps and 11-14 points.

Cue bid the opponent's suit and raise partner's suit to game with 15-17 points. This is a slam try and responder can have three or four card support.

Assume the bidding has proceeded: (Neither side vul.)

West	North	East	South
1H	1S	Pass	?

(1) S. AJ876	(2) S. KQ42	(3) S. AJ7	(4) S. KJ84	(5) S. K87
H. 2	H. 54	H. 43	H. 32	H. 54
D. Q10876	D. AK87	D. AK765	D. AQ64	D. A98765
C. 54	C. A76	C. 543	C. 1075	C. 53

Solutions

(1) 4S Just as if partner had opened 1S.

(2) 2H Intending to raise spades to game to differentiate from hand (1) which also raises to game. This differentiation is made for slam purposes. You simply can't bid 4S immediately with both hands (1) and (2).

(3) 2H The cue bid followed by a non-forcing raise to 3S shows this type hand. (A response of 2D would not be forcing.)

(4) 3S Promising 11-14 points with four trump. Notice hand (3) eventually bids 3S but cue bids first to show three card support.

(5) 2S Not 2D. You have found a fit. If you bid diamonds you deny three card spade support.

A New Suit in Response to an Overcall

What does it mean when bidding goes like this?

West	North	East	South
1H	1S	Pass	2C

If South is bidding properly he does not have three card spade support and probably has six clubs. The 2C bid is not forcing and has a range of 8-12 points. If the spade bidder has club support he raises.

92

Typical South hands would be:

(1)	S. 4	(2)	S. 76
	H. A65		H. 7643
	D. Q43		D. 2
	C. QJ10876		C. AKJ876

A Jump in a New Suit in Response to an Overcall

What does it mean when bidding goes like this?

West	North	East	South
1H	1S	Pass	3C

South's jump to 3C is not forcing, simply invitational. It promises a six card suit minimum and 13-16 points. It is a hand that can stand to hear partner bid 3NT and it does not have spade support.

Typical South hands for this sequence would be:

(1)	S. 65	(2)	S. 3
	H. 654		H. J105
	D. A4		D. K4
	C. AKQ765		C. AKJ10982

Overcalls in No Trump

The One No Trump Overcall.

East	South
1D	1NT

South shows the same strength as an opening bid of 1NT, promises at least one stopper in diamonds and a balanced hand. Expert players do not promise stoppers in each of the unbid suits and might have a long minor in reserve along with a diamond stopper.

Any of the following hands overcall an opening bid of 1D with 1NT:

(1)	(2)	(3)	(4)
S. 65	S. K6	S. AJ8	S. AQ7
H. AJ9	H. 765	H. 54	H. K87
D. AQ87	D. AJ9	D. K7	D. AJ7
C. KQJ5	C. AK1098	C. AK7654	C. QJ76

Hand (1) Does not have a spade stopper but that's life.

Hands (2) Have only 15 H.C.P. but 1NT is still the most descriptive over-
and
(3) call, particularly with (2).

Hand (4) Is the kind you see in books but seldom at the table.

Responses to 1NT Overcalls

Not too much has been written about this. One method is to use 2C as Stayman with a balanced or semi-balanced hand and a cue bid of the opponent's suit as Stayman with an unbalanced hand - almost always showing a singleton or void in the opponent's suit.

West	North	East	South
1H	1NT	Pass	?

(1)
S. KJ87
H. 54
D. K76
C. J987

(2)
S. QJ76
H. 54
D. AK87
C. 654

(3)
S. AJ76
H. 2
D. KJ9876
C. 43

(4)
S. K98
H. 2
D. AJ87
C. K7654

Hand (1)   Responds 2C looking for a spade fit and then rebids 2NT to show 8-9 points if partner does not have four spades.

Hand (2)   Responds 2C and then rebids 3NT if partner does not have four spades.

Hand (3)   Cue bids 2H and then bids diamonds if partner does not have four spades. Partner is warned of the singleton heart.

Hand (4)   Also cue bids 2H and then bids 3C even if partner does bid 2S. When responder cue bids opener should not persist in no trump without a double stopper in the opponent's suit.

If East doubles partner's 1NT overcall, all responses are natural. If South has a good hand, he must redouble.

Responses at the two level in unbid suits are sign offs and jumps to the three level when not preceded by either 2C or a cue bid are invitational.

No Trump Responses to One Level Overcalls

As a one level overcall can be relatively weak partner must be stronger to respond 1NT to an overcall than to an opening bid. The scale goes like this:

To respond 1NT: 9-11 or 12 H.C.P. with a singleton or small doubleton
                  in partner's suit.

To respond 2NT: 12-15 (12 with a doubleton honor in partner's suit;
                  15 with a singleton in partner's suit).

To respond 3NT: 15-18.

It goes without saying that you must have at least one stopper in the opponent's suit but you <u>do not</u>, repeat, <u>do not</u> promise stoppers in each of the
unbid suits.

Assume the bidding has proceeded:

West	North	East	South
1H	1S	Pass	?

What should South bid with each of the following hands?

(1)	S. A5	(2)	S. 2	(3)	S. J4	(4)	S. K5
	H. KJ8		H. AQ65		H. KQ8		H. AJ9
	D. 7654		D. KJ87		D. AQ87		D. KQ109
	C. Q1076		C. A965		C. 10965		C. Q1076

Solutions

Hand (1)   1NT   Not forcing.

Hand (2)   2NT   Bidding conservatively because of the apparent misfit.

Hand (3)   2NT   A borderline case. 1NT if partner is a passed hand.
                 With 12 H.C.P. use your judgment. The 2NT response is not
                 forcing.

Hand (4)   3NT   A "good" 15. Look at your tens and nines.

The Cue Bid in Response to the One Level Overcall

Some hands are so powerful that the only way to force the overcaller to bid
again is to cue bid the opponent's suit. A cue bid is forcing until the
cue bidder either raises the overcaller's suit or bids no trump. If the cue
bidder mentions a new suit the overcaller must bid again. Study these sequences:

quences:	(1)	West	North	East	South		South
		1H	1S	Pass	2H		S. K2
		Pass	3C	Pass	3D		H. 3
							D. AKQ10876
							C. K54

(2)	West	North	East	South	South
	1H	1S	Pass	2H	S. K104
	Pass	3C	Pass	3S	H. 73
					D. AQJ84
					C. Q74
(3)	1H	1S	Pass	2H	S. Q6
	Pass	2S	Pass	2NT	H. A42
					D. A10862
					C. K84

Hand (1)   Is forcing because South has mentioned a new suit after his cue bid.

Hand (2)   Shows 11-14 with 3 card trump support.

Hand (3)   Shows 12-15 with only one heart stopper as opposed to a direct jump to 2NT which usually shows two stoppers.

Sequences (2) and (3) are not forcing because the cue bidder has raised partner's suit or bid no trump.

The Two Level Overcall

The requirements for a two level overcall, particularly in a minor, are more stringent due to the increased probability of a penalty double.

A typical two level overcall will have:

   (1) A six card suit, usually headed by three of the top five honors.

   (2) Between 11-15 points.

Typical overcalls of 2C look like:

(1)		(2)		(3)	
	S. A5		S. 8765		S. 4
	H. 765		H. K4		H. A76
	D. K4		D. 2		D. Q108
	C. KJ10765		C. AQJ987		C. AK10765

A two level overcall does not need the strength of an opening bid but at least 50% qualify as opening bids. This cannot be said for the one level overcall.

Overcalling on Five Card Suits at the Two Level

There are at least four times when it pays to overcall at the two level on a five card suit.

96

(1) Holding two five card suits.

Overcall 2H after a 1S opening with:

    S. 5
    H. AJ986
    D. KQJ87
    C. 54

(2) With a reasonable five card heart suit and a little side distribution.

    S. K4
    H. AQ1076
    D. 43
    C. KJ76

Overcall an opening bid of 1S with 2H.

But <u>do</u> <u>not</u> overcall 2H with this type of hand:

    S. Q76
    H. AQ765
    D. K43
    C. J4

You have the points, but not the tricks. The suit is not strong
enough and the distribution is the worst possible.

(3) With a five card minor, 100 honors in the bid suit or close to
it, and at least 10 H.C.P.

    Suits that look like this qualify:

        AKQJx, AKQ10x, AKJ10x, KQJ10x, AQJ10x.

    Or even: AKQ9x, AQJ9x, KQJ9x, AQ109x, KQ109x,

        AJ109x, AK109x, AKJ9x.

Don't cheat on your suit strength if you are overcalling on a
five card minor suit at the two level! (See rule (4).)

(4) After partner has passed originally and thus cannot hold a good
hand, it often pays to overcall on a good five card suit for
lead directing purposes with less than the required point count.
This type of overcall is most commonly made when not vulnerable.
For example: Sitting South you hold:

    S. 43
    H. 876
    D. 976
    C. AKJ105

If the bidding proceeds:

East	South
1S	?

you should pass. Your suit is strong enough but you do not have
enough high card strength to overcall 2C.

However if the bidding proceeds:

West	North	East	South
Pass	Pass	1S	?

Now there is more to be said for a 2C overcall. Clearly the opponents have the balance of strength with your partner unable to open
the bidding. The opponents may wind up playing hearts or no trump
from the West seat and you do want a club lead badly. This is the
time to stick your neck out. But remember when sticking your neck
out with under strength overcalls at either the one or two level:

(1) Partner must be a passed hand.

(2) You must be not vulnerable.

(3) Your suit must be strong.

Responding to a Two Level Overcall

Keep in mind that a two level overcall will usually have the strength of an
opening bid and raises can be made in competition with a doubleton if necessary. This is only possible because the overcaller is supposed to have a
strong suit.

Raising a Two Level Overcall

The most common raise, of course, is the single raise from two to three.
Again this is very similar to raising an opening bid from one to two or a
one level overcall from one to two. Strength varies from 8 to 11 support
points. (If raising in competition on a doubleton the maximum (10-11)
should be held.)

Assume the bidding goes:

West	North	East	South
1S	2D	2S	?

(1) S. 65   (2) S. 84   (3) S. 7654
    H. AQ87   H. K765   H. A2
    D. 543   D. A4   D. K65
    C. K765   C. A5432   C. 9876

Each of these hands raises to 3D. Unless partner has an unusual overcall
(good distribution) your raise will either end the bidding or push the opponents to 3S which you might have a chance to defeat. In almost no case
does responder reraise the overcaller! After the single raise the rest
is up to the overcaller because you have limited your hand. Occasionally
the overcaller may be able to compete further or even go to game after
hearing about support, but usually passes.

The Double Raise of an Overcall

Here we have a slight problem. Should the double raise of a minor be preemptive or constructive? Which of these two hands should bid 4D on this
sequence?

West	North	East	South
1S	2D	Pass	?

(1) S. 95   (2) S. 4
    H. AK76   H. A765
    D. Q1087   D. KJ72
    C. KJ3   C. 10762

Clearly the first hand is too strong to bid 3D and the second hand is very
sacrifice oriented (more so than a single raise would indicate) and if
partner knew which type of raise (strong in high cards, mild distribution
or weak in high cards, wild distribution) he could better judge what to do
when the opponents bid on (as they inevitably do).

One solution is to play the jump to four as preemptive as in the majors.
With the stronger raises, those hands that are worth opening bids, cue bid
the opponents' suit and then raise partner to the four level or perhaps end
up in 3NT if partner has a spade stopper.

In other words with (1) bid 2S and if partner bids 3D raise to 4D. With
(2) raise to 4D directly. The cue bid has the additional advantage of getting more information from partner. For example, if partner has a stopper
in the opponent's suit he will respond to your cue bid in no trump. This
will help you find no trump games after two level overcalls in the minors.

Take another look at (1). Assume you cue bid 2S and partner rebids 2NT.
Forget your diamond support. Partner has a spade stopper and nine tricks
are easier than eleven. Raise to 3NT.

Thus the cue bid is more flexible than the double raise and should be
used with strong hands that have support for partner's suit. The double
raise should be preemptive.

The Cue Bid in Response to the

Two Level Overcall

We have already seen some uses for the cue bid. It can be used in looking
for a stopper for no trump purposes after a minor suit overcall. It can be
used to show a strong raise (12-15) by cue bidding and then supporting.
Are there any other uses:

    (1) Whenever the responder is strapped for a forcing bid he must

        fall back on the cue bid because that is his only force!

Assume the bidding has proceeded:

West	North	East	South
1S	2D	Pass	?

(1)	S. ---	(2)	S. 5	(3)	S. 543
	H. A876		H. AK8765		H. A87
	D. K7654		D. A4		D. AQ7
	C. A543		C. KQJ7		C. K876

Hand (1) Would cue bid 2S because there is a good chance for a slam. Of
           course when later raising diamonds South would bid at least five
           rather than the non-forcing four after a cue bid.

Hand (2) This hand wants to force the bidding. We know that neither 2H
           nor 3H is forcing in this sequence. South must cue bid 2S and
           then bid hearts to force.

Hand (3)   Is our old friend who is trying to ferret out a spade stopper

for no trump.   If partner bids 2NT, (3) raises to 3NT.

The cue bid is not used as frequently in response to a two level overcall
in hearts.   One does not usually go searching for a no trump contract with
a heart fit (although it is possible).   In general most cue bidding is done
in response to minor suit overcalls.

Responses in No Trump to a
Two Level Overcall

Assuming at least one stopper in the opponent's suit and at least two cards
in partner's suit the scale goes something like this:

$$2NT = 10\text{-}13 \text{ H.C.P.}$$

$$3NT = 14\text{-}17 \text{ H.C.P.}$$

The better the fit in partner's suit the fewer the points that are needed.
Assume the bidding has proceeded:

West	North	East	South
1S	2C	Pass	?

(1)	A. AJ76	(2)	S. Q987
	H. 1087		H. K875
	D. Q1087		D. AJ32
	C. K5		C. 2

Hand (1) is a better bet to bid 2NT than (2).   It will be difficult to
establish partner's six card club suit holding a singleton club but with
Kx the suit is probably ready to run for six tricks.   The smartest course
of action is to pass with (2) and hope the opponents bid again.   Hand (2)
is better suited to defensive play.

In order to bid no trump in response to partner's overcall you do not need
stoppers in each of the unbid suits.   You do need at least one stopper in
the suit bid by the opponents.

As a matter of fact a 2NT response to an overcall usually has one suit
where the stopper is shaky, but partner frequently has a stopper.   Besides,
if you lead a clean life the weak suit is not always led.

Bidding a New Suit in Response to a

Two Level Overcall

If the overcall is in hearts and partner bids three of a minor he cannot
have three card heart support and he must have at least six cards in his
suit. This bidding for example:

West	North	East	South
1S	2H	Pass	3D

shows a powerful diamond suit with no heart support. It is not forcing and
the 2H bidder must be careful about proceeding further with a singleton or
void in diamonds. If the hand is obviously a misfit the best bet is to get
out as quickly and quietly as possible.

If the 2H bidder has a secondary diamond fit and a spade stopper he might
risk 3NT. A raise is also possible.

There is a more delicate problem when the overcall is in a minor and partner bids two of a major.

West	North	East	South
1H	2C	Pass	2S

In the first example South switched from a major to a minor. As no one in
his right mind switches from a major to a minor with major suit support it
wasn't hard to figure out that South did not have major support.

Switching from a minor to a major is a horse of a different color. South
may have a club fit with five good spades, fearing there is a double fit
and the hand may make game in a major and fall one short in a minor. On
the other hand, South may have spades without clubs and simply want to show
his long suit. Let's look at a few examples of possible South hands on the
above sequence.

(1)	S. AQJ87	(2)	S. AQJ87	(3)	S. AKJ1032
	H. A4		H. A43		H. 543
	D. J10943		D. 54		D. 1098
	C. 2		C. J98		C. 3

Hand (1)   Has no support for clubs but might find a spade fit.

Hand (2)   Has a club fit but would like to check out a possible spade fit.

Hand (3)   Simply has spades and is not interested in any other contract.

To tell the truth there is no real solution to the problem. The 2C bidder cannot be clairvoyant enough to know partner has clubs when he bids spades.

The 2C bidder should not assume club support but with a singleton spade and a fine six card suit he tends to rebid his suit. With three card spade support he either passes or raises, and with a doubleton spade he usually passes unless he has a strong overcall and wishes to try for game. The 2S bidder has 9-13 points. The better the spade suit the fewer the points. This is a tough sequence as you can see.

The Jump in a New Suit in Response to a
Two Level Overcall

This sequence:	West	North	East	South
	1H	2C	Pass	3S

Here South is showing at least six and possibly seven spades and is very interested in a spade game if the overcaller has a suitable hand. (Usually two quick tricks without a complete misfit.) The jump is not forcing. North can pass with a completely unsuitable hand.

If responder wishes to force unconditionally he cue bids the opponent's suit and then bids spades.

Tips to the Overcaller

1. Take some liberties with your overcalls at the one level particularly after partner has passed. All you really need is a good suit.

2. Be very careful about your two level overcalls in a minor. The suit must be strong, usually six cards. A vulnerable two level overcall in a minor is very apt to be doubled by good opponents so be sure to have intermediate cards in your suit (tens and nines).

3. Two level overcalls should be able to take five tricks not vulnerable; closer to six tricks vulnerable.

4. Unless partner makes a cue bid the overcaller should not rebid his five card suit. Partner already knows about that five card suit.

5. If partner raises your overcall with a single raise do not compete further unless your overcall reevaluates to 15-16 points.

6. The only response that is forcing to an overcall is a cue bid. Jumps in new suits and jumps to 2NT are invitational.

7. An overcall that takes away bidding space from the opponents is more effective than one that does not. For example an overcall of 1S over a 1C opening takes away the red suits from the responder at the one level. An overcall of 1D would not make it difficult for the responder at all. For this reason overcalls of 1S over a minor opening and overcalls of 2H over 1S are particularly effective.

8. A one level overcall will usually have between 1-1/2 - 2 defensive tricks. A two level overcall will usually contain two defensive tricks. If your overcall is completely lacking in defense you probably have a W.J.O. (if you play them) or perhaps a preemptive overcall (an overcall which skips two levels of bidding and is very similar to an opening three bid).

9. With a defenseless hand avoid making a simple overcall. Either make a W.J.O. or pass and come in later if partner shows signs of life. Passing and then overcalling at your second or third opportunity is rare. But if you do, you will generally have a six card suit with very little high card strength.

You are South and hold: S. QJ10654
                               H. 543
                               D. 2
                               C. K65

West	North	East	South
1D	Pass	1H	Pass
2H	Pass	Pass	2S

South shows a long spade suit and a weak hand. This type of bidding is used mainly when playing I.J.O.'s, as the weak jump overcall usually can be used in this situation directly over 1H.

10. With two five card suits overcall in the higher ranking suit first even if it is the weaker suit. One possible exception is when holding five good clubs and five weak spades over a red suit opening - it often works out better to overcall clubs first.

Tips for the Partner of the Overcaller

1. If partner overcalls and you have a weak hand with a long suit it is
    better not to mention the suit unless your partner gets doubled. Don't
    stir up trouble with bad hands.

2. If partner overcalls with a major do not bid another suit if you have
    three or more cards in partner's suit. Remember a new suit in response
    to an overcall is not forcing and denies support for partner's major.

3. If partner overcalls at the one level and you respond with a new suit
    at the one level it is just barely possible that you have a strong four
    card suit; however, partner always assumes five, just as you always
    assume five when he overcalls at the level of one.

4. A change of suit by the responder at the two level promises a five card
    suit and 80% of the time a six card suit.

5. A change of suit by the responder from the two level to the three level
    promises a minimum of six cards.

6. The strongest response to an overcall is a cue bid.

7. If the cue bid is followed by a raise of overcaller's suit or by 2NT
    the overcaller may pass with a minimum. If the cue bid is followed
    by a new suit the overcaller may not pass.

8. A jump raise or a double jump raise of an overcall is best played as
    preemptive. With strong raises (opening bids or better) cue bid and
    then raise. The preemptive raise of an overcall with four trumps and
    some side distribution is devastatingly effective against all but the
    most expert of opponents.

9. No trump responses to overcalls are constructive bids. Do not bid no
    trump to run away from partner's suit. A singleton in partner's suit
    is no reason for panic, particularly if he has overcalled at the two
    level.

10. When raising an overcall tend to bid the full value of your hand at
    once and let partner make any future decisions unless you find your-
    self in a position to double the opponents for penalties.

6. DEFENSIVE BIDDING

(THE TAKEOUT DOUBLE)

Along with the overcall the takeout double is the most common form of immediate entry into the auction. The requirements for an immediate takeout
double are more rigid than the requirements for an overcall.

Assume the bidding begins:

East	South
1D	Dbl.

What type of hand does South hold? If South is bidding properly he will
have:

1. 11 or more H.C.P.

2. Support for the unbid suits particularly the unbid majors.

3. Fewer than three diamonds (85% of the time).

The Eleven Point Takeout Double

As most doubles will have more than 11 H.C.P. it might be wise to see which
type of hand can double with so little. It is invariably a hand with a
singleton or void in the bid suit and typically 4-4-4-1 distribution, or
possibly 5-4-3-1.

After a 1D opening any of these hands would double:

(1)	S. AJ87	(2)	S. A10976	(3)	S. J1075
	H. KQJ8		H. A965		H. AQ76
	D. 2		D. 2		D. ---
	C. 10976		C. K86		C. A7654

So much for the eleven point double. Excluding that one case, doubles can
be classified into three categories. Knowing this will help us rebid after
partner responds to the double.

Doubles will be subdivided by high card points:

(a) The minimum takeout double 12-15 H.C.P.

(b) The intermediate takeout double 16-18 H.C.P.

(c) The powerful takeout double 19-21 H.C.P.

The Minimum Takeout Double

Most doubles fall into this category. Typically most doubles in this group do not have a five card major (although it is possible). They tend to be balanced hands with shortness in the bid suit.

Holding length in the opponent's suit makes it impossible to have support for all the other suits. Therefore when holding three or four cards in the opponent's suit one must be very careful about doubling PARTICULARLY IF PARTNER IS FORCED TO RESPOND AT THE TWO LEVEL.

In other words if the opening bid is 1C it is proper to double with:

```
S. AJ87
H. K87
D. AJ9
C. 654
```

But if the opening bid is 1S it is lunacy!

Doubles of 1S with minimum hands typically guarantee four hearts or three good hearts and a singleton or doubleton spade.

Double 1S with all of these hands:

```
(1)  S. 7          (2)  S. 85         (3)  S. 65
     H. AQ8             H. KQ73            H. KQ5
     D. KJ876           D. A42             D. AJ87
     C. A765            C. A1075           C. A987
```

But this hand passes 1S:

```
                   S. K98
                   H. A87
                   D. K876
                   C. QJ8
```

Doubles of 1H are similar with regard to spade support. Normally a double of 1H, particularly with a minimum hand, has four card spade support. However, it could have three spades with a singleton heart, or even three spades and a doubleton heart.

Double 1H with any of these hands:

```
(1)  S. AJ98       (2)  S. AK7        (3)  S. KJ9
     H. 543             H. 2               H. 43
     D. AK7             D. J10765          D. A9865
     C. 1087            C. AQ87            C. KQ4
```

1. Do not make takeout doubles with minimum hands and two five card suits.

East	South
1H	?

(1)	S. AJ987	(2)	S. K4
	H. 4		H. 4
	D. KQ876		D. AJ987
	C. K4		C. KJ987

Hand (1) Overcall 1S and bid diamonds later if feasible.

Hand (2) Overcall 2D; if using the unusual no trump - overcall 2NT.

2. Avoid making takeout doubles with 5-3-3-2 distribution when the five card suit is a major and the hand minimum.

    After a 1C opening, overcall 1S with these hands:

(1)	S. AK765	(2)	S. J10965
	H. K54		H. AQ4
	D. K76		D. AK3
	C. 54		C. 65

The reason: If you double and then bid your suit you are describing a double in the intermediate range (16-18 H.C.P.). BUT IF YOU OVER-CALL AND THEN DOUBLE YOU ARE SHOWING THIS TYPE OF HAND. This is a new concept to some; however, it is effective in actual play.

For example:

East	South	West	North
1C	1S	2C	Pass
Pass	Dbl.		

South is showing a takeout double in the minimum zone with five spades. North will act accordingly. For an overcaller to make a later takeout double the opponents must have bid one suit and one suit only, or stopped in precisely 1NT.

3. Overcalling and later doubling for takeout is not restricted to hands with five card majors and 5-3-3-2 distribution. Hands with six card minors and 6-3-3-1 distribution also bid this way.

After a 1H opening:	S. K76	S. Q106
	H. 4	H. 3
	D. AJ9876	D. AKJ765
	C. AJ7	C. K98

Overcall 2D. If the opponents now stop at 2H reopen with a double.

For years players have doubled originally with this type of hand and have had trouble showing their long suit, particularly if opener's partner makes a preemptive raise.

Now the bidding will go along these lines:

East	South (you)	West	North
1H	2D	2H	Pass
Pass	Dbl.		

or even

East	South (you)	West	North
1H	2D	3H*	Pass
Pass	Dbl.		

*Limit Raise.

True, the higher the level, the greater the risk and the better the 2D bidder's hand must be. However partner will know your strength and distribution and can usually make a good decision, particularly if he happens to have a long weak black suit. Certainly he knows he can bid his suit with safety. He also knows that a doubleton in your minor is adequate support as the double after a two level overcall in a minor typically guarantees a six card suit.

Assume you are South and the bidding has proceeded:

West	North	East	South
1H	2D	2H	Pass
Pass	Dbl.	Pass	?

You hold:

(1) S. QJ876	(2) S. KQ87	(3) S. J765
H. K765	H. J87	H. Q109
D. 2	D. 654	D. ---
C. J76	C. J76	C. QJ8765

Hand (1) Bid 2S. Partner has exactly three spades.

Hand (2) Bid 3D. Partner has six diamonds.

Hand (3) Bid 3C. Partner has three clubs.

Most reopening doubles by a two level overcaller will be made if the opponents peter out at the two level. The overcall must be extra strong to reopen with a double at a higher level.

110

4. Before leaving this topic let's not overlook the following sequence in which the double is also for takeout (by agreement).

East	South	West	North
1S	2D	Pass	Pass
2S	Dbl.		

Here we do not have a sequence where one player has supported another so a case could be made for a penalty double. However, if you and your partner agree that in this auction South's double is for takeout South will have something like:

S. 4
H. AQ4
D. AQ10876
C. J54

The Takeout Double
on the Intermediate Hand (16-18 H.C.P.)
and the Powerful Hand   (19-21 H.C.P.)

These types of hands double and bid again even if partner makes a minimum reply. The minimum takeout doubler does not bid again after a minimum reply. This is the basic difference. Compare these two sequences:

	East	South	West	North
(1)	1H	Dbl.	Pass	2C
	Pass	Pass	Pass	

	East	South	West	North
(2)	1H	Dbl.	Pass	2C
	Pass	2S	Pass	?

In the first case South doubles and passes, informing North of a minimum hand. In the second case South doubles and then bids, showing a five card suit (conceivably six) and 16-18 H.C.P. Five-five hands in this range also double first and then bid the two suits rather than overcall directly.

With hands in the 19-21 H.C.P. range, the takeout doubler makes a jump bid at his next opportunity.

Raising the Response to a Takeout Double

When it comes to raising the response to a takeout double we are dealing with support points. Assume the bidding has proceeded:

East	South	West	North
1H	Dbl.	Pass	1S
Pass	2S		
	3S		
	4S		

All raises of forced responses in non-competitive auctions show four trump. North's response was forced.

The raise to 2S shows 15-17 support points.

The raise to 3S shows 18-19 support points.

The raise to 4S shows 20-22 support points.

No Trump Rebids

As all minimum hands automatically pass a forced response (a non-jump response) to a takeout double, it stands to reason if the doubler bids again he must have extra values. If the doubler rebids no trump this is the scale:

1. A rebid of 1NT = 16-18 H.C.P.

   This is similar to an original overcall of 1NT but indicates the possession of at least one four card major.

East	South	West	North
1C	Dbl.	Pass	1D
Pass	1NT		

South might have either of these hands:

S. AJ87	S. K98
H. KJ87	H. AK98
D. A9	D. J876
C. K98	C. AQ

2. A rebid of 2NT = 19-20 H.C.P. with a balanced or semi-balanced hand.

East	South	West	North
1H	Dbl.	Pass	1S or 2C
Pass	2NT		

A direct jump to 2NT is considered "unusual" for the minors so the doubler has no other way of showing that he really wants to bid 2NT.

3. A jump rebid to 3NT shows 21-23 points but I can assure you it never happens.

The Jump Rebid After a Takeout Double

Compare these sequences:

	East	South	West	North
(1)	1H	Dbl.	Pass	1S
	Pass	2C		

	East	South	West	North
(2)	1H	Dbl.	Pass	1S
	Pass	3C		

In (1) South has doubled and bid again showing 16-18 H.C.P. and at least a five card club suit. ANYTIME THE DOUBLER MENTIONS A NEW SUIT HE MUST HAVE AT LEAST FIVE CARDS IN THAT SUIT. ANYTIME THE DOUBLER JUMPS IN A NEW SUIT HE MUST HAVE AT LEAST SIX CARDS IN THAT SUIT.

In (2) the doubler has jumped. This shows 19-20 H.C.P and a six card suit. Neither the 2C bid nor the 3C bid is forcing but once aware of the strength of the doubler's hand responder often bids again, particularly after sequence (2).

The Cue Bid by the Takeout Doubler

The only way the doubler can unconditionally force his partner to bid again is to cue bid the opponent's suit:

East	South	West	North
1H	Dbl.	Pass	1S
Pass	2H		

South must have a fantastic hand and does not want the bidding to die. For practical purposes the 2H rebid is forcing to game unless South rebids 2NT (22-23) or raises spades to the three level which North may pass only if completely busted.

Typical South hands for this sequence are:

S. KJx	S. AJxx	S. AKx	S. AKx
H. Ax	H. ---	H. xxx	H. ---
D. AKxx	D. AKxxx	D. AKx	D. AKxxxx
C. AKxx	C. AQxx	C. AKQx	C. AQxx

Now let's see how well you do on this quiz.

	East	South
	1H	?

What action should South take with each of the following hands?

1. S. AKxxx	2. S. AKxxx	3. S. A10xxx	4. S. AQ10xx
H. xx	H. xx	H. xx	H. x
D. KJx	D. AKx	D. KQxxx	D. AKJxx
C. Qxx	C. Qxx	C. A	C. Kx

5. S. Ax	6. S. x	7. S. AJxx	8. S. Ax
H. AQx	H. Kxx	H. x	H. KQx
D. Kxxx	D. AJ10xxx	D. KQxx	D. Axxxx
C. Jxxx	C. AQx	C. J10xx	C. Kxx

9. S. AQx	10. S. AJ10
H. AQx	H. x
D. KJxx	D. AKx
C. A10x	C. KJ10xxx

Solutions

1. 1S   Not strong enough to double and then bid spades.

2. Dbl.   Strong enough to double and then bid spades.

3. 1S   Not strong enough to double and then bid both suits.

4. Dbl.   Strong enough to double and then bid both suits.

5. Pass   Not enough support for spades to double with such a minimum
        hand.

6. 2D   And then double if the opponents stop in 2H.

7. Dbl.   Minimum but the perfect distribution.

8. 1NT   The equivalent of an opening 1NT bid.

9. Dbl.   And then bid 2NT over any response.

10. Dbl.   And then bid clubs. If the hand were slightly weaker it would
        be better to bid clubs immediately and perhaps double for take-
        out later.

Now try this one:

East	South	West	North
1D	Dble.	Pass	1H
Pass	?		

What should South rebid with each of the following hands? Keep in mind that North has been forced to respond and his failure to jump or cue bid places him in the 0-8 point range.

1. S. KQxx
    H. AQx
    D. xx
    C. Kxxx

2. S. AKxxx
    H. KQx
    D. Ax
    C. Jxx

3. S. AQxx
    H. Jxx
    D. AQ
    C. Kxxx

4. S. KQx
    H. Axx
    D. xx
    C. Axxxx

5. S. KQx
    H. Axx
    D. xx
    C. AKxxx

6. S. KQx
    H. AKxxx
    D. ---
    C. AQJxx

7. S. AQxx
    H. AKx
    D. AJx
    C. Q10x

8. S. AKxx
    H. AKxx
    D. x
    C. xxxx

9. S. Axxx
    H. AKQx
    D. x
    C. AJ10x

10. S. Axxxx
    H. KQxx
    D. x
    C. AQx

Solutions

1. Pass   Minimum doubles do not bid again if partner does not jump or cue bid.

2. 1S   Showing an intermediate double with five spades.

3. 1NT   Same as an opening bid of 1NT. The reason for doubling and not bidding 1NT immediately was the possibility of finding a 4-4 spade fit.

4. Pass   Same as (1).

5. 2C   Same as (2).

6. 2D   A slam is in the air and we need some bidding room. We don't want partner to pass.

7. 2NT   Shows 19 or 20 points and a balanced hand.

8. 2H   15-17 support points. This is a maximum.

9. 4H.   20-22 support points.

10. 3H   18-19 support points. With four card support for a MAJOR suit it is better to support partner immediately than to bid one's own suit.

Delayed Takeout Doubles

Frequently a player will pass at his first opportunity and double at his second. What does it mean?

East	South	West	North
1H	Pass	2H	Pass
Pass	Dbl.		

South's double is for takeout showing slightly less than the requirements for an original takeout double. South will normally have 10-12 H.C.P. with a singleton or doubleton heart. It is not inconceivable that South could have as little as 9 H.C.P. with a perfect hand pattern. Perhaps:

```
S. A1098
H. 4
D. A1076
C. J987
```

Notice that South has doubled <u>after</u> the bidding has died out and both East and West have limited their hands. South's double in this case can be compared in strength to this sequence:

South	West	North	East
Pass	Pass	Pass	1H
Dbl.			

A REOPENING DOUBLE AFTER BOTH OPPONENTS HAVE LIMITED THEMSELVES IS EQUIVALENT IN STRENGTH TO A DIRECT TAKEOUT DOUBLE MADE BY A PASSED HAND.

South can also double for takeout at his second opportunity before both opponents have limited themselves. This requires the strength of an opening bid plus a singleton in the last bid suit.

East	South	West	North
1D	Pass	1S	Pass
2S	Dbl.		

South is not an original passed hand and is doubling at his second opportunity in front of an unlimited hand. What kind of hand does South hold? South is, in fact, making a takeout double of one suit - spades. He must, therefore, have some hand that looks like this:

```
S. 4
H. A1076
D. AQ98
C. K1032
```

South might have the same hand on this bidding:

East	South	West	North
1D	Pass	1H	Pass
1S	Dbl.		

South is making a takeout double of 1S. However, do not confuse this sequence (where South is doubling for takeout even though three suits have been bid) with this one:

East	South	West	North
1H	Pass	2C	Pass
2D	Dbl.		

In this case South's double is for penalties because the first response was made at the two level.

Summary of Delayed Takeout Doubles

1. Passing and then doubling at one's second opportunity after the opponents have found a fit can show either as little as 9-11 H.C.P. or as much as a good opening bid. How is partner supposed to know?

   (a) If the doubler is in the "dead position" (the bidding has gone pass, pass, to him) his double shows 9-11.

   (b) If the doubler enters in the midst of the opponents' bidding he has an opening bid or better. The reason he didn't double originally was because he had too much strength in opener's first bid suit. However, now that the opponents have found a fit in another suit he can double for takeout provided he is short suited in the opponents' agreed suit, a criterion for almost all takeout doubles.

2. When the opponents have bid three suits a delayed double is for takeout if the original response was made at the one level. It is for penalties if the original response was made at the two level.

Responding to a Takeout Double

The main point to keep in mind here is that you must let your partner know how strong you are. You do not automatically bid your longest suit and wait to hear what partner does.

A minimum response in a suit to a takeout double shows a total evaluation of less than 9 points. With more a jump bid or a cue bid must be made immediately.

Also when responding in a suit to a takeout double the responder must bear in mind that queens and jacks in the opener's suit are not counted, and that five and six card suits are counted heavily. As support for all unbid suits (particularly majors) is guaranteed by the doubler, the responder evaluates his hand as if his suit had already been supported. If an eight card fit is assured (the doubler is assumed to have at least three card support) use the one, two, three long suit count and then add 1 point for each doubleton, 2 for each singleton and 3 for a void.

Assume the bidding has proceeded:

West	North	East	South
1C	Dbl.	Pass	?

(1)	S. A8765	(2)	S. Q108765	(3)	S. J8765
	H. 54		H. A43		H. 43
	D. 543		D. 43		D. J76
	C. Q54		C. 43		C. J87

(1)   Is worth approximately six points in response to a takeout double. The five card spade suit is worth one extra and another for the doubleton with the assured eight card spade fit. But the queen of clubs is not counted. (If partner bids no trump later then the queen of clubs is counted because it would fit in with some club strength in partner's hand.)

(2)   This hand is worth 10 points. Six H.C.P. and two for the six card spade suit and one each for the doubletons. Hands in the 9-11 range jump immediately. The proper response is 2S - not forcing.

118

(3) This hand is worth a shabby four points. (The jack of clubs is not counted.) The five card suit is worth one, the doubleton heart is one and the two jacks make up the other two. Just about the worst four point hand imaginable!

More on Responses with Minimum Hands

Responder tries to respond in a major to a takeout double rather than in a minor.

If partner doubles 1C and next hand passes, respond 1H with either of these hands:

(1)	S. 65	(2)	S. 3
	H. J1087		H. KQ107
	D. A876		D. 108765
	C. 1087		C. 976

No matter how weak you are do not pass unless your right hand opponent takes you off the hook by bidding or unless you have five or six good cards in the opponent's suit.

West	North	East	South
1D	Dbl.	Pass	?

(1) S. 876   Respond 1H. Do not pass! The overtricks they make
    H. 1087
    D. 97632   will make their score read like a telephone number.
    C. 104

(2) S. A5   This is the hand that passes 1D doubled.
    H. 765
    D. KJ10876
    C. 54

Bidding Over Interference With Minimum Hands

Assume the bidding proceeds:

West	North	East	South
1C	Dbl.	1H	?

Now that East has bid South no longer need respond. Nevertheless South will make life much easier for North if he does respond. Six to eight points is sufficient at either the one or two level.

```
(1)  S. QJ876              (2)  S. K5
     H. 65                      H. 876
     D. Q65                     D. QJ108
     C. 876                     C. 8765
```

By all means respond 1S with (1) and 2D with (2) over the interference. If
interference forces you to the three level your minimum should be 9 or 10
points.

The 1NT Response to the Takeout Double

The response of 1NT to a takeout double is considered constructive. It is
never done with a bust hand. The normal range after partner has doubled a
minor is 7-10 H.C.P. (Some 10 H.C.P. hands jump to 2NT if they have good
intermediate cards and/or a five card suit.)

After a major suit has been doubled, particularly 1S, a response of 1NT
might be a shade weaker. The range in this case is usually six to nine.
Of course all no trump responses guarantee at least one stopper in the opponent's suit, and usually two since partner is marked with shortness. If
the doubler bids a new suit after the 1NT response it is not forcing. He
wants out! If your hand is too weak to respond 1NT, bid your longest suit
even though it means bidding at the two level.

West	North	East	South
1S	Dbl.	Pass	?

```
S. J543        Respond 2C; not 1NT!
H. 76
D. 743
C. J1086
```


Responding to a Double With 9-11

If your hand reevaluates to 9-11 points you are too strong for a minimum
suit response to a takeout double. Jump even with a four card suit.

West	North	East	South
1D	Dbl.	Pass	?

	(1) S. AJ98	(2) S. K4	(3) S. 76
	H. 43	H. J10876	H. A4
	D. 8765	D. 876	D. 8765
	C. A87	C. K98	C. KJ1098

Hand (1)   Respond 2S holding nine points.

Hand (2)   Respond 2H also holding nine points (one for the five card suit and one for the doubleton because of the assured eight card fit).

Hand (3)   Respond 3C holding 11 points.

The 2NT and 3NT Responses to the Takeout Double

2NT is a positive, non-forcing response showing 10-12 points and usually two stoppers in the opponent's suit. It is highly invitational and only a player with a minimum double in H.C.P. should pass. If the doubler bids over 2NT the partnership is committed to game.

A response of 3NT shows 13-16 H.C.P. and a double stopper in the opponent's suit.

Preemptive Responses to a Takeout Double

Assume the bidding begins:

West	North	East	South
1D	Dbl.	Pass	?

South is allowed to jump to 3S or 4S. Both bids tend to show six card suits or longer and no slam interest - indeed the response of 3S can be passed!

(1) S. QJ10976   This is the type of hand that responds 3S to a take-
    H. 2
    D. 7654   out double. It invites four if opener has controlling
    C. Q4
                  cards (quick tricks).

The doubler should discount side jacks and queens when partner preempts like this. It can be paralleled to evaluating your hand after partner opens 3S. In order to raise to 4S you must have quick tricks, not a heap of kings, queens and jacks.

121

(2)   S. QJ10876   This is the type of hand that leaps to 4S in response
       H. 43
       D. 2   to a double of any suit (except a double of 1S which
       C. A987
                       is passed).

It is a hand weak in high cards but strong in distribution and has a chance
to make 4S opposite a minimum double. In a way it is stronger in playing
strength than the jump to 2S which is not forcing. The jump to two shows a
more balanced hand - a hand that needs extra values by the doubler to produce game.

The Cue Bid in Response to the Takeout Double

This is the strongest response that can be made to a takeout double. It is
forcing until the cue bidder either repeats a suit, bids no trump or supports one of the doubler's suits.

It normally will have a total evaluation of 12 or more points but in some
cases (holding two four card majors, for example) a total count of 9-10-11
is acceptable.

West	North	East	South
1D	Dbl.	Pass	?

(1) S. AQ5   (2) S. KQ987   (3) S. K4   (4) S. KQ76   (5) S. A104
      H. AQ87   H. A   H. A76   H. K876   H. A104
      D. 765   D. 7654   D. 654   D. 54   D. Q32
      C. J76   C. Q87   C. AQ876   C. J87   C. J987

(1)   Responds 2D to the double to find out more about the doubler's
      hand. Obviously this hand wants to play in game and is search-
      ing for the best spot. Doubler may have five spades and only
      three hearts for example.

(2)   There may even be a slam here. Cue bid 2D and then bid spades
      to force the bidding.

(3)   This hand is too strong for a jump to 3C which is not forcing.
      Cue bid 2D and then bid clubs, which is forcing.

(4)   This hand cue bids 2D and then raises partner's probable major
      suit response to three. This is not forcing but invitational.

If responder tries to guess which major to bid he may guess wrong. With a reasonable hand and both majors a cue bid is best.

(5) The hand is worth a jump to 2NT. However, the diamond stopper is rather tenuous. A cue bid followed by a rebid of 2NT shows the same strength as a jump to 2NT but warns partner of but a single stopper in the opponent's suit.

Quiz on Responding to Takeout Doubles

Assume the bidding has proceeded:

West	North	East	South
1C	Dbl.	Pass	?

What do you respond with each of the following hands:

1. S. K876
    H. 54
    D. A765
    C. 876

2. S. KQ87
    H. A65
    D. 7654
    C. 54

3. S. J87
    H. 654
    D. A98
    C. AQ87

4. S. 876
    H. 1087
    D. 876
    C. K876

5. S. A5
    H. AKQ87
    D. 976
    C. 876

6. S. Q87
    H. J765
    D. 2
    C. QJ765

1. 1S   Major rather than minor in response to a takeout double.

2. 2S   Not forcing. (9-11)

3. 2NT   Not forcing. (10-12 H.C.P.)

4. 1D   Bid the cheaper or cheapest three card suit you own when your longest suit has been bid. Do not faint, do not pass go and do not bid 1NT which is a positive response.

5. 2C   Intending to bid hearts next. Remember, with more than 11 points make a cue bid. There may even be a slam here.

6. 1H   Do not pass the double unless you have five or more likely six good cards in the opponent's suit. With a broken five card holding bid another suit with 7-10 H.C.P. or conceivably 1NT.

Responding to Partner's Opening Bid After a Takeout Double

North	East	South	West
1D	Dbl.	?	

Seems strange that we need devote a section to responding to partner's opening if our right hand opponent doubles. The reason is we have another bid at our disposal now...the redouble... and this colors everything.

The fact that we can and should redouble with almost all hands that have eleven or more H.C.P. makes it possible for partner to infer that if we don't redouble we cannot possibly have a strong hand.

Therefore any bid made over a takeout double other than redouble will deny 11 or more H.C.P. We can now subdivide the remaining hands in the 5-10 H.C.P. range as follows (hands with less than five can safely pass):

> The weak responding hand.............5-8 H.C.P.
> The intermediate responding hand.....9-10 H.C.P.

Responding to Partner's Opening After a
Takeout Double With 5-8 H.C.P.

The options here are:

    (1)   Bid a suit at the one level (forcing).

    (2)   Bid a suit at the two level (not forcing).

    (3)   Jump in a new suit (not forcing).

    (4)   Raise partner to two, three or four.

    (5)   Bid 1NT (shows at least two cards in partner's suit).

    (6)   Pass.

(1) Bidding a new suit at the one level.

It is very easy to lose a major suit fit after a takeout double. With a strong four card major or any five card major it is usually good tactics to bid the suit early before it gets lost in the shuffle.

Assume the bidding proceeds:

North	East	South	West
1D	Dbl.	?	

With any of these hands South responds 1H:

(1)	S. K4	(2)	S. J87	(3)	S. A5
	H. QJ106		H. K10876		H. J87654
	D. 765		D. Q54		D. 43
	C. J765		C. 76		C. Q43

This response is forcing for one round and partner rebids as if there had been no takeout double. In other words opener simply makes a natural rebid keeping in mind that South was not strong enough to redouble.

(2) Bidding a new suit at the two level.

Here we have something else to think about. Normally a new suit at the two level shows 10 or more H.C.P. Because hands in this range usually redouble, the two level response after a takeout is not considered a strong response. It simply shows a good five or, more typically, six card suit and little else.

Assume the bidding has gone:

North	East	South	West
1H	Dbl.	?	

South responds 2C with any of the following hands:

(1)	S. K76	(2)	S. 65	(3)	S. 10765
	H. 2		H. 54		H. ---
	D. J76		D. 987		D. J765
	C. A109876		C. AJ10972		C. KQJ98

This response is not forcing and opener must be particularly careful about rebidding his own suit as responder is marked with shortness from his failure to raise.

(3) Jumping in a new suit.

Again this does not show a hand strong in high cards. It merely shows a strong suit, at least six cards, and little else. The bid is made primarily in a major. Jumping to three of a minor tends to show a seven card suit, or perhaps six to three or four honor cards.

Assume the bidding has gone:

West	North	East	South
Pass.	1D	Dbl.	?

With hands (1) and (2) South jumps to 2S; not forcing:

(1) S. KQ10987
     H. 54
     D. J76
     C. 54

(2) S. AJ10976
     H. 3
     D. 76
     C. 10876

With hands (3) and (4) South jumps to 3C; also not forcing:

(3) S. 654
     H. 8
     D. 1082
     C. AQJ1097

(4) S. J765
     H. 2
     D. 2
     C. AJ108765

Opener should be careful about suggesting an alternate trump suit as the jump shows a dominant one-suiter.

(4) Raising partner.

The most common raise is from one to two. It shows 5-8 SUPPORT POINTS, no more. It is a weak response.

Assume the bidding has started:

North	East	South	West
1H	Dbl.	?	

South responds 2H with each of the following hands:

(1) S. A876
     H. J106
     D. 54
     C. 8765

(2) S. K4
     H. 876
     D. QJ87
     C. 10987

(3) S. J8765
     H. K76
     D. 2
     C. 9876

Opener must be careful not to compete too strenuously after an auction with this beginning. The jump raise to three of partner's suit shows 8-10 support points, at least four trumps and a weak defensive hand (never as many as two defensive tricks).

Assume the bidding has proceeded as follows:

North	East	South	West
1S	Dbl.	?	

The following hands would respond 3S:

(1)	S. K876	(2)	S. AQ98	(3)	S. A8765
	H. 2		H. 76		H. K5
	D. K765		D. J8765		D. 765
	C. 7654		C. 87		C. 654

This is a non-forcing response and opener needs about 17 points to go further.

The jump raise from one to four is also preemptive and looks very much like the raise from one to three only a bit more distributional. Vulnerability is also a consideration when it comes to selecting the proper raise. One has to be a little more careful when vulnerable, particularly against opponents who are not afraid to open their mouths and shout "double".

The following sequence has taken on a special meaning in recent years:

North	East	South	West
1H	Dbl.	2NT	

South obviously doesn't have 13-15 H.C.P. or else he would have redoubled. So what does he have? The best usage for 2NT in this sequence is to show a defensive raise to three of partner's suit.

In other words you are trying to show partner that you not only have four card support but your hand has defensive prospects as well. If the opponents compete, your partner will have a better idea of whether or not to sacrifice. The jump to 2NT usually shows 8-10 H.C.P., a balanced hand and close to two defensive tricks.

North	East	South	West
1H	Dbl.	?	

(1)	S. A4	(2)	S. KQ6
	H. AJ87		H. KJ87
	D. 10987		D. 54
	C. 765		C. 8765

Both these hands respond 2NT. With a minimum opener simply returns to three of his original suit; but with extra values he jumps to four.

(5) The response of 1NT.

This is similar to a 1NT response to an opening bid. The most common range is 7-8 H.C.P. With 5 or 6 it is wiser to pass. The only stipulation here is that you have at least two cards in partner's suit. With a singleton it is better to pass and let the opponents get into trouble.

Assume the bidding has gone:

North	East	South	West
1H	Dbl.	?	

(1)	S. K76 H. 765 D. KJ7 C. 10976	(2)	S. A97 H. J6 D. Q1087 C. 8765	(3)	S. Q987 H. 2 D. K765 C. Q876

Hands (1) and (2) respond 1NT. Hand (3) passes as it has better defensive than offensive prospects.

(6) It is no great crime to pass with 5-8 H.C.P. if your hand does not meet any of the requirements we have discussed here.

Bidding Over the Double With 9-10 H.C.P.

Hands in this range are just shy of a redouble. They are best described by PASSING and then bidding.

Compare these sequences:

North	East	South	West
1S	Dbl.	2S	Pass
?			

North	East	South	West
1S	Dbl.	Pass	2C
Pass	Pass	2S	

In the first case South raised immediately and in the second he passed and then raised. HE IS STRONGER IN THE SECOND SEQUENCE.

There are other parallel sequences:

North	East	South	West
1C	Dbl.	1NT	Pass
?			

North	East	South	West
1C	Dbl.	Pass	1H
Pass	Pass	1NT	

Again South is stronger in the second sequence because he passed and then bid.

More parallel sequences:

North	East	South	West
1H	Dbl.	2D	Pass
?			

North	East	South	West
1H	Dbl.	Pass	1S
Pass	Pass	2D	

South is stronger when he passes first and then bids 2D.

Yet none of these stronger sequences is forcing. They merely describe hands that are a point or two shy of a redouble.

Bidding Over the Double With 11 or More H.C.P.

These hands with few exceptions redouble first and then either bid their own suit or support partner's. The redouble does not in any way, shape or form promise support for opener's suit. In fact most redoubles have short-ness in partner's suit and are hunting for penalties. The opponents are often in trouble. For a further look at the redouble see Chapter 13.

Quiz on Bidding Over a Double

Assume the bidding has proceeded:

North	East	South	West
1H	Dbl.	?	

What should South respond with each of the following hands?

1. S. J87
   H. J76
   D. Q876
   C. 1087

2. S. 7
   H. 76
   D. KQJ10876
   C. 765

3. S. A98
   H. AJ7
   D. 765
   C. 6543

4. S. KJ87
   H. 2
   D. A876
   C. QJ76

5. S. 6
   H. AQ876
   D. J7654
   C. 54

6. S. 87
   H. KQ87
   D. A876
   C. 654

7. S. AJ8
   H. 54
   D. Q1076
   C. 7654

8. S. K8765
   H. K876
   D. 2
   C. 1087

9. S. K87
   H. 54
   D. 54
   C. AKJ987

10. S. K10
    H. 6
    D. QJ9876
    C. 7654

Solutions

1. Pass   No reason to bid on this piece of garbage.

2. 3D   Strong suit; weak hand.

3. Pass   And then raise hearts to show 9-10 H.C.P.

4. Rdbl.   And then double for penalties any suit the opponents bid.

5. 4H

6. 2NT   A defensive raise to 3H. Promises four trumps and about two defensive tricks.

7. 1NT   7-8 H.C.P. and at least two cards in partner's suit.

8. 3H   An offensive raise. Usually one defensive trick and at least four card support.

9. Rdbl.   And then bid clubs.

10. 2D   Get those long suits in early. 2D is not forcing.

7. FORCING OR NOT FORCING

If you and your partner wish to play a cohesive system, that system should be outlined so that you know which bids are forcing and which are not.

Here is a chart which should help you.

I. Opening Bids

The only forcing opening bid is a strong two bid. If using weak two bids the only forcing opening bid is 2C. An opening bid of 2NT is not forcing.

II. Responses (By a Non-Passed Hand)

All new suit responses are one round forces unless opener rebids 1NT.

A jump shift or a jump to 2NT is forcing to game.

If the opponents overcall, a cue bid in the opponent's suit is forcing to game.

Direct raises, including a jump from one to three, are not forcing. But any jump raise in a minor which bypasses 3NT is forcing to game.

Opener	Responder
1H	1S
2C	4C

Responder's 4C bid is a game force.

III. Overcalls

Simple or jump overcalls are not forcing.

A direct cue bid can be used as a game force but the most popular treatment is to use it as a two-suiter which makes it forcing for one round only.

IV. Takeout Doubles

Partner is allowed to pass a takeout double under two conditions:
    (1) An intervening bid to the right.
    (2) Great length and strength in the opener's suit.

A takeout double followed by a cue bid by the takeout doubler is forcing until the takeout doubler either bids no trump or raises partner's suit.

V. Responses to Overcalls

The only forcing response is a cue bid in the opponent's suit.

VI. Responses to Takeout Doubles

The only forcing response is a cue bid.

VII. Rebid by the Opener after Partner has Made a One Level Response

The only forcing rebids are reverses, jump shifts and cue bids if the opponents have bid.

A reverse is a one round force.

A jump shift is forcing to game.

VIII. Rebid by the Opener after a Two Level Response

All new suits are forcing.

A reverse is forcing to game as is a new suit at the three level.

All jumps are forcing to game.

A rebid of 2NT is forcing for one round.

General Rules to Remember

1. No bid either partner makes is forcing on the other if there has been an intervening bid to the <u>right</u>.

2. If either player makes an invitational jump (a bid which can be passed) and the partner of that player bids, the partnership is forced to game.

Opener	Responder	
1H	1S	The 3S bid is forcing to game.
3H	3S	The 3H bid was not forcing.

3. A new suit beneath the game level in response to a preemptive bid is forcing.

Opener	Responder	
3D	3H	The 3H bid is forcing.

4. The only forcing responses a passed hand can make are either cue bids (if the opponents have bid) or jump shifts (usually from a major to a minor).

5. Jump raises to the three level are not forcing but jump raises to the four level in a minor are.

Opener	Responder	
1D	1H	Responder can pass.
3H		

Opener	Responder	
1D	2C	Responder cannot pass.
4C		

   The general idea is that any jump in a minor that bypasses 3NT is forcing to game. Of course these sequences are not forcing:

Opener	Responder
1C	4C

Opener	Responder
1D	4D

6. Jump preferences after a one level response are not forcing but after a two level response are forcing.

Opener	Responder
1H	1S
2C	3H

Responder's last bid is not forcing. However if opener bids again the partnership is forced to game.

Opener	Responder
1H	2C
2D	3H

Responder's last bid is forcing to game.

7. An original jump to 2NT by the responder is forcing to game but a second round jump to 2NT is not forcing.

Opener	Responder
1H	2NT

Game force.

Opener	Responder
1D	1H
1S	2NT

Not forcing.

8. Delayed support is forcing; immediate support is not.

Opener	Responder
1S	2C
2H	2S
3C	

The 3C bid is forcing. Had opener raised directly to 3C responder could pass.

9. Raises to 4NT that are not Blackwood but simply show strong balanced hands are not forcing.

10. A jump to game in one's own major or in partner's major is not forcing. A jump to 3NT is never forcing.

8. A LITTLE COMMON SENSE CAN GO A LONG WAY

This little essay may not apply to you but it may to your partner. Remember in this game it is not how weak or strong you are but rather the combined strength of the partnership that counts.

Nobody likes to hold a five point hand but if partner opens 2NT it is not so terrible.

Partner's bidding is supposed to show you both strength and distribution. Most players think about strength but few ever consider distribution. For instance, when partner bids two suits and supports a third he almost surely has a singleton in the fourth suit. You should not go plunging ahead in no trump unless you are quite secure in partner's singleton suit.

Rebids normally show six card suits, not five. Jump rebids promise six card suits. If both opponents have shown strong hands during the bidding be careful about competing too strenuously. Partner simply can't have a good hand.

Don't overcall at the two level on points. Have tricks - which means good intermediate cards in the suit you are bidding.

Don't, and this is so important, tell your partner what you have already told him. If you have shown the strength of your hand with your previous bidding let your partner make the final decision.

Be sure to discount jacks and queens in suits the opponents are bidding. They seldom carry their weight. Singletons and voids in partner's suits are seldom valuable - don't make the beginners' mistake of counting points for them. Only count points for short suits when you have trump support.

Be very careful with hands that have wild distribution until you find a fit. Then the sky is the limit.

In most situations it pays to support partner's suit rather than to rebid your own. This is doubly true if his suit is a major and yours is a minor. Good partners support quickly.

If you have a two-suited hand and one of your opponents bids one of your suits your hand is never quite as strong as it looks. If you play the hand you will usually have problems disposing of your losers in the suit bid by the opponents.

After your partner has bid and the opponents have intervened consider doubling with length in the opponents suit and shortness in your partner's. Many players simply bid no trump and never consider the possibility of a low level penalty double.

If your partner has shown a weak hand with a long suit it is usually better to let him play the hand in his suit rather than have you play it in yours. The reason is that if you play the hand his hand will be worthless to you as a dummy, but if he plays the hand he can use some of your high cards as well as his long suit to take tricks.

Perhaps by concluding with some examples you will understand the futility of being a point counter to the exclusion of all else.

I. The Fit and the Misfit

Opener	Responder (1)	Responder (2)
S. AKxxx	S. x	S. x
H. AJxxx	H. KQxxx	H. xx
D. Kxx	D. Axx	D. xxxx
C. ---	C. xxxx	C. AKQxxx

Opener and Responder (1) make at least six and more likely seven hearts.

Opener and Responder (2) are probably down at any contract at the three level.

Both responding hands have exactly 9 H.C.P. But responder (2)'s points are in clubs where they are not helping the opener.

Lesson: When a hand fits well, the wilder the distribution the better.
When there is a misfit, the wilder the distribution the worse.

II. The Right Singleton

Opener	Responder (1)	Responder (2)
S. xxxx	S. x	S. xxx
H. AKxxxx	H. 10xxxx	H. 10xxxx
D. AK	D. xxx	D. xxxx
C. A	C. xxxx	C. x

Opener and Responder (1) are a laydown for six hearts.

Opener and Responder (2) are apt to go down in 4H with a spade lead if the suit breaks 4-2.

Both responding hands have zero H.C.P. and the same distribution but responder (1) has a singleton in spades which takes care of opener's losing spades and responder (2) has a singleton in clubs which does not help opener take care of his losing spades.

Lesson: Whenever partner has a singleton in a suit in which you have length and weakness the sky is the limit if partner has good trump support.

Whenever partner has the same short suit you do - be careful.

III. The Right Void

Opener	Responder (1)	Responder (2)
S. ---	S. xxx	S. AKQ
H. xxx	H. AKx	H. AKxx
D. AQJxxxx	D. Kxx	D. Kxx
C. xxx	C. AKQ	C. xxx

Opener and Responder (1) are a spread for 6D.

Opener and Responder (2) cannot even make 5D with a club lead.

Both responding hands have the identical point count but responder (1) has his strength in clubs opposite partner's length and responder (2) has his strength in spades opposite partner's void.

Lesson: Do not become immediately enamored of your void even
if the hand has a fit. If the void is facing weakness
in partner's hand the sky is the limit. If the void
is facing great strength there is almost always duplication of values and often quick losers in another
suit.

IV. The right honor cards

Opener	Responder (1)	Responder (2)
S. xx	S. Ax	S. Ax
H. Axx	H. xxx	H. Qxx
D. AKJxxx	D. Qx	D. xx
C. Qx	C. AKJxxx	C. AKJxxx

Opener and responder (1) have fourteen tricks at no trump, clubs or
diamonds.

Opener and responder (2) are in some jeopardy at the five level in
a minor.

Both have the identical count but the difference is the queen of
diamonds vs. the queen of hearts.

Lesson: Honor cards in partner's long suits are worth their weight
in gold. Honor cards in partner's short suits are seldom
valuable, particularly jacks and queens.

V. The Wrong Honor Cards

Opener	Responder (1)	Responder (2)
S. x	S. Qxxxx	S. xxxxx
H. xxx	H. Axx	H. Axx
D. AKxxxx	D. xx	D. Qx
C. AJx	C. Kxx	C. Kxx

Opener and responder (1) have no makeable game.

Opener and responder (2) are almost certainly cold for 3NT.

Both have the point count but responder (1) has a wasted queen of spades and responder (2) has a golden queen of diamonds.

Lesson: Long suits headed by secondary honor cards are usually valueless at a suit contract if another suit is trump and partner is marked with shortness in your long suit.

For example, responder (1) counts his hand at ten points before the bidding begins. But after opener rebids diamonds, denying spade support, responder should drop three points from his count! The queen of spades figures to be worthless as does the fifth spade!

Responder (2), on the other hand, should add a point or two to his hand because of the increased value of the queen of diamonds.

It is certainly true that each of the preceding examples cannot always be bid to the perfect contract, but for there to be any chance at all of arriving at the best contract the partnership must be aware of what is really important...and it isn't entirely the number of points (unless both hands are balanced) but rather the location of those points.

9. THE PENALTY DOUBLE

Most players abuse the one bid that can win them the most points......the penalty double. The penalty double can be used at any level with devastating results - if used properly.

Perhaps we can simplify the discussion with a definition.

A double is for penalties if:

a) Partner has made a positive bid of any kind at any level.

   Example: | South | West | North | East |
   |---|---|---|---|
   | 1C | 1D | Dbl. | |

   North's double is for penalties. South has made a positive bid.

b) The double is of a No Trump bid at any level.

   Example: | South | West | North | East |
   |---|---|---|---|
   | 1NT | Dbl. | | |

   West's double is for penalties.

   Except: | West | North | East | South |
   |---|---|---|---|
   | 1H,1S | Pass | 1NT | Dbl. |

   South's double is used as a takeout double of opener's suit.

c) The doubler has remained silent until the opponents have reached the three level or higher.

   Example: | South | West | North | East |
   |---|---|---|---|
   | 1H | Pass | 1S | Pass |
   | 2H | Pass | 3H | Pass |
   | 4H | Dbl. | | |

   West's double is for penalties because he had a chance to double for takeout earlier.

d) The opponents have bid three suits and the first response was at the two level.

   Example: | South | West | North | East |
   |---|---|---|---|
   | 1H | Pass | 2C | Pass |
   | 2D | Dbl. | | |

   West's double is for penalties showing long diamonds because the opponents have bid three suits and North's first response was at the two level.

If North had responded 1S, West's double would be for takeout.

Perhaps:
S. AJ4
H. AQ87
D. 2
C. K10865

e) The double is of an artificial bid such as Stayman or a reply to Blackwood.

Example:

South	West	North	East
1NT	Pass	2C	Dbl.

East's double is for penalties because the 2C response is artificial asking South to name a four card major.

f) The opponents have opened the bidding with 4S or higher and either player doubles.

Example:

South	West	North	East
4S	Dbl.		

or

South	West	North	East
4S	Pass	Pass	Dbl.

In either case the double is for penalties. If the opponents open 4C, 4D or 4H and either player doubles it is optional although partner passes more often than not.

Now we can study some of these situations separately.

For example: Partner opens 1C and the next hand overcalls 1H.

What do you need to double?

In order to judge when to double an overcall, keep these basics in mind:

1. A partner who has opened the bidding will usually contribute between two and three defensive tricks.

2. You must be able to add your defensive tricks to your partner's assumed defensive tricks to see whether the partnership will be able to take enough tricks to defeat the opposing contract.

3. The best time to double is when you are short in partner's suit (two or fewer cards). The worst time is when you have four or more cards in partner's suit. One opponent will surely be short suited and partner's defensive tricks will go down the drain.

4. If you are considering a double of a No Trump contract, add your points to partner's. Remember it takes about 25-26 points to make 3NT. If you and partner have 16 or more H.C.P. between you, the opponents should not be able to make 3NT unless they have a long suit to run or their honor cards are well placed.

5. It is important when considering a penalty double to ask yourself if your honor cards are well placed. For example, holding KJx of clubs in back or to the left of a club bidder, you probably have two defensive tricks. However, if the club bidder is to your left, you may not take a single trick.

6. The lower the level of the contract you are doubling, the stronger your trumps should be. If you are contemplating a double at the level of one, have five trumps (four good ones is an exception but possible). At the two level four good trumps is sufficient and at higher levels you may double with fewer trumps provided you don't have excessive length in partner's suit or suits that he doesn't know about.

7. Opponents are bound to make some doubled contracts against you. Don't let it bother you. If the opponents never make a doubled contract against you, you are not doubling often enough!

To return to our sequence:

North	East	South	West
1C	1H	?	

South should double 1H with a hand that has heart length and contains four or more defensive tricks. To help you count defensive tricks here is a spot guide:

a. Any Ace is one defensive trick. An Ace-King would be considered two defensive tricks unless you have a six card suit in which case you might take only one trick. An AQ is considered 1-1/2 tricks.

b. A King is considered half a defensive trick but in back of the bidder is worth a full trick more often than not. The King and Queen together in one suit is worth at least one defensive trick and might well turn out to be two.

c. In the trump suit the fourth card is worth one-half trick and every card thereafter is worth one full trick regardless of size. AKxxx in the opponent's suit should be counted as 3-1/2 defensive tricks. Back to our model sequence. Partner opens 1C and next hand bids 1H.

S. A54 = one defensive trick

H. KQ876 = three and a half defensive tricks

D. K54 = probably one defensive trick

C. 32 = no defensive tricks

You have roughly five to six defensive tricks against a heart contract! Partner has opened the bidding promising at least two to three defensive tricks. If your side can take eight defensive tricks, how are they to make 1H? They are not. Double 1H.

If an opponent wanders into the bidding with an overcall at the two level, double with four or more defensive tricks. You might even try it with three!

North	East	South	West
1H	2C	?	

You, South, hold:

S. AK7
H. 43
D. 10876
C. QJ87

You have two defensive tricks in spades and two more in clubs. Your four defensive tricks along with partner's two or three spell a two trick set. Double.

What if the opponents overcall 1NT?

North	East	South	West
1H	1NT	?	

North is assumed to hold at least 12-13 points. There are 40 H.C.P. in the deck. If South has eight or more points, he should consider a penalty double. North-South will have more points than East-West and should, therefore, take more tricks.

If South has:

S. A102
H. J4
D. QJ87
C. 10987

South doubles 1NT.

With a singleton in partner's suit, it pays to have a little extra when doubling 1NT. Nine points minimum.

Doubles of eventual No Trump contracts can even be made on relatively weak hands! Assume South holds this hand:

S. A1054
H. 32
D. J765
C. 432

The bidding proceeds:

North	East	South	West
1H	1S	Pass	1NT
Pass	2NT	Pass	3NT
Pass	Pass	?	

Partner has opened and you have five points plus a double stopper in dummy's long suit. Together you have about 18 points, leaving the opponents 22. They should have 25 or more to make 3NT. They must be overboard. Teach them a lesson. Double.

Sometimes all you have to do is sit and wait. Let's say you hold:

S. AJ984
H. AQ10
D. 432
C. 32

Sitting West this is what you hear:

South	West	North	East
1S	Pass	2C	Pass
2D	Pass	3S	Pass
4S	?		

Don't wait any longer! The opponents have reached game and have run into a horribly breaking trump suit. Make them pay. Double.

Sometimes the opponents run into stacked hands. Again, you are West and you hold:

S. 4
H. AQ1032
D. QJ98
C. A106

The bidding proceeds:

South	West	North	East
1H	Pass	1NT	Pass
2H	Dbl.		

You have declarer's suit and there is no need to let him off the hook. If you pass, the hand may pass out in 2H and you won't get enough. Double.

Be on the lookout to double artificial bids.

You are South: S. 43
                                   H. A54
                                   D. 543
                                   C. KQ1087

The bidding proceeds: | West | North | East | South |
                        |------|-------|------|-------|
                        | 1NT | Pass | 2C | ? |

Double! This will alert your partner to lead a club regardless of the final
        contract.

or   S. 74
                                   H. KQJ8
                                   D. 753
                                   C. 6543

West	North	East	South
1S	Pass	3S	Pass
4NT	Pass	5H	?

Double to alert partner to lead hearts against the eventual slam contract.
Remember the 5H response is artificial; so, your double is for penalties.

A Final Word

1. Count your defensive tricks before doubling a suit contract and add them
   to partner's assumed defensive tricks.

2. Count your H.C.P. and add them to partner's H.C.P. when contemplating a
   double of a no trump contract.

3. Do not make a low level penalty double with four or more cards in partner's suit.

4. Holding four or five cards in the opponents' suit is usually worth one
   or two defensive tricks even if they are small cards.

5. Beware of the sucker double! Partner opens 1C, next hand overcalls 1S,
   and you hold:
                                   S. Q1097532
                                   H. 2
                                   D. Q75
                                   C. 32

Even though you have enough defensive tricks against spades you should pass! The opponents or partner are sure to run and you have no defense against any other contract. Once you have made a low level penalty double, partner will be inclined to double a run-out leaving you in a ticklish spot. The answer is to either have a little outside strength or high honor cards in the suit you are doubling.

6. Doubles of game contracts are the least risky; doubles of 2H or 2S are the most risky because if made you have doubled the opponents into game. Doubles of 2C and 2D are good gambles because the opponents make only an extra 90 points if they just make their contract.

10. WHEN PARTNER MAKES A PENALTY DOUBLE

When your partner makes a penalty double (particularly at the lower levels) he is not commanding you to pass, he is merely suggesting you do so. And unless you are playing with your husband or wife you do not automatically pass! If you have distributional values that your partner cannot possibly know about you normally remove the double.

The most obvious example is removing a penalty double at the one or two level with a void in the opponent's trump suit and a two or three-suited hand.

South	West	North	East
1H	1S	Dbl.	Pass
?			

South holds:

(1)		(2)		(3)	
S.	---	S.	---	S.	---
H.	AQ10xx	H.	AQ10xxxx	H.	AJxxx
D.	KQ10xx	D.	xxx	D.	KQxx
C.	xxx	C.	KQx	C.	QJxx

With (1)   South rebids 2D to show a two suiter.

With (2)   South rebids 2H to show a dominant one suiter with a singleton or void in spades.

With (3)   South either rebids one of his minor suits or by agreement bids 1NT to show a three suited hand.

Keep in mind that South must automatically (99% of the time) pass a penalty double with any balanced hand or with any hand that has at least two cards in the doubled suit. Therefore whenever South pulls the double he is announcing a marked shortness in the opponent's suit even if he himself bids no trump.

Furthermore, South should be very reluctant to rebid his original suit as partner is trying to tell him by doubling that the hand is a misfit. The doubler will seldom, if ever, have more than a doubleton in opener's first suit and usually has a singleton.

Opener has his biggest problem when holding a singleton in the doubled suit. With a void he usually pulls the double, with two or more cards in the opponent's suit he sticks out the double but with a singleton he must use his judgment. If he has an offensive hand he should remove the double but with a defensive hand he should pass.

South	West	North	East
1D	1S	Dbl.	Pass
?			

South holds:

(1) S. x	(2) S. x	(3) S. x	(4) S. x
H. Axx	H. Kxx	H. Axx	H. Axx
D. KQJxxx	D. QJ10xx	D. KQJxx	D. AKxxxx
C. J10x	C. KQJx	C. A10xx	C. Kxx

With hands (1) and (2) South should remove the double as his hand is not defense oriented. With (1) the rebid is 2D and with (2) 2C. With hands (3) and (4) South has excellent defense (remember partner is short in diamonds) and South should pass the double.

Penalty Doubles at Higher Levels

This is a sticky subject. The bidding can go in so many different ways before either player makes a penalty double that it is quite difficult to lay down any general rules; however:

1. One tends to leave in high level penalty doubles with any balanced or semi-balanced hand.

2. If one has hidden four card support or longer for one of partner's suits one tends to remove the double.

3. With freak hands that partner does not know about one tends to remove the double.

South	West	North	East
1H	1S	2D	4S
Pass	Pass	Dbl.	Pass
?			

South holds:

(1) S. x	(2) S. xx	(3) S. x
H. AKxxx	H. AQxxxx	H. AJ10xxx
D. KJxx	D. Jxx	D. x
C. Jxx	C. KQx	C. KQJxx

With (1)   South should pull the double to 5D because of his hidden four card support. Had South supported diamonds earlier he could safely pass the double.

148

With (2)   South should pass.

With (3)   South should bid 5C. He has a freak that his partner
          couldn't possibly know about.

Keep in mind that when partner doubles a high level
contract he seldom has excellent trumps. He is merely
in a bind having no real fit with any of your suits
and does not feel disposed to rebid at the four or
five level his own suit which has not been supported.

11. COMPETITIVE BIDDING AND BALANCING

The best tournament and money bridge players know when to fight tenaciously for part scores. The money bridge player realizes the significance of preventing the opponents from making a part score and is prepared to sacrifice up to 200 points to prevent one.

The tournament player knows he cannot win tournaments unless he frequently pushes his opponents from the two level, where they may wish to play, to the three level where he has a better chance to defeat the contract.

Certain basics must be realized before deciding when to compete or how much to push opponents who do not seem to be going any place in the bidding. They are:

A. If the opponents have an eight card fit or longer in one suit, you and your partner will almost always have a similar fit in another suit. Alternately, if the opponents have no eight card fit and their bidding suggests a misfit it is quite likely that you and partner also do not have an eight card fit and are similarly misfitted.

B. If the opponents voluntarily stop at the two level their total high card count will usually range between 18-23 H.C.P. which means that you and partner will usually be as strong as your opponents even though neither of you has entered the bidding!

C. Because it is to your advantage to compete against opponents who have died out at the lower levels you must have a method of doing so which will not confuse partner. In other words, he must realize that you are simply trying to push the opponents one level higher and do not have normal strength for your bid.

Consider these sequences:

(1)	South	West	North	East
	1H	Dbl.		

	(2)	South	West	North	East
		1H	Pass	2H	Pass
		Pass	Dbl.		

In (1), West has doubled directly at his first opportunity. This is called doubling in the direct position and shows normal values. West should have an opening bid or better. However, in case (2) West did not double immediately but waited until the bidding would have died out before he doubled. This is called doubling in the "dead" or "balancing" position.

Balancing doubles show 9-12 H.C.P. and can be equated to takeout doubles by a passed hand. A typical West hand for (2) might be:

S. AJ54
H. 54
D. K876
C. QJ9

The most common balancing sequence is the one just described. Responder raises opener who, in turn, passes. The player in the "dead seat" knows there is an opposing fit and has three ways of reentering the bidding:

1. The first and most common is the takeout double. The doubler should have support for each of the unbid suits, preferably two or fewer cards in the suit he is doubling.

   Using our model sequence (2) these are examples of reopening or balancing doubles:

	(a)			(b)			(c)	
		S. A765			S. K108			S. J1065
		H. 4			H. 43			H. 4
		D. K876			D. A765			D. AJ876
		C. Q654			C. K1087			C. K98

Notice the first hand (a) has only 9 H.C.P. One should seldom dip lower if partner is to have any confidence in balancing doubles. The second hand (b) is actually weaker offensively than (a) because it has only three card support for the other major, the suit your partner is most likely to bid. Your partner will not be disappointed in (c) which is the best of the lot. Remember - if you are weaker than 9 H.C.P., even with the proper distribution, pass.

2. Another method of reentering the bidding in the balancing seat is by
    bidding a new suit.

	South	West	North	East
	1D	Pass	2D	Pass
	Pass	2H		

Why didn't West overcall 1H originally? Why didn't West double originally in our other examples? He wasn't strong enough! But now that
he sees that the opponents have a fit and have voluntarily stopped at
the two level he knows his partner must have something and was not
quite strong enough to bid in the direct position where full values
are needed.

Here are some typical West hands for the bidding:

	(a)	(b)	(c)
S.	A4	K8	73
H.	J107654	A10976	KQ109
D.	Q43	543	A765
C.	J6	J76	J106

Notice that West was not strong enough to make an original overcall
on any of these hands. The third hand (c) is an exception. The balancer will almost always have a five card suit or longer. An exception can be made with a strong four card suit along with four cards
in the opponent's suit suggesting shortness in partner's hand.

3. A third method of reentering the auction after a major suit opening
    has been supported is with 2NT. A balancing bid of 2NT is considered
    a two-suited takeout for the minors denying the strength or distribu-
    tion of an original 2NT overcall which is also considered "unusual"
    For example, assume West holds either of these hands:

S.	4	S.	54
H.	32	H.	K2
D.	A8765	D.	AJ107
C.	K10876	C.	K9876

	South	West	North	East
	1H	Pass	2H	Pass
	Pass	?		

With either of these hands West balances with 2NT. The bid describes
a hand with at least 5-4 in the two lower unbid suits, preferably 5-5
vulnerable.

Another common balancing act occurs when your left hand opponent opens and this is passed around to you:

West	North	East	South
1H	Pass	Pass	?

How much do you need in this situation to bid?

As it is quite clear the responder has less than six points, you need not worry about the opponents having passed out a game (although they will occasionally), but rather about competing for the partial which may rightfully belong to you.

You may double with as little as nine or ten H.C.P. if you have the proper distribution; bid a suit with a fairly good suit and little else, say a minimum of 8 H.C.P.; or bid 1NT.

The 1NT bid in this situation has a range of 11-15 points. With 16-18 points double and then make a minimum rebid in no trump. With more, double and jump in no trump. Of course, all these no trump bids describe balanced hands with at least one stopper in the enemy suit. A direct jump to 2NT is unusual.

Other points to consider before reopening are whether or not the opponents are vulnerable, in which case it might be best to let them play at the one level with a strong holding in opener's suit, and whether the opening bid on your left has been a major or a minor. If it is a minor suit and partner has not been able to overcall, one should think twice about reopening and conceivably allowing the opponents to find a better spot. Remember, if partner couldn't overcall a minor suit opening bid, he can't have too terribly much unless he happens to be loaded in opener's suit and is making a trap pass.

Assume the bidding has gone with both sides vulnerable:

West	North	East	South
1C	Pass	Pass	?

What should South do?

1. S. A76
    H. K76
    D. KJ98
    C. Q107

2. S. KJ87
    H. AJ87
    D. J98
    C. 54

3. S. KJ8
    H. A987
    D. K87
    C. AJ8

4. S. KJ876
    H. A76
    D. Q87
    C. 43

5. S. K8
    H. J876
    D. K7
    C. AQ876

6. S. AQJ876
    H. A
    D. Q87
    C. 1087

7. S. 5
    H. A8765
    D. Q76
    C. K876

1. 1NT   In the balancing position this shows 11-15 points. If you are
          a passed hand it shows 10-12.

2. Dbl. You might even have a point less for a reopening double, but
          if you do you should have 4-4-4-1 distribution.

3. Dbl. You are intending to bid 1NT over any response partner makes.
          By bidding this way you show 16-18 points and are distinguishing
          between hands (1) and (3).

4. 1S   Fairly normal. Might even be done with slightly less.

5. Pass You have too much defense against clubs to disturb the contract.
          Partner must be weak as he is obviously short in clubs and could
          neither overcall nor double.

6. 2S   Showing a good six card suit and an opening bid. This is not
          forcing but tells partner you have a good hand (similar to an
          intermediate jump overcall).

7. Pass Where, oh where, are the Spades? One must be careful about bal-
          ancing without spades having a partner who had a chance to bid
          the suit at the one level and did not.

Other common balancing situations:

West	North	East	South
1H	Pass	1NT	Pass
2H	Pass	Pass	Dbl.

Frequently, South will have a hand that is short in hearts with support for
the other suits. For example, South may hold:

S. AJ87
H. 4
D. K876
C. Q1095

154

South was unable to double earlier as he was in the direct position and his double would have shown a full opening. However, in the balancing position South can double with as little as 10 points and the proper distribution. For balancing doubles the point count is not as important as the distribution.

Incidentally, if North had doubled 2H on the same auction it would be considered a penalty double. North is over the bidder (not in the balancing position), did not double but passed at his first opportunity and would be doubling opponents who have not found a fit - all criteria for a penalty double.

Returning to:

West	North	East	South
1H	Pass	1NT	Pass
2H`	Pass	Pass	?

South is also at liberty to bid a suit provided it is a good suit.

With:

```
S. KJ10876    or    S. 1098
H. 43               H. ---
D. 32               D. J1076
C. K87              C. KQJ987
```

South should mention his long suit. North will not be misled as South did not overcall at his first opportunity (in the direct position) and has denied normal values.

A somewhat similar sequence is the following:

West	North	East	South
1H	Pass	1NT	Pass
2D	Pass	Pass	?

East appears to like diamonds but neither East nor West has shown any oomph. South should be reluctant to sell out if he has the proper distribution for reentering the bidding.

With:

```
S. AJ87
H. 43
D. 32
C. KQ876
```

South doubles - a takeout double asking for the unbid suits. If partner happens to be loaded in diamonds he passes but will usually bid. Notice

155

that you are doubling because you have support for the two unbid suits (at least four cards in each).

With:

S. Q76
H. KJ76
D. A87
C. K76

South passes 2D. A double would be misleading. With a defensive type hand (a balanced hand) it is better to let the opponents play the contract. Besides, South's heart strength is misplaced under the heart bidder.

When is it dangerous to balance? In rubber bridge it is dangerous when the opponents have a partial, as you can no longer tell if they are simply completing their partial with strength to spare or are really weak. Once the opponents have a part score it is better to get in early and forget about balancing unless you have just the right hand.

Also, it doesn't pay to balance against opponents who are having a tough time finding a fit. The bidding:

North	South
1D	1H
2C or 2D	2H

is a risky sequence to contest as there is no fit in the North-South hands.

Consider these sequences:

North	East	South	West		North	East	South	West
1C	Pass	1D	Pass		1C	Pass	1D	Pass
1H	Pass	1S	Pass		1H	Pass	1NT	Pass
1NT	Pass	Pass	Dbl.		Pass	Dbl.		

When the opponents have bid three or four suits and land in no trump, any double is for penalty and would only be made if you thought your honor cards were well placed or that you had more high card strength than the opponents.

Also in the No Trump family is the following:

East	South	West	North
1H	Pass	1NT	Pass
Pass	?		

156

East-West have no fit so South must be careful. Yet the opponents have stopped at the level of one. What does South need to bid?

If South doubles he would be showing an opening bid or better with the majority of his strength in hearts! It would be silly for South to make a balancing double on 10-12 points against misfitted opponents.

South should have something like:

```
S. 54
H. AQ98
D. AK107
C. J87
```

for his double. North will be inclined to pass unless he has a long suit and a weak hand defensively. If South bids a suit rather than doubling, it should be a strong six carder with little else, perhaps:

```
S. 74
H. Q942
D. 3
C. AQ10976
```

To repeat: Doubles of 1NT in the balancing seat are primarily for penalties. Typically they show balanced hands with strength in opener's suit or suits and 13-15 H.C.P. An exception in the direct position is:

West	North	East	South
1H or 1S	Pass	1NT	Dbl.

Typically South will be doubling for takeout. Atypically he will have a balanced hand with 15-17 H.C.P.

As you have noticed, the balancer makes an assumption that when the opponents die out at the one or two level his partner has some high cards that he has not been able to bid for any one of a number of reasons: a balanced hand, too much strength in the opponent's suit, a long broken suit, etc. So you balance hoping partner has those cards which will usually be enough to help your side make something or at most be down one trick at the two level. The problem arises when your partner suddenly thinks he has a few cards that he has not bid. He now undoes all the good you have done by bidding on after you have balanced.

The typical situation is:

West	North	East	South
1H	Pass	2H	Pass
Pass	2S	3H	?

South holds:

    S. K54
    H. 32
    D. KJ87
    C. K765

Suddenly South now thinks he should bid 3S. After all, his partner bid 2S, didn't he? But North bid 2S on the assumption that South had 10-12 points and some spade support. In other words, North already bid all of South's cards with that 2S bid! South must have additional distributional values to contemplate competing further after partner has balanced - a singleton and usually four trumps.

If South held:

    S. Q1087
    H. 3
    D. A765
    C. K1076

he would be justified in a 3S bid, but not with less.

Because it is so important to compete for the part score, there are a few standard competitive situations with which every bridge player must be familiar. The first is:

South	West	North	East
1H	1S	2H	2S
3H			

South is not really trying to get to game. True, he doesn't have an absolute minimum, but if he has a good five card suit (reducing the chances of an adverse penalty double) it is usually to his advantage to try to push the opponents up one higher. North should not bid 4H on the auction.

Before we leave this sequence, let's consider East's raise to 2S. This may not be quite the same type of hand that would have raised to 2S had North not bid 2H. East may be worried that the bidding will die in 2H and may be raising with a doubleton honor and 10-12 points to prevent North-South from stealing the hand. West therefore should have extra values or a good six card suit to compete to 3S.

Tip: <u>Competitive</u> <u>raises</u> do not guarantee the same trump support that non-competitive raises do.

East might have:
```
S. Q7
H. 543
D. AJ73
C. K765
```

Another sequence that causes difficulty is:

South	West	North	East
1NT	2H	2NT	Pass
?			

What does North's 2NT bid show in this sequence? The normal meaning of 2NT as a raise is 8-9 points. However, in competition it might be made on a hand that would have passed a 1NT opening! North may have:
```
S. J43
H. 32
D. AJ1087
C. 1097
```

Therefore South must have an absolute maximum to bid 3NT on this sequence and North must raise directly to 3NT with 9 points.

A word of caution when bidding competitively. With a defensive hand opposite a partner who has overcalled and opponents who are making forcing bids, do not raise partner immediately even with support for his suit. You will simply encourage him to take a phantom sacrifice.

For example, you, South, hold:
```
S. 1087
H. KJ106
D. 43
C. AJ76
```

and the bidding has proceeded:

West	North	East	South
1H	1S	2C	?

Do <u>not</u> bid 2S with this type of hand. Your strength is in the opponents' suits. Do not slow them down or mislead your partner by giving immediate raise.

12. THE PASSED HAND

What is the difference between a responder who has passed originally and one who has not? The main difference is that the responder has already limited his hand by passing. Partner can not expect an opening bid. Partner can pass new suit responses!

One of the problems of a passed responder is worrying about light third or fourth hand opening bids. This in turn causes him to bid unnaturally. The everpresent fear opener will pass in the middle of an auction is obsessive.

My idea is that you should not open light in the third or fourth position. Playing Weak Twos eliminates the need for most light opening bids that have long suits - and balanced hands that have 10-12 points can just as profitably pass as open in third or fourth seat.

Knowing partner has a sound opening makes passed hand bidding a delight rather than a chore.

What do responses by passed hands mean?

Example I.	Responder	Opener
	Pass	1C
	1H	

Responder must have 6 points and his upper limit is 12. Opener should seldom pass this 1H bid, but if he does he must have at least three hearts and a hand he probably should not have opened in the first place.

Example II.	Responder	Opener
	Pass	1H
	2C	

Responder should have between 10-12 count and is not expecting a pass from the opener (unless there is a part-score). Opener is not forced to bid again but should keep in mind that responder can have a secondary fit in hearts (three cards) and he should pass only with a poor heart suit, a minimum hand, and preferably three clubs - a hand where game in hearts is out of the question.

Example III.   Responder   Opener

                Pass   1H
                2NT

Responder has 11-12 points and has made a non-forcing response. If, for example, opener rebids 3H, responder can pass if the pair is not using Weak Two Bids as opener is signing off. If the pair is using Weak Two Bids, the 3H rebid is forcing as opener must have a good hand or else he would have opened 2H in the first place. Any new suit by the opener is forcing in this sequence.

Example IV.   Responder   Opener

                Pass   1H
                3H

Responder is showing 10-12 points in support of hearts with at least four card support. Playing five card majors, responder can have three card support. (Even playing four card majors many players jump to three of partner's major with three card support for fear of being dropped in a new suit.) If you and partner open light in third or fourth seat, this is a problem. However, playing sound openings, four trumps for your jump raises please!

The Jump Shift by a Passed Hand

Example I.   Responder   Opener

                Pass   1D
                2S

Again this type of sequence depends upon whether or not you are using Weak Two Bids. If you are not, the 2S bid is the equivalent of a Weak Two Bid - a good six card suit and almost an opening bid. Opener is allowed to pass a jump to two of a major with an absolute minimum hand.

Using Weak Two Bids the 2S bid is a one round force - probably a hand with a good diamond fit.

161

Example II.   Responder   Opener

                    Pass   1S
                    3C

All experts consider a jump to the three level a one round force. Responder might have a big spade fit with a distributional hand or a good club suit inviting 3NT.

Passed Hand Quiz

Assume you have passed originally and partner opens 1H. What is your response?

1. S. AJ876   2. S. AJ87   3. S. A   4. S. AJ4
    H. K76   H. KQ87   H. 109876   H. K4
    D. Q53   D. 32   D. 2   D. 10987
    C. 32   C. 543   C. KQ5432   C. QJ87

5. S. 54   6. S. K4   7. S. AJ10987
    H. A76   H. A8765   H. 2
    D. 543   D. J9865   D. A87
    C. KQJ87   C. 2   C. 1098

Solutions

1. 1S   Try to bid as naturally as possible after you have passed unless you have a four card major fit with partner. Then raise immediately or force with a jump shift.

2. 3H   Not forcing.

3. 3C   Forcing. Intending to bid hearts on the next round. Hands like this produce slams if partner has good controls.

4. 2NT Not forcing.

5. 2C   Save your heart support for the next round.

6. 4H   A jump to 4H over 1H has the same meaning whether you are a passed hand or not.

7. 2S   Unless you use Weak Two Bids in which case this is an opening 2S bid.

13. REDOUBLE

The average player knows little about this useful tool. His knowledge is generally limited to remembering that if his partner opens and the next hand doubles, he should redouble with 10 or more points. Or if the opponents double and he thinks he can make the contract he should redouble. However, he is seldom sure or brave enough to do so. As a result the redouble is used infrequently and as often as not incorrectly.

In order to discuss the redouble intelligently we revert to basic sequences and discuss standard expert practice.

The Redouble after a Takeout Double

North	East	South	West
1H	Dbl.	Rdbl.	

What does South mean? Does he promise hearts? Does he deny hearts? Does he promise another bid? Does he have any other strength showing bid at his disposal?

The actual meaning of a redouble in this sequence is that South has a GOOD HAND. South promises a minimum of 10 H.C.P. but very likely has more. (Many 10 point hands do not redouble - the ones that have many queens and jacks, for example.)

South neither promises nor denies hearts although in an expert game he is likely to be short. Most experts with four card support disdain the redouble for other strength showing bids such as 2NT or 3NT. These responses conventionally show primary support (four or more cards), 2NT (10-12), 3NT (13-15) and are forcing to three of opener's suit and to game respectively. The theory behind these no trump jumps is that with a big fit it is unlikely that East-West can be punished at a low level and the redouble allows them to find their possible sacrifice suit. Immediate raises to three and four are preemptive; thus the need to distinguish.

Therefore, barring these artificial jumps to 2NT or 3NT, the redouble is the main strength showing bid at the responder's disposal.

Leaving the redoubler for a moment, let's move to West. West no longer need bid once South redoubles. What should West do over the redouble? As a general rule West mentions a four card major at the one level. However, at the two level, in most cases, he is promising a five card suit and conceivably six! The point count can be zero as either East or West must bid so it pays to have the player with the long suit bid his suit at the lowest possible level before trouble sets in. Remember, the doubler's side is outgunned and is simply looking for a safe landing place. The side that redoubles will either play the hand or double any opposing contract nine times out of ten.

Study a simple deal illustrating this point.
East-West vul.
Dealer South

North

S. QJ7
H. QJ96
D. AQ93
C. 74

West

S. 92
H. AK753
D. KJ102
C. KJ

East

S. 1065
H. 8
D. 765
C. 1098653

South

S. AK843
H. 1042
D. 84
C. AQ2

The bidding:

South	West	North	East
1S	Dbl.	Rdbl.	2C
Pass	Pass	2D	Pass
2S	Pass	4S	All Pass

Opening lead: King of hearts

The defense starts with three rounds of hearts, East ruffing the third. East shifts to a club and South is going to have to play very well to make his game contract. He must rise with the club ace, play two trumps ending in dummy, cash his good heart discarding a minor suit card and then play all his trumps squeezing West in the minors. In actual practice South would probably go down in 4S.

Now let's take a look at what happens to East-West if East does not make the key bid of 2C over the redouble. If East passes, South, with any balanced or semi-balanced hand, also passes as a courtesy to the redoubler. South does not know whether or not the redouble was based on spade support.

The doubler, West, has to extricate himself from his own takeout double. West, in this case holding a five card heart suit, bids it as his partner has announced a balanced hand by passing the redouble.

Assuming West bids 2H, North holding four trumps doubles. East now has to bid 3C. At the three level the requirements for a penalty double after a redouble are not so severe - three reasonable trumps are sufficient. If South doubles 3C his side reaps a harvest of 800 points. Nor will it do West any good to run to 3D as that will be doubled by North with the penalty running in four figures. And we have all seen these auctions where first one player then the other starts running as if being chased by a snake when the doubling starts.

How much easier if the doubler's partner shows his long suit at the lowest possible level rather than waiting for his partner to be doubled and then running to his suit at a higher level.

Incidentally, East could conceivably have a weak hand with a strong suit. For example, give East the AQ10874 of clubs and he jumps to 3C over the redouble to show a good suit.

Once we concede that the doubler's partner must bid a long suit regardless of strength we understand that if he does not it is because he has no long suit. In other words, he has a balanced hand. That is why the doubler should feel secure in mentioning his five card suit after a redouble has been passed back to him. His partner must have at least two cards in each unbid suit.

What happens when the doubler does not have a five card suit? Usually this presents no grave problem. If the doubler can show a four card suit at the one level he does so by bidding his lowest ranking four card suit.

For example, West holds:

S. AJ87
H. K65
D. AQ65
C. 43

and the bidding proceeds:

South	West	North	East
1C	Dbl.	Rdbl.	Pass
Pass	?		

West bids 1D, his cheaper four card suit.

The big worry from the doubler's viewpoint is the following common position:

South	West	North	East
1S	Dbl.	Rdbl.	Pass
Pass			

Naturally, if West has a five or six card suit he bids it. But what if he doesn't? What if West holds:

S. 4
H. AJ87
D. K1076
C. A865

If West bids 2C, for example, and gets doubled does he run to diamonds? Remember, his partner thinks he has a five card club suit and will not rescue with a doubleton club and four diamonds to the jack. In this situation the doubler is supposed to bid 1NT! Then, after the inevitable double he redoubles asking partner to pick any suit at the two level. If his partner has something like:

S. J8653
H. 104
D. Q532
C. 74

he bids 2D over the redouble and the partnership is at least in its best suit.

Another sticky situation dealing with the same sequence is:

South	West	North	East
1S	Dbl.	Rdbl.	?

166

East holds: S. KQ1085
                               H. 43
                               D. 1076
                               C. 543

East knows if he passes his partner will bid some suit at the two level and
his hand will not be a very suitable dummy. East should bid 1NT to tell
partner his entire hand is spades and that perhaps 1NT, probably doubled,
is the best spot, all things considered.

Now watch a little blood flow.

North-South vul.

Dealer East   North

                               S. J752
                               H. 1062
                               D. 10743
                               C. 63

              West   East

              S. 94   S. KQ1086
              H. KQ87   H. 53
              D. J86   D. A952
              C. AQ97   C. K4

                               South

                               S. A3
                               H. AJ94
                               D. KQ
                               C. J10852

The bidding:
              East   South   West   North

              1S   Dbl.   Rdbl.   Pass
              Pass   2C   Dbl.   Pass
              Pass   Pass

Opening lead: Nine of spades

South is down at least 800 and more likely 1100 with adequate defense. It
is simply a case of East-West knowing how to capitalize on a common situation.

If, for example, on the same sequence, North chooses to bid 2D after his
partner is doubled in 2C, East doubles. WITH ANY BALANCED OR SEMI-BALANCED
HAND EITHER THE OPENER OR THE REDOUBLER DOUBLES ANY RUN OUT AT THE ONE OR

TWO LEVEL WITH FOUR TRUMP. This, of course, presumes that the redoubler does not have four or more cards in his partner's suit. Penalty doubles are not made at low levels with undisclosed trump support.

Summing Up

1. A redouble promises two things: 10 points in high cards and one more bid. The redouble neither affirms nor denies support for partner's suit. It simply announces a good hand.

2. After a redouble the doubler's partner bids any four card suit at the one level but only a five or six card suit at the two level. One exception. Assume East holds:

   S. 10874
   H. 2
   D. Q876
   C. J432

The bidding:

South	West	North	East
1S	Dbl.	Rdbl.	?

If East passes, his partner may bid 2H which will probably be doubled. In this one case, with a singleton heart, East bids at the two level with a four card suit. With a strong six card minor or five card major the doubler's partner jumps in his suit over the redouble.

The bidding:

South	West	North	East
1H	Dbl.	Rdbl.	?

Hand 1. (East)

S. KQ984
H. 10874
D. 42
C. 103

Hand 2. (East)

S. 8
H. 10762
D. J4
C. KQ10874

With Hand 1, East jumps to 2S; with Hand 2, 3C. This jump makes it easy to find sacrifices and at the same time tells partner you are not completely broke.

3. In the case of a double to his left, a redouble and a pass to his right, opener passes with all balanced or semi-balanced hands, but bids immediately with unbalanced hands.

For example:

South	West	North	East
1C	Dbl.	Rdbl.	Pass
?			

South holds:

```
S. 5
H. AJ98
D. 54
C. AQ10764
```

South bids 1H to show unbalanced distribution before the bidding gets out of hand.

If South holds:

```
S. 65
H. A
D. 875
C. AQJ8762
```

he rebids 2C.

In no case does South bid with a balanced hand - unless it be to double his right hand opponent if that opponent happens to bid.

4. If the bidding is passed back to the doubler he mentions his five or six card suit if he has one or, barring that, any four card suit he can show at the one level. In the case where 1S is doubled and re-doubled and the doubler has three four card suits he migrates to 1NT and if this gets doubled, redoubles for takeout.

Furthermore, if the doubler has an exceptionally good double with a strong suit he jumps in his own suit. If West holds:

```
S. AJ4
H. KQ6
D. AQ10964
C. 2
```

West bids 2D over 1C doubled and redoubled to alert partner to the offensive potential of the hand.

5. After a double and redouble, either the opener or the redoubler nor-mally doubles any opposing runout at the one or two level with four or more trumps. Furthermore, each should give the other an opportu-nity to do so.

South holds:

```
                    S.  AK54
                    H.  54
                    D.  KJ654
                    C.  105
```

The bidding:

North	East	South	West
1H	Dbl.	Rdbl.	Pass
Pass	2C	?	

South must pass, and by so doing tells North that he's interested in hearing a penalty double. If North has four clubs he obliges.

If South on the same bidding has:

```
                    S.  A876
                    H.  QJ10
                    D.  K107653
                    C.  ---
```

he bids 2D directly over 2C telling partner that he is not interested in hearing a double of 2C because he has either a long suit of his own, a good fit or extreme shortness in clubs.

The Redouble by the Opening Bidder

Compare these two bidding sequences:

(1)	South	West	North	East
	1C	Dbl.	Pass	Pass
	Rdbl.			

(2)	South	West	North	East
	1C	Pass	Pass	Dbl.
	Rdbl.			

See any difference?

In the first case if South passes he plays 1C doubled; in the second, this is not the case at all. The bidding is not over if South passes.

Therefore, it stands to reason that in sequence (1) if South has good clubs he will pass and play 1C doubled perhaps making with overtricks.

But what if South has weak clubs and this is the full deal?

c

6-7-08

Both vul.

Dealer South

<pre>
                              North

                              S. 863
                              H. 752
                              D. J9643
                              C. 85

           West   East

           S. AKJ4   S. 952
           H. A983   H. K106
           D. A107   D. 82
           C. 94   C. KQJ107

                              South

                              S. Q107
                              H. QJ4
                              D. KQ5
                              C. A632
</pre>

If South passes 1C doubled he will take exactly two tricks against average defense and suffer a loss of 1400 points! If, on the other hand, he senses a catastrophe from the emaciated looks of his club suit he can redouble - asking, begging, partner to run to another suit. In this case North runs to 1D and this can only be defeated one trick while East-West have a no trump game. Presumably East-West will not double 1D as neither one has four diamonds and will go on to bid their game - but that is better than going down 1400.

Therefore, the rule is IF PARTNER IS DOUBLED TO HIS LEFT AND THE DOUBLE IS LEFT IN, A REDOUBLE IS FOR RESCUE. This usually occurs after a minor opening, particularly when opener has a three card suit or a weak four carder.

Now consider the other sequence:

South	West	North	East
1C	Pass	Pass	Dbl.
Rdbl.			

Is South running again? No! 1C doubled has not been left in and, even if it is, North still has a chance to bid. Let's reverse the East-West cards:

North

S. 863
H. 752
D. J9643
C. 85

West   East

S. 952   S. AKJ4
H. K106   H. A983
D. 82   D. A107
C. KQJ107   C. 94

South

S. Q107
H. QJ4
D. KQ5
C. A632

The bidding: | South | West | North | East |
| --- | --- | --- | --- |
| 1C | Pass | Pass | Dbl. |
| Pass | Pass | ? | |

In this sequence North still has a chance to rescue his partner if he has
two or fewer clubs and a five card suit of his own. Therefore, South need
not redouble to be rescued. The double will only be left in a small per-
centage of the time and when it is partner still has a chance to escape.

Ergo, it stands to reason that the redouble in this sequence shows a powerful hand and alerts North that simply because he has passed South's opening
bid he should not give up. North-South might still have the balance of
power. Indeed, North-South might even get to game!

Both sides vul.   North

S. 86
H. QJ983
D. J76
C. 754

West   East

S. Q943   S. J10
H. 2   H. 1054
D. 1052   D. KQ98
C. QJ1092   C. AK86

South

S. AK752
H. AK76
D. A43
C. 3

172

The bidding:

South	West	North	East
1S	Pass	Pass	Dbl.
Rdbl.	2C	2H	3C or pass
4H	All Pass		

Opening lead: King of clubs

In this case South's redouble is not for rescue. In fact it announces a powerful hand, typically 18-20 H.C.P. and asks for a little assistance from North, particularly if he has a little support for South's suit or a suit of his own. In this case North's 2H bid allows South to bid game which should be made against any defense.

When a Stayman Response of 2C is Doubled

Assume South has opened 1NT and the bidding has proceeded as follows:

South	West	North	East
1NT	Pass	2C	Dbl.
?			

With four clubs to two honors South must redouble. With a four card major and not four clubs to two honors South bids the major. With three clubs to an honor and no four card major South passes. With two or three small clubs and no four card major South bids 2D. In this case North knows that South does not have a club stopper.

Here are some sample South hands on the above bidding:

(1)	S. A4	(2)	S. AJ84	(3)	S. AJ9	(4)	A74
	H. K108		H. K4		H. K54		H. KJ8
	D. AJ86		D. AK8		D. AJ98		D. AK876
	C. KJ94		C. J874		C. A43		C. J9
	Redouble		Bid 2S		Pass		Bid 2D

In this way North will have a chance to play 2C redoubled with a suitable hand. Furthermore he knows for a certainty that no trump is not the right contract if opener bids 2D over the double and responder has no club stopper either.

The same method of handling the double is also employed after an opening bid of 2NT followed by a double of a 3C Stayman response.

The Redouble of a Doubled Cue Bid

After a suit agreement the partnership often tries for slam via a cue bidding sequence. This gives the defenders a chance to double the various cue
bids for leads...but it also gives the cue bidders an opportunity to redouble to show second round control.

North

S. AQ76
H. 10976
D. A65
C. 76

West

S. J1042
H. QJ
D. J8732
C. Q10

East

S. K98
H. 5
D. KQ109
C. J9842

South

S. 53
H. AK8432
D. 4
C. AK53

The bidding:

North	East	South	West
Pass	Pass	1H	Pass
3H	Pass	4C*	Pass
4D*	Dbl.	Rdbl.	Pass
4S	Pass	6H	All Pass

*Cue bid

Both 4C and 4D are cue bids. When East doubles 4D for a later lead against
a heart contract, South seizes the opportunity to redouble, conventionally
showing second round control of diamonds - either a singleton or the king.
North confidently cue bids the ace of spades and a nice slam is reached.

By passing or bidding over the double of 4D South denies second round diamond control. This knowledge might be important to North.

The Redouble by the Player Who Has Made a Single Raise

South	West	North	East
1H	Pass	2H	Pass
Pass	Dbl.	Rdbl.	

West did not have the values for an original double of 1H but backs in with a balancing double of 2H. West is counting on his partner to have some cards as North-South have not shown too many signs of life.

Frequently North will have a fine 2H raise. Perhaps a maximum with nine or ten H.C.P. and a hand well suited to defense. North redoubles alerting South that perhaps the opponents are in trouble. South should then be willing to double any two level runout with four trumps and any three level runout with three trumps to an honor and a hand reasonably well suited to defense.

Both sides vul.

Dealer North

North

S. A1082
H. J104
D. 54
C. KJ72

West

S. QJ64
H. 76
D. AJ8
C. Q1054

East

S. 953
H. Q532
D. K732
C. A3

South

S. K7
H. AK98
D. Q1096
C. 986

The bidding:

North	East	South	West
Pass	Pass	1H	Pass
2H	Pass	Pass	Dbl.
Rdbl.	Pass	Pass	2S
Dbl.	Pass	Pass	Pass

Opening lead: Jack of hearts

This is not one of life's happier moments for West. He will struggle but will never get out for less than 500 and conceivably may pay 800 for his adventure. Yet these types of adventures are the heart and soul of tournament bridge as is battling for the part score, particularly against a partial at rubber bridge.

Everyone knows the best bid in bridge is "pass"...but redouble is where the action is!

14. THE REVERSE BY THE OPENING BIDDER

Any time the opening bidder bids two suits in such a fashion that his partner, the responder, must bid to the three level to take him back to his original suit, he has "reversed".

Opener	Responder	Opener	Responder	Opener	Responder
1D	1S	1C	1H	1H	2D
2H	?	2D	?	3C	?

In each of the above sequences the opener has reversed. What does this mean? It means that the opening bidder must have a strong hand - a minimum of seventeen or eighteen points (H.C.P. plus distribution); often more. It means that the opener has five or six cards in his first suit and almost always four cards in his second suit and the responder must answer a reverse.

A REVERSE FOLLOWING A ONE OVER ONE RESPONSE FORCES THE RESPONDER TO BID AT LEAST ONE MORE TIME. A REVERSE FOLLOWING A TWO OVER ONE RESPONSE IS FORCING TO GAME.

Reverses must be planned in advance by the opening bidder. He must have the proper distribution and strength. If he is lacking one or the other, he must not reverse!

Assume you are the dealer and hold each of the following hands:

1.	S. AJx	2.	S. x	3.	S. x	4.	S. x
	H. AKxx		H. AKJxx		H. KQxx		H. AJxx
	D. AQxxx		D. AQJxxx		D. AKQx		D. AKQxxx
	C. x		C. x		C. Axx		C. Kx

Each of these hands is strong enough to reverse and each has more diamonds than hearts. Each of these hands should be opened with 1D and hearts rebid at the next opportunity.

Now let's look at some hands that have the same distribution but not the same strength.

1.	S. AJx	2.	S. x	3.	S. x	4.	S. x
	H. AKxx		H. AJ10xx		H. KQ10x		H. AJxx
	D. J10xxx		D. KQ10xxx		D. AKxxx		D. KQxxxx
	C. x		C. x		C. xxx		C. Qx

If these hands are opened with 1D, the hearts cannot be rebid without lying about the strength of the hand. There are two solutions. Open 1D, rebid the diamonds and not mention the hearts; or open 1H and rebid 2D. This is not a reverse but tends to give partner a mistaken idea of your distribution as he will assume hearts is the longer suit.

I feel strongly that 1H is the proper opening bid with the first three hands but that 1D should be opened and the diamonds rebid with the fourth hand.

Naturally players who open five card majors must open each of these hands with 1D but our discussion assumes that a good four card major suit will be opened if common sense dictates. Here it clearly dictates.

What about hands that have the strength for a reverse but not the proper distribution?

1.	S. AJx	2.	S. x	3.	S. x	4.	S. x
	H. AKxxx		H. AKJxxx		H. KQ10xx		H. AKxxxx
	D. AQxx		D. AQJxx		D. AKQx		D. AKxx
	C. x		C. x		C. AJx		C. Kx

Each of these hands is strong enough to open 1D and then bid hearts. But remember the rule: when the opener reverses he must have MORE cards in his first suit. OPENER SHOULD NEVER FORCE A REVERSE BY OPENING THE SHORTER SUIT. Simply open the longest suit and jump, if you must, in your secondary suit. The above hands are all opening bids of 1H. If partner is strong enough to respond, a jump shift to 3D will portray the strength.

A JUMP SHIFT IS NOT NECESSARY IF THE DISTRIBUTION IS PROPER FOR A REVERSE. HOWEVER, IF IT IS NOT, THE JUMP SHIFT IS USED TO SHOW THE ADDITIONAL STRENGTH OF THE OPENER'S HAND.

Responding to a Reverse

Until Monroe Ingberman published a comprehensive method for responding to a reverse in the November 1970 issue of the A.C.B.L. Bulletin the literature in this field was practically non-existent.

In truth few writers wanted to tackle the subject. For a time a reverse was not even considered a one round force. Now it is universally accepted to be one. But how does one answer a reverse?

Ingberman described a very workable method for handling this situation and here it is, although I must admit to having made a few simplifications.

Keep in mind before reading his method that a normal minimum reverse will have at least sixteen or seventeen H.C.P. and a normal hand evaluation of at least eighteen points. Therefore, any reverses in the 17-19 range are considered minimum. Reverses in the 20-21 range are considered maximum. With a larger count, opener has a strong two bid.

If the average reverse has about eighteen points then the responder thinks in terms of game with eight or more points. If the responder has an opening bid of his own facing a reverse there is a great likelihood of a slam. If the responder has five, six or seven points chances are opposite a minimum reverse, if there is no fit, the hand does not belong in game. It is up to the responder to stop the bidding short of game with these hands. Here is how it is all done.

We will use this model sequence for our discussion:

Opener	Responder
1D	1S
2H	?

Responder is forced to bid again. How does he describe hands with eight or more points? WITH EIGHT OR MORE POINTS FACING A REVERSE THE RESPONDER HAS OPTIONS.

He can:

1. Rebid his own suit.

Opener	Responder	Opener	Responder
S. x	S. KQxxx	1D	1S
H. AKxx	H. Qx	2H	2S
D. AKxxx	D. Jx	2NT	3NT
C. AJx	C. 10xxx	Pass	

Responder with a total hand evaluation of nine points rebids his five card suit. Opener rebids 2NT to show a minimum reverse (for no trump purposes opener has but nineteen points) and no spade support. Responder raises to 3NT.

2. Prefer opener's first suit.

Opener	Responder	Opener	Responder
S. x	S. KJ10x	1D	1S
H. AKxx	H. Qxx	2H	3D
D. AKxxx	D. QJx	3NT	Pass
C. AJx	C. xxx		

Responder returns to opener's first suit which is forcing. Rather than try for game in diamonds opener takes the short cut and rebids 3NT which responder is grateful to pass.

3. Support the second suit with a single raise (slam try) or give jump support to the second suit to show a concentration of strength in his two suits.

Opener	Responder	Opener	Responder
S. x	S. Axxxx	1D	1S
H. KQxx	H. A10xx	2H	3H (slam try)
D. AKxxx	D. xx	4NT	5H
C. AQx	C. Kx	5NT	6D
		6H	Pass

Actually the hand has a reasonable play for seven but six is the best contract.

Opener	Responder	Opener	Responder
S. x	S. AQxxx	1D	1S
H. KQxx	H. A10xx	2H	4H
D. AKxxx	D. xx	4NT	5H
C. AQx	C. xx	5NT	6C
		6H	Pass

The 4H raise is not as strong as the 3H raise and perhaps opener is being a bit exuberant. However the contract is reasonable and if the opponents are polite enough to lead the unbid suit (clubs), the hand should make.

4. Give jump preference to opener's first suit to indicate a four card fit and an interest in slam.

Opener	Responder		Opener	Responder
S. Kx	S. Axxxx		1D	1S
H. AQxx	H. x		2H	4D
D. AKxxxx	D. QJxxx		4NT	5D
C. x	C. xx		6D	Pass

5. Jump to 3NT with ten to twelve points and at least one stopper in the unbid suit.

Opener	Responder		Opener	Responder
S. Ax	S. KQxx		1D	1S
H. KJxx	H. xxx		2H	3NT
D. AKQxx	D. xx		Pass	
C. xx	C. KQ10x			

6. Jump in your original suit to show a one loser suit.

Opener	Responder		Opener	Responder
S. x	S. KQJ10xx		1D	1S
H. AKxx	H. Qxx		2H	3S
D. AKxxxx	D. xx		4S	Pass
C. Qx	C. xx			

7. Bid the fourth suit to show a two-suited hand.

Opener	Responder		Opener	Responder
S. Kx	S. QJ10xx		1D	1S
H. QJxx	H. Ax		2H	3C
D. AKJxxx	D. x		3S	4S
C. K	C. Qxxxx		Pass	

It's great fun to have a strong hand and then hear partner reverse. You know you are going to game and there may even be a slam. But what do you do with a terrible hand? You can't pass - the reverse is forcing!

The idea in the text was to have the responder rebid 2NT with all terrible hands in the five to seven range. If the opener has a minimum reverse lacking three card support for responder's original suit or six-five distribution, he is forced to rebid his original suit. Responder can then pass if he wishes.

Opener	Responder		Opener	Responder
S. x	S. K10xxx		1D	1S
H. AQxx	H. xx		2H	2NT (forces 3D)
D. AKxxx	D. Jxx		3D	Pass
C. AJx	C. Qxx			

Responder forces opener to rebid his original suit and then passes the rebid knowing responder cannot have three card spade support.

Opener	Responder		Opener	Responder
S. AJx	S. K10xxx		1D	1S
H. AQxx	H. xx		2H	2NT
D. AKxxx	D. Jxx		3S	4S
C. x	C. Qxx		Pass	

Responder intends to play the hand in 3D and forces the opener to rebid his suit with his 2NT rebid. Opener double crosses responder by showing three card spade support. Responder decides to gamble on 4S. He might even make it!

Opener	Responder		Opener	Responder
S. x	S. Axxxx		1D	1S
H. AKJxx	H. xxx		2H	2NT
D. AQJxxx	D. xxx		3H	4H
C. x	C. Qx		Pass	

Again opener double crosses the responder by not rebidding his original suit after being asked to do so. The reason this time is an unusual six-five hand that the responder could not possibly know about. Responder takes a shot at 4H on the basis of the eight card fit. This one almost certainly will make.

Opener	Responder		Opener	Responder
S. x	S. Axxxx		1D	1S
H. AKxx	H. J10x		2H	2NT
D. KQxxx	D. x		3D	3H
C. AJx	C. 10xxx		Pass	

Responder tries to get out as cheaply as possible. First he forces the opener to rebid his diamonds and then he signs off at 3H. Opener knows that responder has only three hearts as he would have jumped to 4H over 3D with four card support which would be considered a sign off.

182

Opener	Responder		Opener	Responder
S. Qx	S. K10xx		1D	1S
H. AQJx	H. xxx		2H	2NT
D. AKxxx	D. x		3D	3NT
C. Jx	C. A109xx		Pass	

Responder forces the opener to rebid his original suit and then persists to 3NT. This sequence shows 7-9 H.C.P. as opposed to a direct jump to 3NT which shows ten to twelve.

We have already seen that the opener does not always rebid his original suit after a 2NT rebid by the responder. If he has hidden support for responder's first suit, a six-five hand or a maximum reverse he must not rebid his original suit!

We have seen examples of the first two situations. Here is the third. Opener has a maximum reverse.

Opener	Responder		Opener	Responder
S. xx	S. AJxx		1D	1S
H. AKxx	H. Jxx		2H	2NT
D. KQJxx	D. xxx		3NT	Pass
C. AK	C. xxx			

Opener overrules the responder with a maximum plus stoppers in the unbid suit. If the diamonds divide in a civilized manner responder will make his contract. What better way to end a chapter?

15.   THE SHORT CLUB OBSESSION

Almost the first words uttered when two strangers sit down to play with one another are, "do you play the short club?" or "I only open with a five card major" or "I play the short club, do you play the short diamond?" Help!

What is the game coming to? First we need a bit of clarification to separate the short clubbers from the five card majorites.

A player who refuses to open the bidding with a four card major will open the following hand with 1D:

                    S. AK108
                    H. AQJ9
                    D. 754
                    C. 94

Reverse the minor suit holdings and the opening bid would be 1C. Thus, if you are a five card majorite you not only play the short club but the short diamond as well. As a matter of fact, it goes without saying that when you announce you will not open the bidding with a four card major you are playing this way. YOU HAVE NO CHOICE IN THE MATTER.

However, if you are a player who will open the bidding with a four card major if your hand seems to call for it, you will nevertheless on rare occasions open the bidding with a three card club suit, but NEVER A SHORT DIAMOND. The short diamond opening simply does not exist for four card majorites.

Everyone who has ever played bridge has at times been forced to open the bidding with a three card club suit so it is meaningless to ask if your partner plays the "short club". The only meaningful question is to find out if your partner will or will not open the bidding with a four card major. If the answer is "I avoid it", you can bet your last cent that he won't unless a gun is put to his head.

Therefore, in this article I would like to discuss the short club opening in relation to those who WILL OPEN WITH A FOUR CARD MAJOR when common sense dictates.

Playing five card majors common sense never enters into the question. Does a robot use common sense? If he does not have a five card major he opens with one of a minor. Period. He has no choice.

Now we will attack the question of when to open the bidding with a three card club suit and how to handle the bidding once you have done so.

First and most important is that you go out of the way NOT to open the bidding with a three card suit if you can possibly avoid it. That is to say that 1C is never opened on either of the following two hands:

```
1.   S. A4                    2.   S. AQ87
     H. KQ106                       H. 65
     D. J876                        D. J1087
     C. K54                         C. AK5
```

Hands with two four card suits, hearts and diamonds or spades and diamonds NEVER OPEN WITH A THREE CARD CLUB SUIT. NEVER. The proper opening bid with the first hand is 1H and with the second 1D. Reverse the hearts and diamonds on the first hand and your major would be too weak to bid and you would open 1D.

In fact, except for a few far out hands the short club is used primarily in first or second seat (rarely after partner has passed) with 4-3-3-3 hands, the four card suit being a major. THE SHORT CLUB IS NEVER OPENED WITH A FOUR CARD DIAMOND SUIT. NEVER.

Do you realize how much needless blood has been shed by players who refuse to heed this advice? Barrels. Vats. Oceans.

Let's take a look at some hands that are forced to open 1C with a three card suit.

```
1.   S. J1032        or       2.   S. A85
     H. AJ7                         H. K976
     D. KQ5                         D. AJ7
     C. Q93                         C. J106
```

but not:

```
                    3.   S. A76
                         H. K87
                         D. Q876
                         C. AJ6
```

In the first two cases opener has 13 H.C.P. and 4-3-3-3 distribution. Hands like this always cause rebid problems. If opened with one of a major, a two level response is always disconcerting. A 2NT rebid by the opener is supposed to show extra values (15-17) and the above two hands simply don't qualify. In order to avoid that problem we inject another. We open the bidding with a three card suit and hope we land on our feet.

It is dangerous to open the bidding with a three card suit. Partner is afraid to support your suit for fear you have only three. In fact this fear becomes so pronounced that the opener will often go out of his way to rebid a mangy five card club suit just to let his partner know that he does not have three! This, incidentally is a big no-no. Opener is not supposed to rebid a five card club suit to let his partner know that he is not opening a short club and THE RESPONDER IS SUPPOSED TO ASSUME THAT IT IS NOT A SHORT CLUB AND BID ACCORDINGLY.

Not only does this fear to support clubs by the responder keep the partnership from nice club contracts it carries over to the diamond suit as well. Once you are afraid to support clubs it is only a matter of time before you will be afraid to support diamonds. Believe me. I have seen it happen.

However, once you come to believe there is no such thing as a "short diamond" and a short club is a rarity you will have some chance at arriving at the proper contract.

Therefore, on the third example the opening bid is 1D and not 1C. Perhaps you remember that we mentioned that a 2NT rebid in this sequence:

Opener	Responder
1H or 1S	2C
2NT	

shows 15-17 points. This means that if the opener has a 4-3-3-3 hand with 15 H.C.P. and a decent four card major there is no harm in opening the major and rebidding 2NT over any two level response other than a raise, which should be passed.

Hands such as these:

```
        S. KQJ6        or        S. A105
        H. A85                   H. KJ108
        D. QJ7                   D. Q87
        C. Q105                  C. AJ4
```

can be opened with one of a major. Furthermore, if you play 15-17 point
opening 1NT bids they can be opened 1NT thus reducing the possibility of a
short club even more. Many players who use 16-18 point no trumps are apt
to open a 15 point no trump on hands such as these if there is an abundance
of intermediate cards. Is is quite common as a matter of fact.

All this means that with 15 points and a 4-3-3-3 hand either 1NT or the major can often be opened to avoid the problem of the three card club suit.

Hands that have 12 H.C.P. and 4-3-3-3 distribution with a weakish four card
major are usually best described by a PASS. Then if partner opens, a response of 2NT portrays the hand exactly. Hands such as these:

```
        S. Q876        or        S. KQ5
        H. A76                   H. J874
        D. K75                   D. K76
        C. K75                   C. QJ8
```

can safely be passed, thus eliminating still another use of the three card
club suit.

Basically hands in the 13-14 and 19-20 range are the ones that use the
short club. 13-14 point hands are the most frequent; hands such as this:

```
        S. K876        or        S. AJ5
        H. A76                   H. Q874
        D. K75                   D. K76
        C. K75                   C. QJ8
```

Hands with 13 H.C.P. should be opened. It is the 12 point hands that are
optional, not the 13ers. As these hands have no rebid if the major is
opened, the proper opening is 1C.

Furthermore, I will go out on a limb and advise you to rebid 1NT over any
one level response when you have opened 1C on a three card suit. (Of
course if your partner responds in your four card major you should raise.)

In the long run you will come out ahead on both of the above hands if after opening 1C and receiving a 1D response you rebid 1NT. If partner is strong enough he can always check back by bidding his four card major before plunging ahead in no trump. For example:

Opener	Responder		Opener	Responder
S. AJ65	S. Q1032		1C	1D
H. K76	H. A4		1NT	2S
D. K105	D. AQ732		3S	4S
C. Q97	C. 84			

Immediately the screams will start. Why not rebid 1S over 1D? What if partner has four spades and is not strong enough to bid again. You will miss your 4-4 fit! Heresy! Hang him!

Hold the rope. We just saw an example of responder checking back with an unbalanced hand and the major was not lost. If responder is too weak to make a second bid he will very often answer in the major the first time if the suit is decent.

For example, responding hands like these:

S. AQ105	S. KQJ9	S. A5
H. 54	H. 32	H. KJ106
D. Q765	D. 87654	D. J765
C. 543	C. J4	C. 765

should respond to a 1C opening with one of a major. The major is strong and the hand is not worth two bids. If the opener raises the major with three card support the "dreaded" 4-3 fit should be manageable. If the opener has four of the major the 4-4 fit has been found.

However, the responder should not automatically answer a 1C opening with a four card major bypassing strong diamond suits, or even go out of the way to respond in the major if the major is weak and the hand is strong enough for two bids. There is no reason to bid unnaturally with good hands.

For example, your partner opens 1C and you hold:

S. Q765	S. 10765	S. 10943	S. A4
H. 43	H. 54	H. J874	H. J875
D. AKQ87	D. AKJ8	D. KQJ7	D. QJ109
C. 43	C. 876	C. 4	C. 654

Respond 1D on all these hands. Your major is weak and you have an alternate suit to show. You wouldn't be happy if your partner raised your major holding three card support (something you wouldn't have minded in the previous examples) so bid 1D.

It is true that if you respond 1D and your partner rebids 1NT and you are not strong enough to bid again you may miss a 4-4 fit. However, you will almost never miss game and in rubber bridge a 40 and a 60 part score are about the same. For a real loss to be suffered you must miss a 4-4 fit, go down in no trump and find that you could have made a major part score. This is the type of parlay that a gambler wouldn't mind betting on all day long.

In return you avoid horrible problems like this that confront the responder daily when the opener rebids his four card major after opening a three card suit:

Opener	Responder		Opener	Responder
S. AJ65	S. 32		1C	1D
H. K76	H. 543		1S	?
D. K87	D. AQ532			
C. Q87	C. K54			

Now what is the responder supposed to do? It is evident that the best contract is 1NT played from the opener's side. Is responder supposed to rebid 1NT? If he doesn't he may be too high. In most cases 2C is the bid. This forces the opener to retreat to 2D, which in this case will be the eventual contract and may well go down one trick.

But that's not the worst of it. Have you ever thought what bidding like this sounds like to the responder?

Opener	Responder
1C	1H
1S	2C
2H	?

Is this really the way for the opener to bid a 4-3-3-3 no trump oriented hand? Never once bidding no trump? From the responder's point of view the opener may really have the suits he is bidding. Heaven forbid. Hands like this:

189

```
       Opener              or        Opener

    S.  AJ87                       S.  AK76
    H.  1087                       H.  A43
    D.  2                          D.  43
    C.  AK654                      C.  QJ98
```

If the responder has to guess whether opener has clubs with an unbalanced
hand or three clubs with a 4-3-3-3 hand he has got to go wrong a good
part of the time.

Therefore, if you are in agreement with these ideas you should be in agreement with the following statement: WHENEVER THE OPENER BIDS TWO SUITS AT
THE LEVEL OF ONE HE HAS AT LEAST FOUR CARDS IN EACH OF HIS SUITS. In other
words the short club does not exist when the bidding goes:

```
       Opener              Responder

    1C                     1D
    1H or 1S               ?
```

If the opener happens to have a three card club suit the rebid should be
1NT. Furthermore if the rebid is 1NT the responder should not fear supporting the clubs anyway! Look at these two hands:

```
    Opener      Responder          Opener      Responder

  S. A43      S. J9752           1C          1S
  H. K742     H. Q53             1NT         ?
  D. A52      D. 10
  C. Q94      C. KJ53
```

At this point the responder usually thinks to himself - what if my partner
has a short club? I had better not support. So he either passes, leaving
the opener to suffer with the inevitable diamond lead, or he bids 2S and
when he finds three spades in the dummy as opposed to a small doubleton or
even a singleton honor he thinks he is a genius.

He is an idiot. If he had simply bid 2C his partner looking at only three
clubs would take him back to 2S. If the opener happened to have four or
five clubs (which would be much more common) he would simply pass 2C or
raise to 3C. For example, the opener might have had a hand like this:

```
    Opener      Responder          Opener      Responder

  S. 76       S. J9752           1C          1S
  H. AJ3      H. Q53             1NT         2C
  D. A52      D. 10              3C          Pass
  C. A10654   C. KJ53
```

The 2C rebid by the responder can show anywhere between 6-10 points. If opener has a maximum he can make one more try. With a minimum he either passes or takes the responder back to 2S.

Once these principles are accepted wholeheartedly by both the opener and responder the opener will nevermore have trouble with hands like these:

	Opener		Opener
S.	AJ86	S.	KQ73
H.	32	H.	3
D.	K5	D.	K4
C.	AJ1065	C.	AJ10543

In each case the opening bid is 1C. Assume partner responds 1D, what is the rebid? In each case the rebid is 1S. Remember this promises clubs. Furthermore if you rebid the clubs in this sequence you tend to have six as partner will assume four or five anyway.

A sequence like this:

Opener	Responder
1C	1D
1S	1NT
2C	

tends to describe hands with six clubs and four spades. With five clubs and four spades opener would normally pass 1NT or raise to 2NT or 3NT with sufficient count and doubletons in the red suits. With a singleton heart, opener supports diamonds over the 1NT rebid.

When the opener is not worried about showing that his club opening is "long" he can concentrate on more important aspects of his rebid. For example:

	Opener	Opener	Responder
S.	AJ5	1C	1S
H.	32	?	
D.	K76		
C.	AJ1076		

Opener has a clear-cut raise to 2S. 2C would be hopeless. We have already seen that in most cases the responder is prepared to have his four card suit raised, but what about the times he has five or even six small cards in his suit? If the opener refuses to support, the suit is often lost

191

because the responder is understandably reluctant to rebid such "robust" suits as: 10 6 4 3 2 or 9 8 6 4 3 2.

OPENER SHOULD THEREFORE TEND TO SUPPORT THE MAJOR WITH THREE CARDS AND A SIDE SINGLETON OR DOUBLETON RATHER THAN REBID HIS OWN SUIT WITH MINIMUM HANDS. WITH 4-3-3-3 HANDS OPENER SHOULD TEND TO REBID 1NT RATHER THAN SUPPORT PARTNER' MAJOR.

The same holds true in most cases when it comes to choosing between rebidding the club suit and rebidding 1NT holding a five card club suit.

(a) Opener	(b) Opener	(c) Opener	(d) Opener
S. 76	S. 5	S. J5	S. 54
H. AQ5	H. AQ76	H. Q1076	H. AK76
D. J109	D. 543	D. AQ	D. 43
C. AK765	C. AK765	C. A10876	C. AK876

Each of the above hands should be opened with 1C. If the response is 1S, (a) and (c) rebid 1NT and (b) and (d) 2C. Why?

(a) is a balanced hand 5-3-3-2 distribution. Whenever responder mentions opener's doubleton it is automatic to rebid 1NT with this distribution.

The other three hands require a little judgment. (b) should not rebid 1NT because of the small singleton in partner's suit. A 1NT rebid normally promises at least two cards in partner's suit or, every so often, a singleton honor. The hand is not strong enough to reverse into 2H so 2C is the answer by elimination. Hands (c) and (d) have the same distribution but it is obvious that (c) is more no trump oriented and should rebid 1NT. (d) is not strong enough to mention the hearts and the lack of any diamond stoppers makes it a better 2C rebid.

ASSUMING EXPERT PLAYERS: IF OPENER REBIDS HIS CLUBS OVER A ONE LEVEL RESPONSE HE WILL HAVE SIX CLUBS MORE OFTEN THAN FIVE....MUCH MORE OFTEN!

Still another responder hangup is the refusal to give an immediate raise in clubs holding a four card major and a weak hand.

For example, partner opens 1C and you hold:

```
S. J876
H. 54
D. J76
C. AQ87
```

Many players stubbornly respond 1S on such hands and then die a thousand deaths when partner raises them to 2S with three trump. If partner happens to have four spades, of course, they are in the right spot but they might have arrived there anyway.

Opener	Responder
S. AK54	S. J876
H. K3	H. 54
D. 1076	D. J54
C. KJ65	C. AQ87

Take the classic case where each player has four cards in both spades and clubs. If the responder bids 1S he gets raised to two, plays it there and makes 2S for a score of 60 below the line. If he raises to 2C the opener passes and he makes that for a score of 40 below the line. Big deal! Furthermore if the responder raises to 2C and the opponents compete the responder can then introduce his spade suit and nothing is lost if opener has four spades. If he has only three he usually returns to clubs.

So, if opener has a weak hand and there is a double fit nothing is lost by supporting clubs right away. Indeed the responder shows a plus by raising immediately if the opener has a minimum hand with four clubs and three spades as he stands a good chance of getting raised in spades and playing in an inferior contract.

In all cases where the opener has a strong hand (upward of 16 points) he will mention his major over the raise to 2C and again nothing is lost.

Opener	Responder	Opener	Responder
S. AK76	S. Q432	1C	2C
H. A2	H. 765	2S	3S
D. 54	D. 105	4S	
C. AQ876	C. KJ105		

The 2S rebid is forcing and shows a good hand with clubs and spades. It denies a short club. With a short club no trump is always the first rebid.

It all amounts to this. With a weak hand (9 points or less) and a weak four card major and four or more clubs the responder stands to gain by raising clubs as opposed to responding in the weakish major.

If the major is strong and can stand a raise on three cards then it should be mentioned. If partner opens 1C and you hold:

S. 765
H. AKJ9
D. 105
C. 9865

by all means respond 1H.

If the major is weak and the hand is strong (upward of 10 points) it is safe to respond in the major because, even if partner raises, responder is strong enough to return to the minor and opener will then be able to judge which is the best contract. Example:

Opener	Responder	Opener	Responder
S. A5	S. 873	1C	1H
H. KQ87	H. J1043	2H	3C
D. 765	D. A2	3H	Pass or 4H
C. A876	C. KQ53		

The responder's 3C rebid is not forcing, by agreement. (Many experts play it forcing.) If not forcing it shows 10-12 points, is invitational and shows that the major response was made on four cards and needs reconfirmation of support. If opener has four hearts he either rebids 3H or 4H depending upon his overall strength. If he has only three hearts he can pass 3C or try 3NT with certain hands.

Opener	Responder	Opener	Responder
S. A4	S. 1087	1C	1H
H. AJ7	H. K853	2H	3C*
D. 765	D. K4	Pass**	
C. K10765	C. AJ92		

*Partner I have a four card heart suit, at least four card club support and an invitational hand. Take me back to hearts with four and either leave it in clubs with three card heart support or gamble 3NT.

**Roger, over and out.

To repeat ad nauseum: Weak hands should raise clubs immediately with four card support and a weak four card major. Invitational hands show the major and then return to clubs. Game forcing hands either jump to 2NT immediately with balanced hands containing a weakish four card major, or bid the major and, after having received support, branch out into 3NT or a new suit for further confirmation of four card support.

Opener	Responder		Opener	Responder
S. 65	S. A9		1C	1H
H. AQ87	H. J654		2H	3NT
D. A43	D. KQ5		4H	Pass
C. K876	C. A543			

Responder is too strong to bid 3C if played not forcing. His 3NT rebid is not a closeout. It simply announces an opening bid with only four hearts. Opener should return to 4H with four card support and pass 3NT with only three hearts.

Opener	Responder		Opener	Responder
S. 65	S. AK94		1C	1H
H. AQ87	H. K543		2H	2S
D. A43	D. 76		4H	Pass
C. A765	C. K98			

Responder is trying to discover whether or not opener has four hearts. Opener not only has four hearts but also a maximum raise. His rebid of 4H confirms this. Had he only three hearts he would either branch off into no trump with a diamond stopper, or rebid a good five card club suit.

Opener	Responder		Opener	Responder
S. 65	S. AK94		1C	1H
H. AQ8	H. K543		2H	2S
D. 654	D. 87		3C	5C
C. AQJ54	C. K98		Pass	

Let's get back to our beloved "short club". Earlier it was mentioned that the bid was used more often in first or second seat. Why? Because in first or second seat you must prepare for a rebid. Your partner is an unpassed hand and any new suit by him will be forcing. In third or fourth seat you are allowed to pass any non-jump response if you wish.

What does this all mean? It means that if you pick up a hand like this:

```
S. AK106
H. Q76
D. K108
C. J76
```

In the first or second seat you are more or less compelled to open 1C.
However, in the third or fourth seat you can comfortably open 1S and pass
any two level response as game is remote.

In the preceding case your four card major was strong. If it were weak and
you were in third or fourth position it would have been optional whether to
open 1C or one of your weakish majors. Nevertheless the short club opening
in third or fourth seat is far less likely than in first or second...where
it isn't too likely.

Players who regularly play rubber bridge are constantly caught in part
score competitive struggles. It is most disconcerting not to be able to
compete for the part score in a minor for fear of a short suit opening.
For that reason a three card opening bid with a partial is for practical
purposes extinct. There is no real purpose, unless you hate your partner
and wish to prolong the rubber, to open a three card suit with a partial.
With any decent four card major and a part score the major suit should be
opened in preference to a three card club suit.

Honesty is now setting in and I feel compelled to discuss hands that I hope
I never hold. Hands with two weak four card majors. Hands like this:

```
S. J932        or worse:        S. 9753
H. 10763                        H. 8743
D. A7                           D. AKQ
C. AKJ                          C. A9
```

I get a case of the shudders just looking these hands, especially the
second one. (All five card majorites are now smiling to themselves.
Finally they are having their day.)

When neither four card major is biddable (QJxx or better) then we must
stoop to opening 1C with a three card suit. That is not so bad. What is
so bad is the second hand where we might actually have to open 1D! 1D on
on a three card suit! Let me say that in my lifetime I have never opened

a three card diamond suit so this hand must be a rarity. But if I ever get dealt that hand my face will turn so many colors that my partner will know my exact holding even if I don't bid at all!

That takes care of the short club with 13-14-15 point hands. All we have left is the 19-20 point hands with that same 4-3-3-3 distribution, the four card suit being a major.

Let me point out at this time that in spite of what you read in your bridge primers the point count range for the 2NT opening bid is not, repeat, not 22-24 points. This is virtually unplayable as too many 20 and 21 point hands get passed out at the one level.

The most common range for the 2NT opening is 20-21-22 or simply 20-21. The stronger hands in no trump are opened 2C (forcing and artificial) and the first rebid is 2NT. All this means is that you get to open 2NT more than ever and you don't have to worry about the short club with 20 or 21 points. Those hands are opened 2NT!

The only problem is the 19 point hand, if 19 point hands can ever be considered a problem. Hands like this:

```
S. AJ8
H. K876
D. AK6
C. A97
```

The best solution is to open 1C and jump rebid 2NT. Again partner should assume you have a club suit on this bidding and support your clubs. If these are the two hands the bidding should go:

Opener	Responder	Opener	· Responder
S. AJ8	S. K10632	1C	1S
H. K876	H. 2	2NT	3C
D. AK6	D. Q98	3S	4S
C. A98	C. QJ43		

So once again you have lost nothing by supporting clubs.

On the other hand, if the two hands were like this:

Opener	Responder
S. A8	S. K10632
H. A107	H. 2
D. AK7	D. Q98
C. K10765	C. QJ32

A nice club game or even a laydown club slam might be reached. Notice that 3NT is going to be defeated with the normal heart lead. Notice also that the opener treats hands with 18 H.C.P. and a five card suit as 19 points and jumps to 2NT after having opened 1C. 18 point hands with a five card suit are too strong to be opened 1NT. Partner will pass with 7 and a game may be missed.

Summing Up

1. If you are a confirmed five card majorite you need not be terribly concerned with the preceding pages. Indeed if you haven't sneered at least five times I would be surprised.

2. If you are a four card majorite you should be very concerned with the preceding pages. Remember you are allowed to use your judgment when it comes to opening the bidding. Such a privilege should not be dismissed lightly.

3. Hands with 4-3-3-3 distribution and 13-14-15 or 19 H.C.P. are awkward to describe, particularly when the four card suit is a weakish major. In general, these hands should be opened 1C and 1NT rebid with 13-14-15 or 2NT with 19. The four card major should not be shown at the level of one with this distribution.

4. Even the above rule has an exception or two. A short club is seldom opened in third or fourth seat and even less than seldom when holding a part score.

5. Hands that have four hearts and four spades should be opened with a spade if the suit is biddable. If not, a heart if that suit is biddable. If neither suit is biddable open your three card minor. This is the only time a three card diamond suit can ever be mentioned.

For practical purposes there is no such animal as a three card diamond opening.

6. Hands that have four hearts and four diamonds, or four spades and four diamonds are never opened with a short club.

7. When responding to a 1C opening it is permissible to pass over a weak longer diamond suit and respond in a strong four card major with a weak hand. With a hand strong enough to make two bids (upward of 10 H.C.P.) the responder bids his longest suit first.

8. In the long run it is better for the responder to give partner an immediate raise to 2C when holding four or more clubs as well as a weak four card major with 9 or fewer points. If opener is strong he will show his four card major over the raise. If opener is weak 2C will be a playable spot.

9. With 10-12 H.C.P. responder can afford to show any four card major over an opening club bid. If opener raises responder can, if he has four card support for clubs, return to 3C, not forcing. Opener then reraises the major with four card support, jumping to four with a maximum. Responder bids the same over an opening 1D bid.

10. With 13 or more H.C.P. the responder can also afford to respond with a weak four card major as he will be strong enough to extricate himself if his partner gives him a single raise. He can, for example, jump to 3NT or bid a new suit. In either case opener will return to responder's original major with four card support or make some other bid with three card support.

11. Opener should not go out of his way to rebid a five card club suit. Rebidding 1NT, raising partner or showing a new suit all take precedence.

12. When opener shows two suits at the level of one he must have at least four cards in each suit. With 4-3-3-3 he rebids 1NT.

13. Responder supports clubs if he has them. Opener can always return to responder's first suit if he happens to have a three card club suit.

14. Start opening 2NT with 20-21-22 points and open 2C and rebid 2NT with 23-24. This will eliminate even more short club openings.

15. The short club is a necessary evil. Do not go out of your way to open 1C on a three card suit if you can help it.

16. Each of the above rules or statements are subject to logical exceptions. Unfortunately it takes an experienced player to recognize most of them, nevertheless they exist. Nothing in bridge is sacred except common sense.

16. MODERN USES OF THE CUE BID

In modern contract bridge the cue bid has come of age. Even the old stand-by of a direct cue bid in the opponent's suit has a new look.

1. The direct cue bid of the opponent's suit.

East	South
1S	2S?

The meaning of this cue bid for some, at least, has remained the same. It shows a gigantic hand with usually, but not necessarily, first round spade control. Perhaps:

```
S. ---
H. AKJ104
D. AKQ987
C. Q4
```

It is forcing to game. However it has been noted that few players ever pick up such gigantic hands after the opponents have opened the bidding and a takeout double followed by a cue bid can handle these hands. Some new ideas on an old subject:

A. The Michael's Cue Bid.

This is a direct cue bid of the opener's suit designed to show a two suited hand. A cue bid of a major suit promises at least four cards in the other major and a five or six card unspecified minor suit. Responder bids 2NT to discover which minor.

A cue bid of a minor suit shows a light major two suiter, typically 5-5 with 8-11 H.C.P.

B. Top and Bottom Cue Bids of the Major Suits.

This convention appeals more than Michael's because it specifically announces the possession of at least four cards in the other major and five or six clubs.

```
Hands like this:    S. 54
                    H. AQ98
                    D. 5
                    C. KQ5432
```

have always been a problem over a 1S opening.

An overcall of 2C runs the risk of losing a heart fit, a
takeout double runs the risk of a diamond response, and a
Michael's Cue Bid sometimes leaves partner in the dark as
to which minor you hold, especially if responder raises
spades. Top and Bottom Cue Bids solve these problems. A
response of 2NT to a top and bottom cue bid asks partner
for further clarification. If the cue bidder has five
cards in his major suit (he could have been 5-5) he must
bid it.

2. Cue bidding after a minor suit fit has been uncovered.

South	West	North	East
1D	Pass	3D	Pass
3H?			

After a minor suit fit has been discovered the first assumption must
be that the partnership is looking for 3NT and all new suits in a
non-competitive auction are simply showing stoppers.

South might well have:

    S. 65
    H. AK4
    D. AQ876
    C. Q104

South is fishing for 3NT. If North bids 3S, showing a spade stopper,
South bids 3NT.

However this auction shows a real suit:

South	North
1C	2C
2H,2S	

South has four cards in his major and if North happens to have four
(unlikely) he raises the major.

A. Cue bidding after the opponent's have bid ONE SUIT.

South	West	North	East
1D	Pass	2C	2S
3C	Pass	3S?	

This type of cue bid (after minor suit agreement) is generally
used as an asking bid for a stopper in that suit.

North might have: S. 876
                                     H. Q104
                                     D. 4
                                     C. AKQ987

If South cannot bid no trump the hand will play in clubs.

B.   Cue bidding after the opponents have bid TWO SUITS.

South	West	North	East
1C	1D	2C	2S
3S			

This cue bid (again after minor suit agreement) shows a
stopper in spades as opposed to asking for one and is fishing for a stopper in diamonds. If partner does not have a
diamond stopper the hand will play in clubs. If South has
both of the opponents' suits stopped he must bid no trump
himself gambling on a heart stopper from partner.

3. The Advance Cue Bid:

South	North
1NT	3S
?	

South holds: S. AJ3
                                     H. A765
                                     D. K3
                                     C. A1076

Admittedly South has a lovely hand for spades but then again it is
not clear whether North's attention is simply directed towards game
or slam. An Advance Cue Bid is the answer.

South rebids 4C. This cannot logically be a long club suit so by
inference it agrees spades, shows a first round club control and
expresses a desire for a slam. If North signs off at 4S opener
passes.

It takes a fairly expert partnership to manage Advance Cue Bids as
both players must understand that the logic of the auction makes it
impossible for the cue bidder to be mentioning a real suit at such a
high level; therefore, a slam try is being made in the last bid suit.

203

Other common examples of Advance Cue Bids as played by practically every expert in the country:

Opener	Responder	
2NT	3H	Opener agrees hearts, indicates an interest in a slam and shows a diamond control. Advance cue bids more often than not show concentrations of strength. Usually AK or AQ. They also show good trump support.
4D		

Opener	Responder	
1H	1S	Again responder's intentions are not clear. Opener announces a strong hand for spades with a club control. If responder really did have slam designs he knows his partner is willing.
2NT	3S	
4C		

Notice how none of these Advance Cue Bids take the bidding beyond the game level.

5. Cue bids in response to overcalls and takeout doubles are covered in Chapters 5 and 6.

17. THE JUMP SHIFT BY THE RESPONDER

Assume your partner opens the bidding and you find yourself gazing at 19 or 20 points. What is your reaction? The average player is programmed to jump shift because the "book" says so. That is one number he never forgets - 19 points for a jump shift.

Forget the book for a moment. Your partner opens the bidding and you have 19 or more points. Where is this hand going to play? In a slam? Of course in a slam. You are strong enough to force the bidding to a slam with that count even if partner has a minimum opening bid.

So it really doesn't matter whether you jump shift or not if you are going to a slam in any event. If you wait stoically until you have 19 or more points, your jump shift has become a wasted bid!

The real reason for making a jump shift is to SUGGEST A SLAM. Hands in the 16-18 point range are ideal. With hands of this strength you need partner's help in deciding whether or not to bid a slam. Your aunt Helen's grandmother can bid a slam with 19 or 20 points facing an opening bid, but how many players can bid slams accurately with 16 to 18 points facing an opening bid? You're right - not too many.

Therefore I am suggesting that most hands in the 16 to 18 point range make immediate jump shifts and furthermore that opener assume that responder has that count! If responder has jump shifted with 19 or 20 he must carry the hand to slam by himself so opener need not concern himself with that type of jump any longer.

16 to 18 point hands fall into the following general categories:

    I.   The balanced hand.

   II.   The one suited hand (with and without a solid suit).

 III.   The hand that has four or more cards in support of partner's suit.

  IV.   Two suited hands.

   V.   Miscellaneous. Hands not covered in any of the above categories.

The Balanced Hand

The balanced hand is subdivided as follows:

1. 16 to 17 point hands that do not have a five card suit.

2. 18 to 19 point hands that do not have a five card suit.

3. 16 to 18 point hands that do have a five card suit.

4. 15 to 17 point hands that have a six card minor suit.

All counts refer to H.C.P.

1. The standard method for dealing with the 16-17 point balanced hands
    that do not have a five card suit (or perhaps have a weak five card
    suit) is to respond 3NT. This is by no means a cure-all but the al-
    ternatives are even worse. By not bidding an immediate 3NT responder
    usually gets tangled up and opener never does quite get the picture.

    So with the 16-17 point balanced hands with stoppers in the unbid
    suits respond 3NT.

    A few examples of 3NT responses to an opening bid of 1C:

S. AJx	S. QJ9x	S. AQ	S. AQx
H. Jxxx	H. AJ9	H. J10xx	H. KJx
D. AKx	D. KJ9x	D. KQ9x	D. Jxxxx
C. Kxx	C. Ax	C. A10x	C. AJ

    Notice that a four card major or a weak five card minor is no deter-
    rent to an original response of 3NT. If the responder bids his long
    suit first it becomes difficult to show the strength of his hand with-
    out destroying the picture of his distribution.

2. Balanced hands in the 18-19 range require special handling. Earlier
    it was mentioned that with 19 points responder has enough to drive the
    hand to slam all by his lonesome. That is usually true but there is
    an exception. A 19 point balanced hand facing a micro mini opening
    does not always produce slam. So for these hands - a special response.
    Respond 2NT and over anything partner bids rebid 4NT. The 4NT rebid is
    not Blackwood. It is simply a slam invitation with 18 or 19 balanced
    points.

Opener	Responder		Opener	Responder
S. Axx	S. KQx		1C	2NT
H. Kxx	H. Axxx		3NT	4NT (18-19)
D. Qxx	D. AKx		Pass	
C. Axxx	C. Q10x			

If opener has more than a minimum hand he either jumps to 6NT or bids another suit on the way. In no case does opener answer aces.

3. A third category of balanced hands are those in the 16-17 point range with five card suits.

Hands like this in response to a 1C opening:

S. AJ9xx	S. AQx	S. KQx
H. Kx	H. KQxxx	H. AJx
D. AQx	D. AJx	D. AQJxx
C. Kxx	C. xx	C. xx

The proper response with hands of this type is a jump shift in the five card suit and then a no trump rebid at the cheapest level possible.

Opener	Responder		Opener	Responder
S. xx	S. AJ9xx		1C	2S
H. AQx	H. Kx		2NT	3NT (16-17)
D. Kxx	D. AQx		Pass	
C. QJxxx	C. Kxx			

What if the responder has 18-19 points with a five card suit? You might consider using the Miles Convention named after Marshall Miles who devised the following method:

Opener	Responder		Opener	Responder
S. x	S. AKJxx		1H	2NT
H. AJxxx	H. xx		3C	4S (18-19)*
D. Kxx	D. AQx		4NT	
C. KJxx	C. A10x			*Five Card Suit

Responder jumps to 2NT and then bids his five card suit at the FOUR LEVEL to show this type of hand. If opener now rebids 4NT it is a sign off. The four level response is forcing for one round.

As you have noticed a response of 2NT when followed by either 4NT or a rebid of a new suit at the four level has an exceptional meaning. Nevertheless opener considers the 2NT response as a natural bid with 13-15 count until he learns otherwise.

Keep in mind that the unusual treatments described here do not come up very often and nineteen times out of twenty a 2NT response is normal.

4. Six card minor suits with 15-16 points are treated the same as hands with five card suits in the 16-17 point range. Jump shift and rebid no trump at the cheapest level possible.

Opener	Responder	Opener	Responder
S. AQxxx	S. xx	1S	3C
H. KQxx	H. Axx	3H	3NT
D. Jxx	D. KQ	Pass	
C. x	C. AQ10xxx		

Of course there is no greater indignity than making a jump shift, stopping in game, and then going down! This just might be the case here but 3NT is the best contract.

Notice how the responder transfers the captaincy to the opener by jump shifting and then rebidding no trump. It is now up to the opener to carry on to slam if he has more than minimum values. Responder has given his all with his jump shift and rebid. Opener must consider the total point count of the two hands, paying particular attention to whether or not the hand has a fit. With no fit a high card count of approximately 33 is required. With a good fit 30 or more points will usually do.

No longer need you worry if partner opens the bidding and you have a strong balanced hand. Jump to 3NT or make your jump shift and rebid no trump and then let him worry.

The One Suited Major Hand

There are three types of major suit jump shifts.

1. The jump followed by no trump has already been discussed.

2. The jump followed by a rebid in the same suit.

Opener	Responder	Opener	Responder
S. Axxx	S. Qx	1D	2H
H. x	H. AKJxxx	2S	3H
D. KQxxx	D. xx	3NT	Pass
C. KJx	C. Axx		

When responder jumps in a major and then rebids the major he must have a six card suit and typically 14 to 16 H.C.P. If responder has more he can still jump shift and rebid his suit but he must carry on beyond the game level.

Opener	Responder	Opener	Responder
S. KJxx	S. Qx	1D	2H
H. Qx	H. AKJxxx	2S	3H
D. AQxxx	D. xx	4H	Pass
C. xx	C. AJx		

Responder has shown his entire hand and opener is in charge. If responder has jump shifted with more than 16 H.C.P. and a six card major he proceeds further.

Opener	Responder	Opener	Responder
S. KJxx	S. Qx	1D	2H
H. Qx	H. AKJxxx	2S	3H
D. AQxxx	D. xx	4H	4NT
C. xx	C. AKx	5D	6H
		Pass	

This time responder takes charge because his hand counts to 19 points including distribution and the hand has a fit.

3. The jump in a major followed by another jump in the same major.

Opener	Responder	Opener	Responder
S. Kxx	S. xx	1C	2H
H. x	H. AKQJxxx	3C	4H
D. AJx	D. KQx	4NT	5D
C. AKxxxx	C. x	6NT	Pass

Two jumps in the same suit by the responder promise an absolutely solid six or seven card suit with an outside ace or king. The key feature of the hand is the solid suit and responder needs little else for the bid. With a six card solid suit an outside ace is usually held but with a seven card solid suit a couple of kings or a king-queen combination on the outside is sufficient.

On the example hand responder plays the hand in no trump to protect his king of spades. At a heart contract a spade lead through the king could defeat 6H. 6NT is indefensible.

Knowing that two jumps in the same suit promise a solid suit we can make the following assumption when the bidding goes like this:

Opener	Responder	
1H	2S	Responder does NOT have a solid suit
3C	3S	as he failed to jump on his rebid.

The One Suited Minor Hand

Some minor one suiters simply cannot be treated as balanced hands (we cannot jump shift and then rebid no trump).

There are two possibilities:

1. Jump in the minor and then jump again.
2. Jump in the minor and then rebid the minor.

Opener	Responder	Opener	Responder
S. AKxxxx	S. Jx	1S	3C
H. xx	H. x	3S	5C
D. KQx	D. 10x	Pass	
C. xx	C. AKQJxxxx		

When responder jumps in his suit and then jumps again to the five level, by-passing 4NT, he is announcing a solid seven or, more likely, eight card suit with no outside aces. Opener needs a hand strong in controls to bid a slam.

Then there is this sequence:

Opener	Responder
1S	3C
3H	4C

This is a stronger sequence by the responder but the suit is probably not solid. Responder might have either of these hands:

	(1)	S. x		(2)	S. xx
		H. Ax			H. AKx
		D. Ax			D. Ax
		C. AQxxxxxx			C. AK109xx

By taking the hand beyond 3NT responder is trying his very hardest to encourage opener to slam.

210

Hands With Primary Support (Four or More Cards)
For Opener's Suit

Hands in this category naturally count points for short suits. This is the type of hand that is best suited for a jump shift, and then return to partner's suit is always the rebid.

Partner assumes you have 16-18 points in support of his suit. He knows that if you have more you will take charge later.

Assume partner opens 1H and you hold:

```
S. xx
H. AQxx
D. AKQxx
C. xx
```

This is a perfect hand for a jump shift. After your jump to 3D your next bid will be 4H and now partner is in control. He knows you have good diamonds with four card heart support.

Opener	Responder	Opener	Responder
S. x	S. xx	1H	3D
H. KJ10xxx	H. AQxx	3H	4H
D. xx	D. AKQxx	4NT	5H
C. AKxx	C. xx	6H	Pass

It looks so simple, but how often have you been stuck with the above responding hand in this predicament or seen someone else there?:

Opener	Responder
1H	2D
2H	?

Now the responder starts wondering what to do. Sometimes in utter despair he says 4H and other times he leaps to 4NT. When partner shows one ace he panics thinking there may be two losers in a black suit and signs off at 5H.

In any case the responder is making life miserable for himself by taking charge when he should be allowing partner to take charge. Change opener's hand to:

Opener	Responder	Opener	Responder
S. xx	S. xx	1H	3D
H. KJ10xxx	H. AQxx	3H	4H
D. Jx	D. AKQxx	5C	5D
C. AKQ	C. xx	5H	Pass

This time opener does not use Blackwood because of the two small spades but cue bids instead. Responder cue bids in diamonds but the hand stops short of slam because neither player has second round spade control.

Many expert players jump shift and then return to partner's major with only three card support because, in truth, many hands are difficult to bid if the return to partner's suit promises four card support.

Many of these players use five card majors and believe that three card support is sufficient. Indeed for game bidding it doesn't matter too much whether declarer is playing a five-three or a five-four trump fit. But for slam bidding it is very important to know how many trumps responder has.

All experienced players are aware of the extra options open to the declarer in the play if he can draw trumps and leave trumps in both hands.

End plays, loser on loser plays, discarding a loser from dummy and then trumping losers in the dummy are all possibilities open to the declarer if dummy remains with trumps after the adverse trumps have been removed.

For accurate slam bidding declarer simply has to know whether he is embarking on a five-three or a five-four trump fit.

Furthermore when playing four card major suit openings it is absolutely essential to know whether the responder has primary (four or more cards) or secondary (three cards) trump support.

We assume, therefore, that if the bidding proceeds:

Opener	Responder
1S	3C
3H	3S

Responder is showing four card spade support.

There is a somewhat similar sequence:

Opener	Responder
1S	3C
3H	4S

Why does the responder jump to 4S instead of bidding only 3S?

There are two possibilities. If you like you can play that the second jump shows four card support and the simple preference only three card support, but perhaps better is that the second jump shows magnificent spades with a control in the jumped suit.

Opener	Responder	Opener	Responder
S. xxxxx	S. AKQxx	1S	3C
H. AKxx	H. xx	3H	4S
D. AJx	D. xx	4NT	5H
C. x	C. AJ10x	5NT	6D
		6S	Pass

Responder jumps to 3C because he has 16-18 points in support of spades. Responder's second jump is reassuring opener that there are no spade losers. It is usually impossible to make partner understand how powerful your trumps really are unless you jump a second time. Once assured about spades opener asks for aces and kings considering the possibility of a grand slam!

Until now we have been discussing jump shifts with primary support for opener's major suit. What if the opening bid is a minor? Here there is 100% agreement that a jump shift followed by a return to opener's minor guarantees primary support.

Furthermore a second jump by the responder shows the same type of super support as it would in response to a major opening.

Opener	Responder	Opener	Responder
S. Qxx	S. x	1C	2D
H. AKx	H. xx	2NT	4C
D. QJx	D. AK10xx	4H	4NT
C. Qxxx	C. AKJ10x	5D	6C
		Pass	

Responder jump shifts and then jumps again to confirm powerful club support. As clubs is the agreed suit opener feels free to cue bid the ace of hearts. Responder now takes charge and bids the club slam.

The key to this hand, incidentally, is the singleton spade in responder's hand. Reverse responder's major suit holdings and responder simply rebids 5C over 4H as neither player can bid the slam without at least second round spade control.

Two Suiters

Two suited hands are troublesome because it normally takes three bids to describe them - higher ranking suit first and lower ranking suit twice.

If the first bid is a jump shift, by the time the responder gets around to showing his distribution he will be in the stratosphere.

FOR A JUMP SHIFT TO BE WORTHWHILE THE STRENGTH AND DISTRIBUTION MUST BE ACCOUNTED FOR IN TWO BIDS.

An impasse. Even our beloved 16-18 point hands cannot be shown accurately in two bids if the distribution is five-five or six-five. What to do?

One solution is not to jump shift at all. This is the expert solution. They usually can untangle themselves - particularly if partner is aware that responder is not going to jump shift with two suited hands.

However, for the average player it is usually better to jump immediately and alert partner as to the strength of the hand, even if the distribution temporarily remains a mystery.

Here are some typical problems:

Opener	Responder	Opener	Responder
S. x	S. AKxxx	1H	2S
H. AJ10xxx	H. x	3H	4D
D. J10x	D. AKQxx	?	
C. AJx	C. xx		

Now what should opener do? A raise to 5D normally guarantees primary support as responder could have a four card suit. But on the actual hand diamonds is the best contract. Should opener rebid 4H and then have responder rebid 5D? It works here but what if the two hands are:

Opener	Responder
S. xx	S. AKxxx
H. AKJ1098	H. x
D. xx	D. AKQxx
C. QJx	C. xx

Now 5D is a horrible contract and 4H is best.

The solution to this is to assume that if responder bids a second suit at the four level he must have two five card suits. If his second suit is bid at the three level he is not assumed to have two five card suits.

(1)

Opener	Responder
1H	2S
3H	4C

Responder has five (or six) spades and five clubs. Opener can support with three clubs.

(2)

Opener	Responder
1D	2S
3D	3H

Opener assumes responder has only four hearts, unless he rebids them, because he has shown his second suit at the three level.

If responder has a monstrous two suited hand (more than 18 points) he still jump shifts, if he wishes, but he must later take charge as opener is not assuming such a strong hand.

Opener	Responder		Opener	Responder
S. Kxx	S. Ax		1C	2H
H. xx	H. AKQxx		3C	3D
D. xx	D. AQJxx		3NT	4D
C. AKJxxx	C. x		4H	4NT
			5D	5NT
			6H	6NT
			Pass	

Responder is planning on bidding a slam from the very beginning. He is actually interested more in a grand slam than a small slam if there is a fit. Opener makes no encouraging sounds so responder settles for a small slam.

Summary

What is being said here is that when your partner opens the bidding and you have 16-18 points slam is possible if partner has more than a minimum.

If you do what millions of others have done in the past, make a simple non-jump shift response, you will find yourself at loose ends on your rebid. You will either have to bludgeon the hand into a slam or meekly settle for game.

However, if you jump shift and then sign off partner can take up the slack if he has more than a minimum.

If you find you actually have a hand containing upward of 19 points you are at liberty to either jump shift and then take the hand to a slam or to simply make forcing bids without jumping and then take the hand to slam.

For practical purposes 19 point hands facing opening bids produce slam unless both hands are disgustingly balanced or there is a huge misfit.

When opener hears a jump shift he makes his normal rebid and waits to hear which type of hand responder has before deciding whether there is a slam or not.

Opener knows that if responder has 19 or more points he is going to slam, so he assumes the jump shift is in the 16-18 point range and bids accordingly.

Miscellaneous

Finally we come to the miscellaneous 16-18 point hands that do not fit into any of our other neat categories. They are:

1. Hands that have three card support for opener's first suit.
2. Balanced hands without a stopper in each of the unbid suits.
3. Some 5-4-2-2 hands.
4. Hands that have four card support plus a void.

Writing about these hands makes me feel uncomfortable because that is the way I feel at the table when I pick one up.

Dissecting the problem hands one by one:

Hands With Three Card Support for Opener's Suit

Partner opens 1S and you hold: S. Axx
                                       H. x
                                       D. AKxxxx
                                       C. Axx

If you jump to 3D and then bid 3S over 3H partner will expect four card spade support. If you bid 2D you are going to have to show the strength of this hand quite delicately without actually committing the hand to a slam.

Many experts would respond 3D and then rebid 3S taking their chances. Certainly that isn't too bad. I prefer 2D and working it out from there.

For the average player using five card majors I would suggest 3D as the least of evils. Even using four card majors it might work out best but it is just not my style. A man must believe in something, you know.

Balanced Hands Without Stoppers in All Suits

Partner opens 1S and you hold: S. xxx
                                       H. xxx
                                       D. AKQ
                                       C. AKJx

You could bid 3C and then rebid 3NT if partner rebids 3H. If, however, partner raises to 4C and you rebid 4S he will think you have better spades. The expert solution is to respond 2C and then bid diamonds and hope for the best.

Another possibility is to respond 3NT.

Some 5-4-2-2 Hands

Partner opens 1H and you hold: S. xx
                                       H. xx
                                       D. AKJ10x
                                       C. AKJx

If you jump to 3D and partner rebids 3H you are forced to rebid 4C. Earlier we said that a new suit by the responder at the FOUR LEVEL promises a five card suit. What to do?

Don't jump shift if you can see that you are going to have to go to the four level to show your second suit. Respond 2D and then bid 3C. That bidding also shows a good hand. If partner rebids 3NT a raise to 4NT by you is not Blackwood in the civilized world.

Opener	Responder		Opener	Responder
S. AKxxx	S. xx		1S	2D
H. AKxx	H. xx		2H	3C
D. x	D. AKJ10x		3NT	4NT
C. Qxx	C. AKJx		6NT	Pass

Responder's raise to 4NT in this sequence normally shows 17-18 points and typically five-four distribution. Responder raises to 4NT with only 16 because of the strength of his diamond suit. Opener accepts the slam invitation gratefully.

Hands That Have Four Card Support Plus a Void

Partner opens 1S and you hold:
   S. A10xx
   H. KQxx
   D. AJ10xx
   C. ---

How are you going to describe such a hand? Keep in mind that the key to the hand may be in telling your partner about your void. He can now evaluate his hand for slam purposes dependent upon his holding in your void suit. If he has the ace or the ace-king he knows he is looking at wasted cards and will be conservative. On the other hand if he is looking at three or four small cards in your void suit a slam or grand slam may be on with very few H.C.P.

Opener	Responder		Opener	Responder
S. KQxxx	S. A10xx		1S	2D
H. Ax	H. KQxx		2S	3H
D. Qx	D. AJ10xx		3NT	5S
C. Q10xx	C. ---		6S	Pass

To begin with responder has so many things to tell his partner that he is better off not jumping. The standard procedure when it comes to showing a void is to bid two suits and then jump in partner's suit.

In this case once opener knows responder has a club void he has no fear of bidding a slam. Indeed the two hands are not far from a grand slam and there are only 27 H.C.P. between them.

218

Now let's take a different hand for the opener but keep the same one for responder.

Opener	Responder	Opener	Responder
S. KQxxx	S. A10xx	1S	2D
H. xx	H. KQxx	2S	3H
D. xx	D. AJ10xx	3NT	5S
C. AKxx	C. ---	Pass	

This time the opener discovers the duplication of values in clubs and passes the invitation to slam. Too much wasted strength.

Perhaps you are thinking that responder's jump to 5S is asking about club losers rather than showing a void.

That would be true if opener had not rebid no trump. Once one player has previously bid no trump the jump to five of the major after previously bidding two suits shows a void and does not ask about anything.

What if the opener does not rebid no trump? How does the responder show a void in that case?

Opener	Responder	Opener	Responder
S. AQxxxx	S. J9xx	1S	2D
H. KQx	H. A10xx	2S	3H
D. x	D. AKxxx	3S	6S!
C. xxx	C. ---		

Not very scientific but once responder knows that opener does not have very much, if any, club strength judging by his refusal to bid no trump, he knows that whatever high cards opener has are in the right places. Sometimes it pays to take the bull by the horns with a void suit and no wasted values.

18. SLAM BIDDING WITH BALANCED HANDS

A difficult topic - slam bidding - can be made easier if it is subdivided
properly. The two subdivisions to be covered in this chapter are:

  I.   Balanced hands facing balanced hands.

  II. Balanced hands facing long powerful suits.

Balanced Hands Facing Balanced Hands

These are the easiest of all slams to bid. You need know only how to add.
If the total count between the two hands falls in the 33-36 range the final
contract should usually be 6NT. 32 H.C.P. between the two hands usually
suffices if either one has an establishable five card suit.

Hands with slightly less count, 31-33, often produce twelve tricks easier
in a 4-4 trump fit rather than no trump. As Stayman is designed to uncover
4-4 major suit fits, we are going to have to design our own methods for uncovering 4-4 minor suit fits in the slam range.

Consider these two hands:

Opener	Responder
S. Axx	S. Kx
H. KQx	H. Axx
D. KJxx	D. AQxx
C. Kxx	C. Axxx

Opener has a count of 16 and responder 17. Until you finish this chapter
your bidding should be:

Opener	Responder
1NT	6NT
Pass	

The responder knows the total count between the two hands is at least 33
points and that both hands are balanced. Anytime he has this information
he should leap to 6NT.

Now take a look at the contract. There are eleven top tricks and it takes
a 3-3 club division (36%) to make 6NT. Now take a look at a contract of
6D. Twelve tricks are there for the taking as a spade can be ruffed in the
responder's hand along with the eleven obvious tricks. How can these two
hands logically be bid to 6D?

The solution offered here is that when one player is definitely going to bid a slam over his partner's previous no trump bid he use the raise to 5NT rather than 6NT. The raise to 5NT asks partner to bid four card suits in ascending order.

Opener	Responder	Opener	Responder
S. Axx	S. Kx	1NT	5NT
H. KQx	H. Axx	6D	Pass
D. KJxx	D. AQxx		
C. Kxx	C. Axxx		

Responder raises to 5NT asking opener to bid four card suits "up the line". Opener complies by bidding 6D, in this case his only four card suit, and responder passes knowing the partnership has located a 4-4 trump fit.

If responder does not have four diamonds he either bids a four card major or 6NT.

THE JUMP TO 5NT AFTER A PREVIOUS NO TRUMP BID IS FORCING TO THE SIX LEVEL. IF A 4-4 FIT CANNOT BE LOCATED THE HAND MUST PLAY IN 6NT.

Playing tournament bridge many experts purposely pass over 4-4 minor suit fits to play the hand in no trump just in case twelve tricks can be made at either contract. Even if the hand happens to produce thirteen tricks in the minor a better score is achieved for bidding and making 6NT than bidding six of a minor and making seven.

However it is quite profitable to be able to locate the 4-4 minor suit fits particularly on hands that have a total count of 31-33 H.C.P. With disturbing frequency these hands seem to take twelve tricks at a suit contract and only eleven at no trump.

A 4-4 minor suit fit can also be uncovered after using Stayman if the responder is strong enough to force the hand to a small slam.

Opener	Responder	Opener	Responder
S. AQx	S. xx	2NT (20-22)	3C
H. Kx	H. QJxx	3D	5NT
D. AJxx	D. KQxx	6C	6D
C. KQJx	C. Axx	Pass	

Responder immediately envisions a slam holding 12 H.C.P. facing a minimum of 20. There are two possible suits where a 4-4 fit may exist - diamonds and hearts.

Responder uses Stayman to check out the possibility of a 4-4 heart fit. No luck! Opener denies a four card major by rebidding 3D. Responder does not give up. He leaps to 5NT forcing opener to bid four card suits in ascending order. Opener bids 6C and responder 6D. Voila the 4-4 fit has been found! Is 6D a better contract?

True enough if the opponents lead spades or if the king of spades is finessable 6NT can be made easily. However if diamonds are trump declarer can make twelve tricks without the spade finesse. A ruff in either hand after trumps are drawn produces the extra trick.

Once it is agreed that a leap to 5NT when there has been no prior suit agreement asks partner to bid his four card suits in ascending order it is child's play to find a 4-4 fit if it exists.

Opener	Responder	Opener	Responder
S. Axx	S. Kxxx	1NT	2C
H. KQxx	H. Ax	2H	5NT
D. KJxx	D. AQxx	6D	Pass
C. Kx	C. Axx		

Again the responder has two opportunities to discover a 4-4 fit. First he uses Stayman hoping opener has four spades. When that fails he leaps to 5NT looking for a 4-4 diamond fit. Sure enough opener has four diamonds and a home is found. 6D is a vastly superior contract to 6NT which needs either a 3-3 spade division or a squeeze. 6D requires that the declarer does not revoke in the play.

Perhaps some of you are wondering why 5NT in this sequence is not the GRAND SLAM FORCE asking opener for two of the top three honors in the last bid suit - hearts. Mainly because it is illogical. Responder would have to have an incredible freak hand to want to find out about heart honors to the exclusion of all else. What about aces? How could the responder know that all the aces were held? Using 5NT after a Stayman bid to ask opener for any unbid four card suit retains sanity in the auction.

What if the opener has no other four card suit to bid when partner raises to 5NT? He simply bids 6NT.

Opener	Responder	Opener	Responder
S. Axx	S. Kxxx	1NT	2C
H. KQxx	H. Ax	2H	5NT
D. KJx	D. AQxx	6NT	Pass
C. Kxx	C. Axx		

As you see there is no 4-4 fit on this hand and both partners know it.

What if the opener has a five card suit?

Opener	Responder	Opener	Responder
S. AJx	S. Kxxx	1NT	2C
H. KQxxx	H. Axx	2H	5NT
D. Kx	D. AJxx	6H	Pass
C. Kxx	C. Ax		

Some players jump to 3H immediately to show a five card heart suit after partner has bid Stayman. Some do not. In case you do not you can still show a five card suit over 5NT if you have previously bid the suit. When opener repeats his hearts, after already having shown four, the reason must be a five card suit. Responder with three hearts and a side doubleton passes.

6NT is a fine contract but 6H is super, making even if both the spade and diamond finesses are wrong because of the club ruff in dummy.

What about balanced hands that need a maximum from partner to produce slam? Hands that are not strong enough to unilaterally leap to 5NT?

Opener	Responder	Opener	Responder
S. AJx	S. Kxx	1NT	4NT
H. Kxx	H. Ax	Pass	
D. Qxxx	D. AJxx		
C. AQx	C. Kxxx		

Responder is not strong enough to force the hand to slam so contents himself with a raise to 4NT which typically shows 15-16 points plus a balanced hand.

Opener proceeds to six with 17 or 18 count but passes with 16. In this case opener passes and although 6NT is a terrible contract 6D is not too bad. However, IF OPENER IS STRONG ENOUGH TO ACCEPT RESPONDER'S SLAM TRY OF 4NT HE CAN, IF HE WISHES, BID HIS FOUR CARD SUITS IN ASCENDING ORDER.

Let's give the opener one more point, responder the same hand and see how the bidding goes.

Opener	Responder		Opener	Responder
S. AJx	S. Kxx		1NT	4NT
H. Kxx	H. Ax		5D	6D
D. Kxxx	D. AJxx		Pass	
C. AQx	C. Kxxx			

Responder invites a no trump slam with a raise to 4NT which is NOT BLACK-WOOD. Opener accepts with a count of 17 and bids his four card suit. This happens to fit responder's four card suit and responder raises to 6D rather than 6NT. 6D is a much superior contract.

ONCE EITHER PARTNER ACCEPTS AN INVITATION OF 4NT THE HAND MUST PLAY AT THE SIX LEVEL UNLESS EITHER PARTNER SUBSEQUENTLY BIDS 5NT WHICH CAN CONCEIVABLY BE PASSED.

Once it is agreed that a jump to 4NT over a previous no trump is natural and not Blackwood (Gerber can be used for aces in these sequences) and a jump to 5NT over a previous no trump bid is forcing to slam asking partner to bid four card suits in ascending order all sorts of beautiful 4-4 fits can be uncovered.

Opener	Responder		Opener	Responder
S. AQx	S. Jxx		1D	1H
H. xx	H. AKQx		2NT	5NT
D. AQxx	D. Jx		6C	Pass
C. AKxx	C. QJxx			

Opener shows 18-19 with the jump to 2NT. Responder with 14 can, if he wishes, simply raise to 6NT but it doesn't cost anything to try to uncover a possible 4-4 club fit. Responder leaps to 5NT asking opener to bid any unbid four card suit in ascending order. (Had opener bid 6D over 5NT it would show a five card suit as he has already bid diamonds.) Opener bids 6C, responder passes and the best contract is reached.

Whenever responder bids 4NT as an invitation to six, opener has many options. Most important is that he must PASS WITH A MINIMUM FOR HIS PREVIOUS BIDDING. However, if he has a maximum or near maximum he can:

(1) Jump directly to 6NT.

Opener	Responder	Opener	Responder
S. AJx	S. Kxx	1C	1D (or 2NT)
H. KJx	H. AQxx	2NT	4NT
D. A10x	D. KQxx	6NT	Pass
C. AQ109	C. xx		

Opener shows 18-19 by jumping to 2NT. Responder invites six by raising to 4NT. Opener accepts with a maximum, good intermediate cards and no other four card side suit.

(2) Bid another four card suit looking for a possible 4-4 fit.

Opener	Responder	Opener	Responder
S. xx	S. AKxx	1D	1S
H. AQx	H. J10x	2NT	4NT
D. AKxx	D. xx	5C	6C
C. AJ10x	C. KQxx	Pass	

Again responder invites with a raise to 4NT showing 13-14 H.C.P. Opener accepts (any bid other than pass is an acceptance) and shows his four card club suit en route. Responder likes clubs and raises to six which is best.

(3) Rebid his original suit at the five level promising a five card suit.

Opener	Responder	Opener	Responder
S. KQx	S. xx	1C	1D
H. AJx	H. Kxxx	2NT	4NT
D. xx	D. AKQx	5C	6C
C. AKQxx	C. J10x	Pass	

This time opener accepts the slam invitation by rebidding his original suit to show a five card suit. Responder raises to six knowing that there is a 5-3 fit and perhaps an extra trick via a spade ruff.

In fact 6C is the best contract but most tournament players would prefer to play a hand like this in 6NT because of the scoring methods. It is interesting to note that tournament players, a notch below expert class, are the worst slam bidders imaginable because

they try to steer every marginal slam hand towards their beloved
no trump.

(4) Jump in the original suit to the six level to show a solid five or
     six card suit or a strong six card suit.

Opener	Responder
S. xx	S. AQxx
H. K10x	H. Ax
D. AKQJxx	D. xxx
C. Ax	C. Kxxx

Opener	Responder
1D	1S
2NT	4NT
6D	Pass

Responder invites, opener accepts and shows a powerful diamond suit.
Responder with a doubleton allows the hand to play in diamonds fore-
seeing a possible heart ruff in dummy.

Obviously responder is allowed to return to 6NT after this type of
jump. However it is nice for the responder to have the option.

On the example hand 6NT depends upon the spade finesse. However 6D
makes even if the spade finesse is wrong by simply ruffing a heart
in dummy.

(5) Support responder's first suit at the five level which shows three
     card support plus a side doubleton.

Opener	Responder
S. Ax	S. Kxx
H. K10x	H. AQxxx
D. AKJxx	D. xx
C. K10x	C. Axx

Opener	Responder
1D	1H
2NT	4NT
5H	6H
Pass	

Responder invites and opener accepts. This time opener has a choice
of acceptances. He can rebid his five card diamond suit or he can
show heart support. Support has the first priority and opener bids
5H. Responder holding five hearts elects to play in the 5-3 fit
knowing that the responding hand has a doubleton somewhere. 6H is
the best contract.

Have you noticed on these bidding sequences that the responder does
not rebid a five card suit after his partner has announced a balanced
hand? Have you also noticed that the responder with two four card

suits does not show the second suit after partner has bid no trump?

The reason is that by rebidding the original suit or showing a second suit the responder is indicating an unbalanced hand. With a balanced hand responder simply raises no trump. The eight card fits can be uncovered easily before the hand is bid to the six level.

Bidding is so much easier if the responder stops bidding suits with a balanced hand once he discovers his partner also has a balanced hand.

The above rule also applies to the opening bidder if responder has indicated a balanced hand.

Opener	Responder	
1H 3H	2NT	Opener is showing SIX hearts.

Opener	Responder	
1D 3S	2NT	Opener does NOT have two four card suits.

(6) Give jump support to responder's first suit at the six level promising FOUR CARD support.

Opener	Responder	Opener	Responder
S. AQx	S. xxx	1C	1D
H. Kx	H. Axxx	2NT	4NT
D. xxxx	D. AKQJ	6D	Pass
C. AKQx	C. xx		

Responder invites and opener accepts because he has a maximum hand for diamonds. His jump to 6D promises four card support. Responder passes and plays in the 4-4 fit rather than 6NT with a bare count of 32-33 H.C.P. and no long suit to work with.

Most of the slam examples showed hands that had 32-33 H.C.P. and illustrated the desirability of playing these hands in a 4-4 or even a 5-3 fit rather than in no trump.

HOWEVER IF THE TOTAL COUNT BETWEEN THE TWO HANDS IS 34-36 IT IS
BETTER TO PLAY THE HAND IN NO TRUMP RATHER THAN SEEK A 4-4 FIT,
PARTICULARLY WITH A WEAK FOUR CARD SUIT.

A bad trump break might ruin the suit slam but no trump should
produce twelve tricks on sheer power.

Opener	Responder	Opener	Responder
S. AJx	S. KQxx	1NT	2C
H. Kx	H. Ax	2D	6NT
D. Axxx	D. Kxxx	Pass	
C. KJxx	C. AQx		

Responder investigates a possible 4-4 spade fit (his spades are
strong) and when that doesn't jell he does NOT look for a 4-4 diamond fit by jumping to 5NT. Why?

Responder has 18 H.C.P. and knows the total count between the two
hands must be at least 34. It is dangerous to play hands of this
type in a 4-4 fit unless the trump suit is strong.

Look at these hands. There are twelve tricks off the top at no
trump but a 4-1 diamond division defeats 6D.

The easiest way to put this is: IF YOU KNOW YOU HAVE 34-36 H.C.P.
BETWEEN THE TWO HANDS, FORGET STAYMAN, FORGET YOUR JUMP TO FIVE NO
TRUMP, FORGET EVERYTHING! SIMPLY OPEN YOUR MOUTH AND BID 6NT!

Stopping at 5NT.

Opener	Responder	Opener	Responder
S. AJx	S. KQx	1NT	4NT
H. K109x	H. AJx	5C	5D
D. Ax	D. K108x	5H	5NT
C. A109x	C. Qxx	Pass	

Opener gambles on accepting in the hopes of uncovering a 4-4 fit. When
one does not exist and responder simply bids 5NT opener is allowed to pass,
which he gratefully does. Now all he has to do is make it!

Balanced Hands Facing Long Suits

You might ask, "Why play a hand with a long suit in no trump? Why not in the long suit?" Take a look at these two hands:

Opener	Responder	Opener	Responder
S. AQx	S. Kx	1NT	?
H. Kxx	H. xx		
D. xxx	D. AKQJxxx		
C. AKxx	C. xx		

Can you see that 6NT makes easily when played from the opener's side of the table but 6D from the responder's side might be defeated with a heart lead through the king?

Clearly there are many hands where one player has a long strong suit, particularly without a singleton or void, when it is advantageous to play the hand at no trump so that the lead comes up to, rather than through, the no trump bidder's hand.

What should responder bid? Should he jump to 6NT and never mention diamonds at all? Not exactly. You see these might be the two hands:

Opener	Responder
S. AQJ	S. Kx
H. Kxx	H. xx
D. xxx	D. AKQJxxx
C. KQJx	C. xx

6NT would hardly be a success story missing two aces! First the problem: The problem is that when one hand has a long solid or even semi-solid suit the partnership does not need 33 H.C.P. to produce 6NT. Notice that the partnership hands in the first example that do make 6NT have a combined count of only 30 but the length or the extra tricks in diamonds take up the slack.

However when there is a possibility that you are going to slam with as little as 28-31/32 H.C.P. you should be sure you are not missing two aces! (You can't be missing two aces if you have 33 H.C.P. because the opponents have only seven.)

Therefore hands that have long suits opposite no trump opening bids usually use the Gerber 4C convention before leaping blindly to the six level.

Opener	Responder	Opener	Responder
S. AQx	S. Kx	1NT	4C (Gerber)
H. Kxx	H. xx	4S (2 Aces)	6NT
D. xxx	D. AKQJxxx	Pass	
C. AKxx	C. xx		

Responder asks for aces with an immediate jump to 4C. Opener shows two aces and responder gambles the slam knowing that the hand cannot be missing two aces and that the lead is coming up to the stronger hand.

What if the partnership is missing two aces?

Opener	Responder	Opener	Responder
S. AQJ	S. Kx	1NT	4C (Gerber)
H. Kxx	H. xx	4H (1 Ace)	4NT
D. xxx	D. AKQJxxx	Pass	
C. KQJx	C. xx		

Responder checks for aces and discovers the hand is missing two aces. Responder signs off at 4NT. After a Gerber bid of 4C responder must bid 5C to ask for kings. A rebid of 4NT is an absolute sign off announcing to the whole world that the partnership is missing two aces.

Of course the opponents could conceivably defeat 4NT with a club lead to the ace and heart lead through the king but if they find that defense you are in too tough a game and you had better cut out as soon as possible.

Jumping to 4C (Gerber) is common in this sequence also:

Opener	Responder	Opener	Responder
S. Kxx	S. xx	1D	1H
H. xx	H. AKQ10xxx	2NT	4C (Gerber)
D. AKQxx	D. xx	4S (2 Aces)	6NT
C. AQx	C. Kx		

Opener shows 18-19 but responder has been around long enough to know that his type of hand facing 18-19 produces slam more often than not if the hand is not missing two aces.

Responder leaps to 4C and opener shows two aces. Responder bids the slam in no trump to protect a possible king of spades in his partner's hand.

Just so you don't think that everything is going to come up roses for you every time, opener could have QJx of spades and the bidding would proceed identically. Instead of missing two aces you would be missing an ace and a king in the same suit!

As scary as this appears it is not nearly as scary as missing two aces. When you are missing two aces most opponents can manage to take their two tricks even if they lead the wrong suit. However if you are missing an ace and a king in the same suit you very often have twelve tricks in the other three suits and if the proper suit isn't led you usually steal the slam. The looks that cross the table when the opponents realize they could have taken the first two tricks had they led the right suit is worth the price of admission.

Sometimes a player can use Gerber, discover the hand is missing two aces, and still play the hand in his long suit if he wishes.

Opener	Responder	Opener	Responder
S. KQJ	S. xx	1D	1H
H. xx	H. AKQ10xxx	2NT	4C (Gerber)
D. AKQJx	D. xx	4H (1 Ace)	Pass or 4NT
C. QJx	C. Kx		

Responder jumps to 4C (Gerber) and discovers the hand is missing two aces. As opener's last bid happens to be 4H responder can pass if he wishes and play the hand in hearts. However at tournament bridge responder would probably bid 4NT which opener must pass and play the hand at no trump.

Certainly at rubber bridge responder passes 4H. In either case the hand is played at a nice comfortable level where nothing can go wrong.

Summary

Hands that contain powerful six or seven card suits facing a strong balanced hand frequently produce twelve tricks with a combined high card count of as little as 28. However when trying for a slam with so few H.C.P. the player with the long suit must be sure the partnership is not missing two aces.

The usual procedure with strong one suited hands facing strong balanced hands is to leap to 4C (Gerber) after partner's previous no trump bid. After the response the Gerber bidder must decide whether to play the hand in his long suit or in no trump.

The usual criteria followed by experts is to play the hand in a suit if the player with the long suit has a singleton and to play the hand in no trump if he does not. This is particularly true when the hand is missing one ace and the Gerber bidder has two or three small cards in one suit. Partner may have the king and by playing no trump partner's king is protected on opening lead.

If the hand is missing two aces the Gerber bidder signs off at 4NT, four of a major or 5D. A follow up bid of 5C by the Gerber bidder is for kings. The Gerber bidder cannot sign off at 5C!

Ideally it would be best to play the hand in the long suit from the no trump bidder's side of the table. Is this possible? Sometimes.

I hope this doesn't scare you but experts have gone to great lengths to devise methods to play suit slams from the no trump side after opening bids of 1NT or 2NT by using the Jacoby Transfer Bid.

Opener	Responder	Opener	Responder
S. AQx	S. xx	1NT	4D (Transfer to 4H)
H. Jxx	H. AKQ10xxx	4H	4NT (Blackwood)
D. QJ10x	D. x	5H	6H
C. AQJ	C. Kxx	Pass	

Responder transfers to hearts (he can also bid 2D to transfer to 2H but then a follow up bid of 4NT would be natural and not Blackwood) and then asks for aces.

Opener shows two aces and responder with a singleton in his hand allows the opener to play the hand in 6H.

The opener can also use Gerber to arrive at good slams and stay out of bad ones.

Opener	Responder		Opener	Responder
S. J	S. Q10x		1D	2NT
H. x	H. AQx		4C (Gerber)	4H (1 Ace)
D. AKQJxxx	D. xxx		6D	Pass
C. A109x	C. KQxx			

Opener checks on aces before bidding the slam in diamonds. Opener knows that the high card count between the two hands is going to be lacking so the ace-asking precaution is necessary.

Opener	Responder		Opener	Responder
S. J	S. K10x		1D	2NT
H. x	H. KQx		4C (Gerber)	4D (No Aces)
D. AKQJxxx	D. xxx		4NT or 5D	Pass
C. A109x	C. KQxx			

This time opener discovers the partnership is missing two aces. In tournament bridge he automatically signs off at 4NT; at rubber bridge at 5D. Either way a slam is not bid missing two aces.

In closing let me say that bridge experts not only are concerned with world affairs but also with uncovering 4-4 fits and playing the hand from the right side of the table. Life's real problems!

19. SLAM BIDDING WITH UNBALANCED HANDS

Hands with singletons, voids and strong trump fits do not lend themselves to no trump play. The problem with these hands is not whether to play in a suit or in no trump but rather whether or not to try for slam in the agreed suit.

Slam bidding is precarious at best. There are numerous pitfalls that have to be avoided before contracting for a slam. The most common are:

1. Missing two or more cashable aces.

2. Each partner having two quick losers in the same suit.

3. Two trump losers.

4. A trump loser and a missing ace.

5. Having a king led through on opening lead. (Playing the hand from the wrong side of the table.)

6. Having to knock out an ace and having the opponents set up a trick for themselves on opening lead that they cash when in with their ace.

7. The opponents leading a singleton and having opening leader's partner turn up with the ace of that suit or the ace of trumps and subsequently giving partner a ruff.

8. Having a slam depend upon making two out of two finesses (25%). If a slam depends upon one finesse it is considered a reasonable slam as it will make about 50% of the time. If a hand depends upon making one of two finesses it is considered a good slam as it will make about 75% of the time.

9. Duplication of values - an ace or an ace-king opposite a void.

Sounds pretty bleak, doesn't it? Well, you should know some of the problems before bursting into six and losing your certain game bonus.

The two main methods for arriving at a slam are the Blackwood Convention and Cue Bidding. The real problem is knowing when to use them.

Blackwood

Easily the most abused convention (outside of marriage) is Blackwood.
Everyone professes to play the convention but in reality only a handful
of players understand it.

What is Blackwood? The Blackwood Convention was designed to keep a partnership out of unmakeable slams off two aces. It was also designed to
inform the partnership how many aces and kings they held jointly.

Opener	Responder	Opener	Responder
S. AKJxx	S. Q10xx	1S	3S (Limit Raise)
H. KQJxx	H. xx	4NT	5D
D. KQ	D. AJ10x	5S	Pass
C. x	C. Kxx		

Responder gives a limit raise and opener "envisions" a slam. How does
opener envision a slam? You see in suit contracts a player need not be
so obsessed with point count. More important are:

1. A good trump fit.
2. An abundance of first round controls (aces and voids) and
    second round controls (kings and singletons).
3. Wild distribution. The wilder the better <u>after</u> a trump fit
    has been discovered.

All of these plusses reduce the number of total points needed between the
two hands. Many a suit slam can be made with as little as 28 points if
everything else is there. However even if there is a good fit but neither
player has a singleton, a void or a five card side suit to establish, you
need almost as much for a suit slam as for a no trump slam!

In our example hand, opener "sees" at most three possible losers - the ace
of hearts, diamonds and clubs. If responder has two of the three aces a
slam should be easy.

Whenever the only problem is <u>how many</u> aces partner has Blackwood is the
answer. In this case responder has only one ace and opener signs off at

5S. Give the responder the ace of clubs instead of the king and there is a laydown slam in spades.

Responses to Blackwood

When partner bids 4NT, Blackwood (and as you know 4NT is not always Blackwood), the responses are as follows:

5C   Either zero or all four aces. (If partner can't tell the difference from your previous bidding you need a new partner...fast!)

5D   One ace.

5H   Two aces.

5S   Three aces.

If the Blackwood bidder follows up his 4NT query with 5NT he is asking for kings. Furthermore he is promising that all four aces are held jointly by the partnership. Why ask for kings if you are missing an ace? You are already in six no matter what your partner answers and you can't go to seven missing an ace. (At tournament bridge some partnerships do not require all four aces be held jointly because of the added possibility of playing 6NT.)

The responses to 5NT asking for kings are:

6C   No kings.

6D   One king.

6H   Two kings.

6S   Three kings.

6NT   Four kings.

In this book it is assumed that if the Blackwood bidder asks for kings he is promising partner the four aces are held jointly. This hand explains why this rule is so important.

Opener	Responder	Opener	Responder
S. KQx	S. Ax	4H	4NT
H. KQ10xxxxx	H. Ax	5C	5NT
D. x	D. Axxxxx	7H or 7NT	
C. x	C. AJx		

Responder asks for aces and opener shows none. Responder asks for kings - at the same time telling opener he has all four aces. Responder can now count thirteen tricks and need not answer for kings. Indeed, any time the partner of the 5NT bidder can count thirteen tricks he must bid seven of the agreed suit or 7NT. By answering kings he denies the ability to count thirteen tricks.

In cases where thirteen top tricks can be counted, 7NT is the better contract as you need not expose yourself to a ruff on opening lead.

Before going any further with the Blackwood Convention it might be wise to have some rules to determine when 4NT is Blackwood. The rules are:

(1)   Any <u>jump</u> to 4NT after a suit agreement is Blackwood.

Opener	Responder		Opener	Responder		Opener	Responder
1D	3D		1D	1H		1D	2C
4NT			3H	4NT		3C	4NT

(2)   Any <u>jump</u> to 4NT when the previous bid has been a suit is Blackwood.

Opener	Responder		Opener	Responder		Opener	Responder
1H	2D		1S	2H		1D	1H
2S	4NT		4NT			2S	3C
						4NT	

(3)   An opening bid of 4NT is Blackwood. (Balanced hands with 27-28 are opened 2C and the rebid is 3NT.)

(4)   Any 4NT bid made by a strong two bid opener is Blackwood.

Opener	Responder
2C	2H
4NT	

(5)   Any 4NT bid made by the responder who has originally made a jump shift is Blackwood.

Opener	Responder		Opener	Responder
1D	2H		1D	3C
2NT	4NT		3NT	4NT

(6) Any 4NT bid after delayed MAJOR SUIT agreement at the four level is
     Blackwood.

Opener	Responder		Opener	Responder
1S	2D		1H	2D
2H	3C		2S	3C
3NT	4S		3H	4H
4NT			4NT	

(7) Any direct response of 4NT to a preemptive opening is Blackwood.

Opener	Responder		Opener	Responder
3D	4NT		4H	4NT

(8) When the last bid has been a jump to 3NT.

Opener	Responder	But not:	Opener	Responder
1S	2H		1S	2H
3NT	4NT		2S	3D
			3NT	4NT

Looking at the chart it seems as if almost every 4NT bid made by either the
opener or the responder is Blackwood. Now let's look at another chart.

When 4NT is Not Blackwood

(1) When no suit has been mentioned.

Opener	Responder		Opener	Responder		Opener	Responder
1NT	4NT		2NT	4NT		3NT	4NT

(2) When no suit has been agreed upon and the previous bid was 1NT or 2NT.
     (Gerber can be used in every one of these cases to ask for aces.)

Opener	Responder		Opener	Responder		Opener	Responder
1H	2NT		1D	1H		1H	2C
4NT			2NT	4NT		2D	2NT
						4NT	

Opener	Responder
1H	1S
1NT	4NT

(3) When there has been delayed support for a MINOR suit at the four level
     and the previous bid by the 4NT bidder was 3NT.

Opener	Responder		Opener	Responder
S. KQJ	S. x		1D	2C
H. Qx	H. AKxx		2D	2H
D. KQJxxx	D. Axx		3NT	4D
C. Jx	C. K109xx		4NT	Pass

Responder makes a slam try showing a singleton spade and opener rejects because of the wasted cards he holds in spades. If opener has Axx of spades he either jumps to 6D or cue bids 4S to show an interest. Responder can then ask for aces if he wishes.

Opener	Responder		Opener	Responder
S. x	S. KQJx		1D	2C
H. AQxx	H. KJ		2H	3NT
D. AKxxx	D. xx		4C	4NT
C. KJx	C. Q10xxx		Pass	

Opener shows an interest in slam in clubs with a singleton spade. Responder is not interested with his wasted strength in spades together with his lack of aces and kings on the side.

(4) When the previous bid has been a non-jump to 3NT.

Opener	Responder		Opener	Responder
S. AKxxx	S. xx		1S	2H
H. xx	H. AKxxx		2S	3D
D. xxx	D. AQJx		3NT	4NT
C. AQx	C. Kx		Pass	

Responder raises no trump to show a semi-balanced hand, 17-18 H.C.P. Opener refuses the invitation.

(5) When there has been in intervening overcall of 4S.

North	East	South	West
1D	4S	4NT	

South is simply asking North to pick any suit at the five level.

South might have: S. x
                       H. AQxx
                       D. Kxx
                       C. KQ10xx

(6) When it is obvious from the bidding that 4NT must be "unusual".

North	East	South	West
1S	Pass	4S	4NT
Pass	?		

West is showing a gigantic two-suiter, probably the minors. However, if East bids 5C and West bids 5D he indicates a red two-suiter. If East bids 5D and West bids 5H he indicates a heart-club two-suiter.

Responding to Blackwood With a Void

The method recommended by Blackwood is the following:

If the void is useful (not in partner's strongest suit) the responses are:

    6C = No aces plus a useful void.

    6D = One ace plus a useful void.

    6H = Two aces plus a useful void.

    6S = Three aces plus a useful void.

Notice that the responder never counts the void as an extra ace but simply jumps to the six level to show the number of aces he has and by jumping announces the possession of a void. The Blackwood bidder is supposed to be able to figure out where that void is.

Roman Blackwood

A slightly more sophisticated and accurate method of showing a void when partner bids Blackwood is a variation called "Roman Blackwood". It goes like this:

With no aces and a void: Simply respond 5C as you do with no aces. If partner then signs off at five of his suit you must use your judgment whether to pass or whether to gamble six of the agreed suit. In order to gamble six your previous bidding must have shown a very weak hand and partner's an unusually strong one (opening two bid, jump shift, etc.).

With one ace and a void:

    (1) Jump to six of the VOID suit if the void suit is lower than the trump suit.

    (2) Jump to six of the TRUMP SUIT if the void is higher ranking than the trump suit.

With two aces and a void: Respond 5NT.

Opener	Responder	Opener	Responder
S. AJxxxx	S. KQxxx	1S	4S
H. AKJxx	H. ---	4NT	5C
D. x	D. Q10xxxx	5S	?
C. x	C. xx		

This is the one time responder must guess what to do. Responder has already shown a weak hand but opener did not open with a strong two or make
a jump shift. In this case a gambling raise would not work. Notice playing regular Blackwood you are supposed to respond 6C showing no aces and a
useful void and the hand is automatically in six. In truth there is no
real solution for hands that have no aces and a void, unless partner has
shown an extremely strong hand and there is little or no danger in playing
at the six level missing two cashable aces.

Things are more serene when responder has one ace.

Opener	Responder	Opener	Responder
S. AQxxxx	S. KJxxx	1S	4S
H. KQxxx	H. ---	4NT	6H
D. A	D. xxxxx	6S	
C. x	C. Axx		

Responder shows one ace (obviously clubs) and a void in hearts. Opener
bids 6S thinking fleetingly of seven.

		(Strong Twos)		(Weak Twos)	
Opener	Responder	Opener	Responder	Opener	Responder
S. KQx	S. ---	2H	3H	2C	2D
H. AKQJxx	H. 10xxx	4NT	6H	2H	3H
D. AKQ	D. xxxxx	7H	Pass	4NT	6H
C. x	C. AKxx			7H	Pass

Responder shows an ace and a higher ranking void. Opener knows that responder has a spade void with the ace of clubs. What is there to lose?
Notice using the regular Blackwood convention the response is 6D showing
an ace and an UNSPECIFIED VOID. Opener does not know what to do as the void
can be diamonds and then the opponents have a black ace to cash.

Holding two aces and a void the responder normally jumps to 5NT even though
he holds a void in one of partner's suits! The partner should be able to
work out the situation. If the 4NT bidder is in doubt he simply settles
for six rather than gambling seven.

Opener	Responder		Opener	Responder
S. KQJx	S. A109x		1C	1D
H. x	H. xxxx		2S	4S
D. KQ	D. AJxxx		4NT	5NT
C. AKJxxx	C. ---		6S	Pass

Responder shows two aces and a void. As the void cannot be in either spades or diamonds it must be in either hearts or clubs. (Clever?) If the void is in hearts the opponents have been silent with twelve hearts between them! Opener assumes the void is clubs and signs off at 6S.

Opener	Responder		Opener	Responder
S. AKxx	S. x		1C	1H
H. J10xx	H. AKxxxx		2S	3D
D. ---	D. QJxxx		4H	4NT
C. AKQxx	C. x		5NT	7H
			Pass	

Opener shows a powerful hand with obvious diamond shortness. When responder inquires for aces he discovers opener is void in diamonds and holds two aces. It is not unreasonable for opener to bid seven on the assumption that responder has four trumps on this bidding.

Blackwood Over Interference

Sometimes the opponents can become downright nasty. They might interfere with a 4NT bid with distributional hands. For example, the bidding may go like this:

North	East	South	West
1S	2H	3S	4H
4NT	5H	?	

Perhaps East-West are not vulnerable and they are sacrificing at 5H. Perhaps they think you do not know how to show aces over an intervening bid. Perhaps anything. The point is - how do you show aces over this type of interference?

One of the simplest and most accurate methods is the following:

Double...Shows no aces.

Pass..Shows one ace.

Next ranking suit including no trump..........Shows two aces.

Skipping a suit including no trump.............Shows three aces.

This method is called DOPI pronounced "dope-ee". If you can remember the word "DOPI" you are home free. Because the "DO" stands for Double with zero (0) aces and the "PI" stands for Pass with one (I) ace.

Go back to the sample sequence and assume South holds:

```
S. AQxx
H. xx
D. KQxx
C. 10xx
```

South passes 5H showing one ace.

.You cannot show a void over interference.

.You should not double for penalties if you have at least one ace as partner will assume you have no aces when you double.

An alternative method for handling Blackwood Interference at the six or
seven level where showing the number of aces you have may put you out of
range is to play "DEPO". This stands for Double with an Even number of
aces (zero or two) and Pass with an Odd number (one or three).

It comes in handy in this twice in a lifetime situation:

North	East	South	West
2S (strong)	3H	3S	4H
4NT	6H	?	

South holds:

```
S. J876
H. A4
D. K876
C. 10876
```

South passes to show an odd number of aces and North decides whether to go
on or whether to double.

Dangers in Using Blackwood

(1) Getting past your trump suit at the five level missing two aces!

Opener	Responder	Opener	Responder
S. x	S. KQx	1C	3C
H. KQ	H. x	4NT	5D
D. KQxx	D. Axx	5S	5NT
C. AKQxxx	C. J10xxxx	Pass	

This problem arises mainly in the club suit when the Blackwood bidder has only one ace and finds only one ace in his partner's hand although his partner's bidding has led him to believe that he probably had more.

In any case if this happens to you there is a way out the back door. You simply bid five of an unbid major (if both majors are unbid, bid spades) and partner is compelled to bid 5NT which you pass. You might not always make 5NT missing two aces but I can assure you it will be easier than making 6C.

You might also remember that it is dangerous to ask for aces when clubs is the agreed suit and you have only one ace. The same problem could conceivably arise if diamonds are the trump suit and the 4NT bidder has no aces and his partner responds 5H showing two aces! Again the 4NT bidder must bid 5S and play the hand at the world's most disliked contract - 5NT.

Perhaps you can understand why the Blackwood bidder should usually be the stronger of the two hands particularly when the fit is in a minor suit.

(2)   Bidding 4NT, prematurely, when holding a void.

	Opener	Responder
S.	AKJxxxx	Qxx
H.	---	KQxx
D.	KQJxx	Ax
C.	A	10xxx

(Strong Twos)		(Weak Twos)		(Weak Twos)	
Opener	Responder	Opener	Responder	Opener	Responder
2S	3S	2C	2NT (Positive)	2C	2D (Automatic)
4C	4D	3S	4D (Cue Bid)	2S	3S
4NT	5D	4NT	5D	4C	4D
7S		7S		4NT	5D
				7S	

The point of this hand is to show you that the opener should not bid 4NT prematurely. If opener bids 4NT directly over the raise to 3S and responder shows an ace, opener will not know which ace it is! However, if the opener CUE BIDS 4C (any new suit after

244

MAJOR agreement is considered a cue bid asking partner to show specific first and second round controls) and responder cue bids 4D, opener can bid 7S directly. However there are two reasons for double checking with Blackwood after cue bidding has started.

(a) Partner may have two aces and 7NT might be the better contract particularly at tournament bridge.

(b) There may have been a mix up and partner does not have any ace in which case you can still sign off at six.

Also in the sequence where 2NT was bid in response to 2C, keep in mind that 2NT is a positive response showing a balanced hand. Therefore when responder bids 4D over 3S he is not showing a diamond suit, but rather cue bidding the ace of diamonds with a spade fit. This type of bidding is only done in expert partnerships and is known as an Advance Cue Bid.

When a cue bidding sequence begins and you have two aces cue bid the cheaper one first if they are not touching in rank but the higher ranking of touching aces first.*

Opener	Responder	Opener	Responder
S. AKxxxx	S. Q10xx	1S	3S (Limit Raise)
H. x	H. A10xx	4C	4H
D. xx	D. Ax		
C. AKQx	C. xxx		

With two aces to show, responder shows hearts first because both aces are touching in rank. If the player who is going to make a cue bid has two aces one of which can be shown at the three level, the other at the four level, the three level ace is cue bid first.

Opener	Responder	Opener	Responder
S. Ax	S. xx	1H	3H (Limit Raise)
H. AKJxx	H. Q10xx	3S	
D. AQxx	D. KJx		
C. xx	C. A10xx		

Opener cue bids spades first as that ace can be shown at a cheaper level. We will return to both of these hands.

*An idea with considerable merit advanced by the British expert Jeremy Flint in his book "Tiger Bridge".

(3) Bidding 4NT prematurely with two or more losers in an unbid suit.

This is the greatest sin of all and the one that is committed daily by practically everyone.

Opener	Responder (1)	Responder (2)	Responder (3)
S. AKxxxx	S. Q10xx	S. Q10xx	S. Q10xx
H. x	H. AKxx	H. Jxx	H. A10xx
D. Qx	D. Jxx	D. AKxx	D. Ax
C. AKQx	C. xx	C. xx	C. xxx

Opener	Responder
1S	3S (Limit Raise)
?	

If opener remembers the general rule of not bidding Blackwood with two or more losers in an unbid suit (unless partner has previously made a strong bid in no trump) he will automatically know that it is not right to bid 4NT over 3S.

What usually happens is that opener does bid 4NT and responder bids 5D showing one ace. Now opener is afraid that the responder holds the ace of hearts as in (1) and that the opponents might take two diamond tricks. If responder does have (1) opener is right. But what if responder has (2)? Now 6S is a laydown and responder still has only one ace. BUT IT IS THE RIGHT ACE and Blackwood can only find out HOW MANY ACES. Cue bidding is used when you want to find out WHICH ACES AND WHICH KINGS!

Therefore with two or more losers in an unbid suit and the scent of slam in the air it is far better to begin with a cue bid.

If partner cue bids the weak suit it is then optional whether to continue cue bidding or switch to Blackwood. However until partner cue bids the suit in which you have two or more losers Blackwood is out and bidding six is also verboten.

Opener	Responder (1)		Opener	Responder
S. AKxxxx	S. Q10xx		1S	3S (Limit Raise)
H. x	H. AKxx		4C	4H
D. Qx	D. Jxx		4S	Pass
C. AKQx	C. xx			

Opener cue bids 4C to show an interest in a slam. Opener does not use Blackwood because of the two small diamonds - an unbid suit. Responder cue bids the ace of hearts. Opener gives up and bids 4S fearing two diamond losers. Had responder a singleton diamond, for example, he could continue cue bidding or even bid Blackwood if he wished. Opener has already indicated a desire to get to slam with his 4C cue so he obviously has a good hand.

Opener	Responder (2)		Opener	Responder
S. AKxxxx	S. Q10xx		1S	3S
H. x	H. Jxx		4C	4D
D. Qx	D. AKxx		4NT	5D
C. AKQx	C. xx		6S	Pass

Again opener cue bids 4C but this time responder cue bids 4D - the suit the opener feared. Opener now is going to bid six and double checks for aces. (It can't hurt to double check but the real reason is that sometimes partner will have two aces and seven might be bid.)

Opener	Responder (3)		Opener	Responder
S. AKxxxx	S. Q10xx		1S	3S
H. x	H. A10xx		4C	4H
D. Qx	D. Ax		5C	5D
C. AKQx	C. xxx		6S	Pass

Opener cue bids 4C and responder cue bids 4H. This cue bid neither affirms nor denies diamond control. Opener decides to cue bid once more to see if he can elicit some sort of diamond cue bid from responder. When he does he bids the slam. Even if opener had signed off at 4S responder would cue bid the ace of diamonds.

Cue Bidding Tips

1. Before cue bidding can begin a suit must be agreed upon and the player who initiates the cue bid must be interested in a slam.

2. You cannot cue bid the ace or king of trumps.

3. Avoid cue bidding voids. Partner usually thinks it is an ace and then thinks that any honor cards he holds in that suit are valuable when in reality they are not.

4. First round cue bids show first round controls (usually aces).
    Second round cue bids show second round controls (kings or singletons).

Opener	Responder	Opener	Responder
S. AKJxx	S. Qxxx	1S	3S
H. x	H. Qxx	4C	4D
D. Jxx	D. AKxx	5C	5D
C. AKQx	C. xx	6S	Pass

    Opener cue bids the ace of clubs and responder the ace of diamonds. Opener tries once more by cue bidding the king of clubs and responder plays along by cue bidding the king of diamonds. Opener gambles 6S hoping that he can figure out something to do with his third diamond. As it turns out he will probably go down one trick. If every slam in this book made even I wouldn't believe the system.

5. Cue bid your cheaper of non-touching aces and kings first, but higher ranking of touching aces or kings first.

6. When a cue bidding sequence has been initiated neither player can bid a small slam in the agreed suit without at least second round control of the unbid suit.

7. After a cue bidding sequence has begun and partner shifts gears into Blackwood show your aces even though you have cue bid them previously.

Besides our beloved Blackwood and cue bidding we have a few more aids which enable us to both get to good slams and stay out of bad ones.

The Raise or Jump to the Five Level in the Agreed Major

A jump or even a raise to the five level in the agreed major in three specific situations asks partner about his holding in a specific suit.

(1) The jump or raise to the five level when there is one unbid suit asks about partner's holding in that suit.

Opener	Responder	Opener	Responder
S. A	S. KQxxx	1H	1S
H. AQ10xxx	H. KJx	3D	4H
D. AKxx	D. Qxx	5H	Pass
C. xx	C. xx		

Opener's raise to 5H asks about the unbid suit - clubs. Opener must be solid in everything else to make this bid and responder must look only at his clubs when responding.

..If responder has two or more quick losers in clubs he must PASS.

..If responder has a singleton club he bids six of the agreed suit.

..If responder has the king of clubs he bids 5NT.

..If responder has the ace of clubs he bids 6C.

Opener	Responder	Opener	Responder
S. A	S. KQJxx	1H	1S
H. AQJxx	H. K10x	3D	4H
D. AKQx	D. x	5H	5NT
C. xxx	C. Kxxx	6NT	

Opener asks about clubs, the unbid suit, and responder shows the king. Opener decides it is probably safer to play the hand at no trump from the responder's side than it is at hearts from the opener's side because of the danger of an immediate attack on the king of clubs. This time the opener is right.

(2) This type of jump or raise is also made after a cue bidding sequence has begun and there is exactly one unbid suit.

Opener	Responder		Opener	Responder
S. Q10x	S. AKJxxxx		1H	2S
H. AKJ10x	H. x		3S	4C
D. Qx	D. xx		4H	5S
C. J10x	C. AKQ		Pass	

This time responder asks opener about diamonds - the unbid suit.
Responder with two quick losers passes. Had opener the king of
diamonds he would rebid 5NT which the responder would convert to
6NT.

(3)   If the opponents have made an intervening bid the jump or raise to
      five of the agreed major asks partner about his holding in the
      OPPONENTS' SUIT.

North

S. xxx
H. AJ109xxx
D. x
C. Jx

South

S. AKx
H. KQxx
D. xx
C. AKQ10

East	South	West	North
1D	Dbl.	Pass	4H
Pass	5H	Pass	6H
Pass	Pass	Pass	

South asks about diamond losers.   North with only one loser raises
to 6H which is a laydown.   Reverse the diamonds and clubs in the
North hand and six cannot be made.   Notice how useless Blackwood
is here where the problem is not aces but rather the nature of
partner's diamond holding.

Once you know what the problem is you are on the road to becoming a good
slam bidder - provided you have the tools to solve your problem, to say
nothing of a good partner.

More Problems - Problems in the Trump Suit

Until this page you might have noticed that everyone has had very robust trump suits. Ha, ha. In real life that is not the case. Indeed sometimes the only problem lies in the trump suit itself!

Opener	Responder (1)	Responder (2)
S. 9xxxxx	S. Q10xx	S. KQJx
H. AKQx	H. xx	H. xx
D. AKx	D. Qxx	D. Jxx
C. ---	C. AKxx	C. Axxx

In both cases the bidding starts out:

Opener	Responder
1S	3S
?	

Opener has very weak spades but would like to be in six if partner has good spades.

There is a solution. A jump to five of the agreed major when there has been no intervening bid and no cue bidding, and there is more than one unbid suit, asks partner to evaluate his trump holding for five or six. In order to bid six the responding hand must decide how good his trumps are in relation to his previous bidding. If they are rather weak as in (1) he passes but in (2) he bids six. Notice that responder need only look at his trump suit. Opener is not interested in anything else.

Opener	Responder (1)	Opener	Responder
S. A109xxx	S. QXX	2C	2D (denial)
H. AKQJ	H. xxx	2S	2NT*
D. AKQ	D. xxxx	3H	3S
C. ---	C. xxx	5S	6S
		Pass	

*Preparing to raise spades later but trying to sound as weak as possible.

Opener finally unearths some spade support. His jump to 5S asks how good responder's spades are in relation to his previous bidding. Considering everything they are pretty good so responder bids 6S like a man.

In bridge you must learn when partner asks a specific question about a specific suit not to worry about what you have in the other suits. Just answer the question!

Opener	Responder	Opener	Responder
S. A109xxx	S. xx	2C	2D (negative)
H. AKQJ	H. xx	2S	2NT
D. AKQ	D. xxxx	3H	3S
C. ---	C. Jxxxx	5S	Pass

The bidding goes the same and once again the opener is interested in responder's trump holding ONLY. No cue bidding has begun and the opponents have not interfered (I wonder why) so the jump to five of the agreed major is asking about trumps for five or six. In this case the responder can safely pass and if trumps are 4-1 the hand is down in five! Nobody is perfect!

The Grand Slam Force

Sometimes the only problem is in the trump suit but the problem is not whether to play five or six, but rather six or seven!

Opener	Responder	Opener	Responder
S. J10xxx	S. KQxxx	1S	?
H. AKx	H. ---		
D. x	D. AKJ10xxxx		
C. AQxx	C. ---		

Don't laugh. I actually held the responding hand and jumped to 7S! This was not a resounding success obviously.

If I ever get that hand again I will know what to do. I will leap to 5NT the GRAND SLAM FORCE!

A leap to 5NT after a previous suit bid asks partner to define his trump holding specifically for small slam or grand slam purposes. The responses are:

6C - The queen or less in the agreed or the last bid suit.

6 of the agreed suit - The ace or king in the agreed or the last bid suit.

7C - Two of the top three honors in the agreed or the last bid suit.

One can even be more precise with the responses, particularly when the suit is spades, as responses of 6D and 6H can be used to show varying degrees of length holding either the ace or king. However, the above is a great improvement on the older method and reasonably easy to remember.

The bidding on the previous hand:

Opener	Responder
1S	5NT
6C	6S
Pass	

Responder asks opener about his holding in the last bid suit - spades. Opener shows the queen or less and responder signs off at 6S.

Now for some less exotic examples:

Opener	Responder		Opener	Responder
S. Qxxxxx	S. AKxx		1S	2C
H. AKQx	H. xx		2H or 3H	4S
D. AKx	D. xx		5NT	7C
C. --	C. KQxxx		7S	Pass

Opener is interested in one thing and one thing only..how good are responder's spades? Responder has two of the top three honors and bids 7C. Why 7C?

On some hands it is possible for a player to make a grand slam force in one suit with the intention of playing in another if partner has two of the top three honors!

Opener	Responder
S. Qxx	S. AKxxx
H. AK	H. xxx
D. AKQJxxxx	D. xx
C. ---	C. Qxx

(Strong Twos)		(Weak Twos)	
Opener	Responder	Opener	Responder
2D	2S	2C	2S
5NT	7C	5NT	7C
7D	Pass	7D	Pass

ALL ROADS LEAD TO ROME!

Opener visualizes a grand slam in _diamonds_ if partner has the ace-king of spades. If responder automatically jumps to 7S to show two of the top three honors the hand will have to play in spades where a 4-1 trump division wrecks the contract. 7D is ice cold. Therefore there are times when it pays to bid 7C to show two of the top three honors in the last bid suit and let the 5NT bidder place the contract in seven of his own choosing.

Sometimes it is possible to use the Grand Slam Force after a cue bid has clarified another problem.

Opener	Responder		Opener	Responder
S. Kxx	S. AQx		1H	2D
H. AKQ10x	H. Jx		4D	4S
D. A10xxx	D. KQxxx		5NT	7C
C. ---	C. 10xx		7D	Pass

Opener forces with a jump raise in diamonds. Responder cue bids the ace of spades and opener can now safely use the Grand Slam Force to discover whether or not responder has both the king and queen of diamonds. Responder confirms two of the top three honors by jumping to 7C. Responder could, of course, jump to 7D also as there is no conceivable chance that opener wants to play this hand in clubs.

Change the responder's hand to: S. AQx
                                             H. Jx
                                             D. Q9xxx
                                             C. Kxx

and the bidding would be the same up to the response to 5NT. With the queen or less the proper response is 6C which the opener converts to 6D - the proper contract.

More Homework

For very serious students of the game an extension of the Grand Slam Force is recommended.

If the player responding to the Grand Slam Force has already promised a powerful suit by his previous bidding the responses are slightly different.
6C - Shows either the ace or king.
6 of the agreed suit (or the last bid suit) - Shows 2 of the top 3 honors.
7C - Shows the ace-king-queen of the agreed or last bid suit.

Opener	Responder		Opener	Responder
S. xx	S. AKQxx		4H	5NT
H. AKQ10xxx	H. xx		7C	7H
D. x	D. AKxxxx		Pass	
C. xxx	C. ---			

Responder is willing to play seven if opener has solid hearts, but not if opener has only two of the top three heart honors. Playing this useful extension responder jumps to 5NT secure that opener, who has shown a powerful suit from his previous bidding, cannot bid seven unless he has the three top heart honors.

What constitutes a powerful suit?

1. Any opening three bid or four bid. (Unless you and your partner play sick three and four bids.)

2. Any jump rebid.

Opener	Responder
1H	1S
3H	5NT

Opener would not bid seven unless he had the three top honors in hearts.

Summary of Slam Techniques

The jump to five of the agreed major has one of three possible meanings depending upon the previous bidding:

1. What do you have in the opponent's suit?

2. What do you have in the unbid suit?

3. How good are your trumps?

How does the partner determine which is which?

1. If the opponents have bid a suit it is asking about the opponent's suit.

2. If a cue bidding sequence has begun it is asking about the unbid suit.

3. If there has been no cue bidding and the opponents have not bid and there is more than one unbid suit it is asking about the quality of the trump suit for small slam purposes. Bid the slam with good trumps for your previous bidding and pass with bad ones.

A jump to 5NT after prior suit agreement, or when the last bid has been a suit, is the Grand Slam Force in the agreed suit, or the last bid suit if there has been no agreement.

Opener	Responder	
1S	2H	
4H	5NT	Grand Slam Force in hearts.

Opener	Responder	
1H	2S	
3H	5NT	Grand Slam Force in hearts.

When responding to the Grand Slam Force you are simply a parrot.

With the queen or less in the trump suit - Respond 6C.

With the ace or king   - Respond 6 of the agreed suit.

With two of the top three honors   - Respond 7C.

By the way, if you can remember all of this give me a ring. I need a good partner who likes to play this way.

E.K.

20. RESPONDING TO A ONE NO TRUMP OPENING BID

Since more and more players are beginning to see the advantages of opening one no trump even when holding a small doubleton, it is necessary to codify the responses so that no disaster comes from this sensible practice.

In my opinion, both Stayman (either Forcing or Non-Forcing) and Jacoby Transfer Bids should be used when responding to one no trump. Basically, Stayman is used with hands that contain either one four card major, two four card majors, or one five and one four card major with at least eight high card points.

Jacoby is used with hands that have either one or two five card majors or one six card major.

For the following examples assume that the opening one no trump bid is in the 15+ - 17+ range.

The Most Common Stayman Sequences

Opener		Responder		Opener	Responder
S.	Axx	S.	Kxxx	1NT	2C*
H.	Kxx	H.	Axx	2D**	3NT
D.	AQxx	D.	xx	Pass	
C.	QJx	C.	K10xx		

* Do you have a four card major?

** No.

Notice that after the Stayman inquiry of two clubs responder never bids a four card major, but simply returns to the same number of no trump he would have bid had he not used Stayman. With 8 or 9 high card points the responder simply rebids 2NT, giving the opener a chance to pass with a minimum.

257

With less than eight high card points the responder does not use Stayman unless he has one of two types of exceptional hands.

Type I - Responder Short in Clubs.

Opener		Responder		Opener	Responder
S.	Kx	S.	xxxx	1NT	2C
H.	Axxx	H.	Qxxx	2H	Pass
D.	KQx	D.	J10xxx		
C.	Axxx	C.	none		

In this case responder is prepared for any rebid opener might make. Opener is forbidden to rebid 2NT. Responder simply passes any rebid opener makes, including 2D. Notice, for the responder to use Stayman with this ultra-weak type hand he must be short in CLUBS, not any other suit. Reverse the clubs and diamonds and responder passes the 1NT opening because he cannot stand a rebid of 2D.

Type II - Two Major Suits, Plus a Side Singleton

Opener		Responder		Opener	Responder
S.	KJxx	S.	109xx	1NT	2C
H.	xx	H.	AKxx	2S	3S
D.	AKxx	D.	x	4S	Pass
C.	KQx	C.	xxxx		

This time responder breaks the eight H.C.P. point rule because he has two four card majors and a side singleton, which means that there might be a good play for game if opener also has a four card major. Responder should have seven H.C.P. to fool with Stayman in this case. (Unless his singleton is in clubs.)

Another important point to remember is not to use Stayman with 4-3-3-3 hands. The disadvantages outweigh the advantages.

Disadvantages

1. Tipping off your partner's distribution to the defenders.

258

2. Giving the opponents a chance to double two clubs for a lead.

3. Finding that you have a 4-4 major suit fit but that partner's distribution is also 4-3-3-3 and that the hand plays just as well in no trump.

Advantages

1. Finding a 4-4 fit which plays one or two tricks better in the major.

Forcing vs. Non-Forcing Stayman

Each partnership must decide whether to play Forcing or Non-Forcing Stayman. Each has its good points, and although most players prefer Non-Forcing Stayman I think Forcing Stayman has slightly more to offer.

Forcing Stayman

Forcing Stayman simply means that when responder bids 2C the auction cannot die until a contract of either 2NT or three of a major is reached.

Opener	Responder
1NT	2C
2D	2H or 2S
?	

Therefore the above sequence is forcing on opener. He must either raise or jump raise the major (depending upon strength) with a three card fit, or rebid 2NT or 3NT with a doubleton in responder's suit. He cannot pass.

Furthermore, if opener rebids 2NT and responder introduces a new suit, a game forcing sequence has been established.

Opener	Responder
1NT	2C
2D	2S
2NT	3C
?	

Responder has a spade-club forcing to game hand. Almost certainly four clubs rather than five. (With five clubs and five spades responder uses Jacoby.)

In order to use the convention, responder should have at least eight high card points. (See exceptions on previous pages.) With less, responder either passes or transfers and then passes -- unless opener shows signs of life over the transfer response.

Non-Forcing Stayman

The major difference between Forcing and Non-Forcing Stayman revolves around our old sequence:

Opener	Responder
1NT	2C
2D	2H

Again responder is showing five hearts, but this time his range is severely limited. He must have between 6-8 high card points and very likely a side four card spade suit. (Otherwise he simply transfers.)

Opener will normally pass this sequence unless he has a maximum with a fit. Obviously if responder has a stronger hand he must jump to three of his major over two diamonds to create a game forcing sequence.

Non-Forcing Stayman caters to weak responding hands that have five cards in one major plus four cards in the other or one suited major hands in the 6-8 high card point range.

Jacoby Transfer Bids

The Jacoby Transfer Bids are becoming more and more a part of the American and worldwide bridge scene.

In essence the responder transfers the play over to the opener, forcing the defenders to lead into the stronger hand -- a tremendous advantage for the declaring side. This is done by simply bidding the suit beneath the major suit you hold.

Opener	Responder	Opener	Responder
S. Axx	S. QJ10xxx	1NT	2H
H. AQx	H. xx	2S	4S
D. Kxxx	D. x	Pass	
C. Kxx	C. AJ10x		

Under normal circumstances the responder would simply leap to four spades, obviously the proper contract. However, the hand should be played by the opener rather than the responder in order to protect opener's red suit holdings from immediate attack.

By bidding the suit beneath the one he holds, responder forces the opener to bid responder's real suit. The responder can then:

a. Pass.   Showing a weak hand and a five or six card major.

b. Raise the major.   In theory showing a six card suit because the opener may well have a doubleton.

c. Rebid 2NT or 3NT.   Showing a five card major and a balanced hand. The 2NT rebid shows 8-9 H.C.P. The 3NT rebid shows 10-14 H.C.P.

d. Bid a new suit.   Forcing, and in theory showing two five card suits. Many players use the new suit to show a four card suit, but playing Forcing Stayman this is not necessary. With a five card major and a four card minor you respond 2C and then bid both suits if you have room.

e. Bid 4NT.   Quantitative. Showing a five card major and 15-16 H.C.P.

f. Jump in a new suit.   Showing a singleton in the jump suit, a six card major, and

                                    a slam try.

Here are examples of these bids -- always assuming the original response was 2H

(promising at least five spades).

a.   S. Axxxxx   Pass opener's 2S rebid.
       H. x
       D. xxx
       C. xxx

b.   S. Axxxxx   Raise 2S to 3S, inviting partner to game and promising <u>six</u>
       H. Kxx
       D. xx   spades. (With five spades responder either passes, returns
       C. xx
                    to no trump, or bids a new suit; but seldom raises.)

c.1   S. Axxxx   Rebid 2NT showing five spades, 8-9 H.C.P., and a balanced hand.
       H. Kx
       D. J10x   (5-3-3-2 or 5-2-2-4.)
       C. xxx

c.2   S. KQxxx   Rebid 3NT showing five spades, 10-14 H.C.P., and a balanced
       H. xx
       D. Axx   hand.
       C. J10x

d.   S. KJxxx   Rebid 3D to show five spades, five diamonds, and a hand strong
       H. Ax
       D. Q10xxx   enough to play in game. (With weaker 5-5 hands transfer and
       C. x
                    pass or transfer and raise, even though you only have a five

                    card suit -- another exception.)

e.   S. KJxxx   Rebid 4NT to show five spades and 15-16 H.C.P. Opener must
       H. Ax
       D. Kxx   decide whether or not to go to slam. It is not Blackwood.
       C. Axx

f.	S. AJxxxx		Rebid 4D to show six spades, a singleton diamond, and slam
	H. Axx		
	D. x		interest. (12-14 H.C.P.)
	C. K10x		

Jump Responses in a Major

Direct jumps to three of a major are slam tries and promise at least six cards in the suit -- never five! Typically the distribution of the responder's hand will be 6-3-2-2 with 13-15 H.C.P. With less, responder simply transfers and raises to game, transfers and jumps in the singleton, or simply bids four of his own major which, by agreement, is natural. (Some players also use four level transfers.)

NOTE: After responder makes a two level transfer opener is allowed to leap to three of responder's suit providing he has a super hand.

The Minor Suits

Until this point all discussion has centered around the major suits and how to handle the responding hand with various major suit holdings. What about the minors?

Jacoby Transfer Bids make provision for many minor suited hands by using the catch-all response of 2S, which is called Minor Suit Stayman. It is used on all hands where responder has two long minor suits of any strength, plus any hand on which responder wishes to sign off in DIAMONDS. (Please keep in mind that this is just one variation of Jacoby.)

A. The Weak Minor Two Suiter (Responder rebids 3C).

Opener	Responder	Opener	Responder
S. KJxx	S. xx	1NT	2S*
H. Axx	H. x	2NT**	3C***
D. Kxx	D. QJxxx	Pass****	
C. KQx	C. J10xxx		

   * Do you have a four card minor?

** No.
                                                 263

*** I have a weak minor two suiter. Pick the minor you like best.

**** O.K.

If opener has three diamonds and two clubs he corrects to 3D over 3C. If opener has a four card minor he bids it over 2S and responder passes. In any case, the hand plays in three of a minor whenever responder rebids 3C over 2NT.

B. The Game or Slam-Going Minor Two Suiter (Responder rebids his singleton).

Opener		Responder		Opener	Responder
S.	KQJx	S.	x	1NT	2S
H.	KQx	H.	xx	2NT	3S*
D.	Axx	D.	KQxxx	3NT**	Pass
C.	Jxx	C.	AK10xx		

* I have a strong minor two suiter (11-14 H.C.P.) and a singleton spade.
Interested in a slam?

** No. Too much wasted strength in your singleton suit.

C. The Diamond Bust (Responder rebids 3D).

Opener		Responder		Opener	Responder
S.	KJxx	S.	xxx	1NT	2S
H.	Q10x	H.	x	3C	3D
D.	Kx	D.	QJxxxx	Pass	
C.	AQxx	C.	xxx		

Whenever responder rebids 3D after an original 2S response he is showing a diamond bust. Opener is supposed to pass. If responder had a two suiter he would either pass 3C with a weak hand or rebid a singleton major with a strong hand. The 2S response doe not cater to hands that are weak and wish to sign off in <u>clubs</u>. It caters to minor two suiters and diamond bust hands.

D. The Strong Balanced Minor Two-Suiter (Responder rebids 3NT).

Minor Suit Stayman also caters to hands that are 4-4 or 5-4 in the minors with no singleton but are interested in a slam because of their point count (14-16).

Opener	Responder		Opener	Responder
S. Axx	S. Kx		1NT	2S*
H. Axxx	H. Kx		3D**	3NT***
D. KQxx	D. Axxx		6D****	Pass*****
C. Kx	C. AJxxx			

* Do you have a four card minor?

** Yes.

*** I have both minors, am balanced, and hold 14-16 H.C.P.

**** I think I have the right hand for a diamond slam in that case.

***** Let's hope you know what you are doing for once in your life.

We now head into muddy waters. We still haven't discussed several other types of hands that responder might hold in response to 1NT. They are:

a. The club bust.

b. 4-4-4-1 hands in the game or slam zone.

c. The one suited minor hands that wish to invite GAME.

d. The one suited minor hands that wish to invite SLAM.

e. Minor-major two suiters in which the minor is the longer suit.

The question now arises as to just how far the reader is willing to go to memorize and play what is going to be suggested.

The Club Bust; The Good 4-4-4-1 Hand.

There are two possibilities with a club bust. One is to pass 1NT, and if the opponents double run to 2C. That is the simplest method, and not impractical because the probability of having a club bust with everyone passing is low.

Alternatively, the response of 2NT can be used to force opener to rebid 3C. Then responder can pass if he has a club bust, or can bid his singleton if he has 4-4-4-1 distribution with game or slam potential. (With a singleton club responder rebids 3NT. If responder really wishes to raise to 2NT he bids Stayman and then 2NT. My advice is to forget the club bust and the 4-4-4-1 hands and simply use 2NT in the natural sense.

The One Suited Minor Hand That Wishes to Invite Game.

Most players now use the jump from 1NT to 3D to invite game. Typically the bid shows a six card suit, usually with two of the top three honors, and 5-7 H.C.P. (If the suit is AKxxxx, though, you should bid 3NT.) It caters to the hands on which opener has a small doubleton in the minor or a weakish one no trump opening. In either case he passes.

The One Suited Minor Hand That Wishes to Invite Slam; The Minor-Major Hand.

The only (simple) way left to show these types of hands is to first bid 2C and then bid the minor.

Examples

Opener	Responder	Opener	Responder
S. AQxx	S. xx	1NT	3D
H. KQxx	H. Jxx	Pass	
D. xx	D. KQxxxx		
C. AJx	C. xx		

Responder invites game by jumping to 3D and opener refuses because he has no diamond fit. If you are the type of player who will always rebid 3NT in this sequence then play another system. You need discipline for this one.

Opener	Responder	Opener	Responder
S. Kx	S. Axxx	1NT	2C
H. Axxx	H. x	2H	3C
D. Kxxx	D. Ax	3H	3S
C. KQx	C. AJ10xxx	4C	4D
		4S	5H
		7C	Pass

This is, of course, fantasy. Everybody is bidding too beautifully. However, the first few bids are worthy of note. When responder bids 3C he shows a strong hand in clubs with possibly a side four card major.

Opener has a club fit plus a hand rich in controls so he bids 3H rather than sign off in 3NT. Responder now cue bids the ace of spades and opener confirms the club fit. The remaining bids are all cue bids until the opener can almost "see" the responder's hand and leaps to seven. Most players would be overjoyed to get to six clubs with these cards.

I suggest a somewhat similar structure as responding to one no trump. In other words, 3C is Stayman, forcing to game; Jacoby is for the major suits; and a direct response of 3S is Minor Suit Stayman.

Stayman

Stayman is used on all hands that have one four card major, two four card majors, or one four card and one five card major and that are strong enough to want to play in game or slam opposite a 20-22 point two no trump opening bid. If you play a stronger 2NT range then you need less to respond with Stayman.

Opener rebids 3D to deny a four card major, or bids his major at the three level with either a four or five card suit. A helpful adjunct to opener's rebids is to play that a rebid of 3NT shows a good club suit while a rebid of 3D tends to show diamond length as opposed to club length.

Opener	Responder	Opener	Responder
S. Axx	S. Q10xxx	2NT	3C
H. Kx	H. Axxx	3D	3S
D. AKxx	D. xx	4S	Pass
C. AQxx	C. xx		

As ever, if responder introduces a major suit after using Stayman he shows a five card suit.

Opener	Responder	Opener	Responder
S. AQx	S. Kxxx	2NT	3C
H. KJx	H. Axx	3NT*	4C**
D. Ax	D. x	4D	4H
C. AQxxx	C. Jxxxx	4S	6C
		Pass	

* No four card major, but a club suit.

** Natural.

After the "raise" to four clubs all other bids are cue bids until responder's final bid.

Jacoby Transfer Bids

Jacoby (3D for hearts and 3H for spades) is used on all hands that have one five or six card major suit. Responder can transfer and then:

a. Return to 3NT or 4NT. Both are natural and show five card suits and balanced hands. The return to 3NT shows 5-9 H.C.P. and the return to 4NT shows 10-12.

b. Bid a new suit. Typically showing 5-5 and giving opener a choice of contracts.

c. Raise the major. Showing a six card suit and no slam intention.

d. Jump in a new suit. Showing a __singleton__ in the jump suit. This is a slam try with a six card major suit.

e. Pass.

Opener	Responder	Opener	Responder
S. Kxx	S. J10xxx	2NT	3H
H. KQJ	H. Axx	3S	3NT
D. Axxxx	D. xx	4S	Pass
C. AK	C. xxx		

Responder transfers and then converts to 3NT, showing five spades and a balanced hand. Opener corrects to four spades because he has a good hand for spades.

Opener	Responder	Opener	Responder
S. Kx	S. Axxxx	2NT	3H
H. KJxxx	H. xx	3S	4C
D. AKx	D. x	4D	5C
C. AQx	C. Kxxxx	Pass	

Responder transfer to spades and then shows his second suit. Opener cue bids 4D (4NT would be to play) and responder, with modest values, bids 5C. (If responder had good spades he would rebid 4S.) Opener makes a good pass.

Opener	Responder	Opener	Responder
S. Qx	S. J10xxxx	2NT	3H
H. AKxxx	H. x	3S	4S
D. KQx	D. xxx	Pass	
C. AQx	C. Kxx		

Responder transfers and raises, showing a six card suit with no slam aspirations.

Opener	Responder	Opener	Responder
S. KQJx	S. x	2NT	3D
H. Kx	H. AQ10xxx	3H	4S
D. AQJx	D. Kxx	4NT	Pass
C. KQx	C. Jxx		

Responder transfers and jumps in spades to show six hearts, a singleton spade, and a slam try. Opener signs off in 4NT. A cue bid at this point would show slam interest

Opener	Responder	Opener	Responder
S. KQx	S. x	2NT	3D
H. Ax	H. Jxxxx	3H	Pass
D. AKxxx	D. xx		
C. KQx	C. xxxx		

Responder transfers and passes, knowing that if opener had a maximum hand for hearts he would have leaped to 4H directly.

NOTE: After a three level transfer opener is permitted to leap directly to four of responder's major if he has a super hand.

Minor Suit Stayman

A direct response of 3S is Minor Suit Stayman. Opener shows a minor if he has one and rebids 3NT if he does not. If responder has slam interest he rebids his major suit singleton. If he does not he either raises opener to game in the minor, bids 4C, or passes 3NT.

Opener	Responder	Opener	Responder
S. AJxx	S. x	2NT	3S
H. KQxx	H. xx	3NT	Pass
D. Ax	D. Kxxxx		
C. AKx	C. Q10xxx		

Responder shows a minor two suiter and opener denies a four card minor. Responder now has options. He can pass, bid 4C if he simply wishes to play game in either minor, or he can make a mild slam try by cue bidding his major suit singleton. On this hand he elects to pass.

Opener	Responder	Opener	Responder
S. xxx	S. x	2NT	3S
H. AKJx	H. xx	4C	4S
D. Ax	D. KQxxx	6C	Pass
C. AKJx	C. Q10xxx		

Responder shows a minor two suiter, opener shows clubs, and responder shows a singleton spade. Opener jumps to six clubs knowing he can lose no more than one spade trick.

Four Level Responses

There are the simple four level responses and there are the complicated ones. First the good news - the simple ones.

4C.	Gerber.
4D.	Natural, slam try.
4H, 4S.	Natural, sign offs.
4NT.	Natural.

Now the bad news - the complicated ones.

4C.	Club suit. Slam try.
4D.	Transfer to 4H. If followed by 4NT it is Blackwood.
4H.	Transfer to 4S. And if followed by 4NT, Blackwood.
4S.	Diamond suit, slam try.
4NT.	Natural.

Using this method a response of 3C, followed by 4C is Gerber (unless opener rebids 3NT showing clubs), but a response of 3C followed by 4NT is natural.

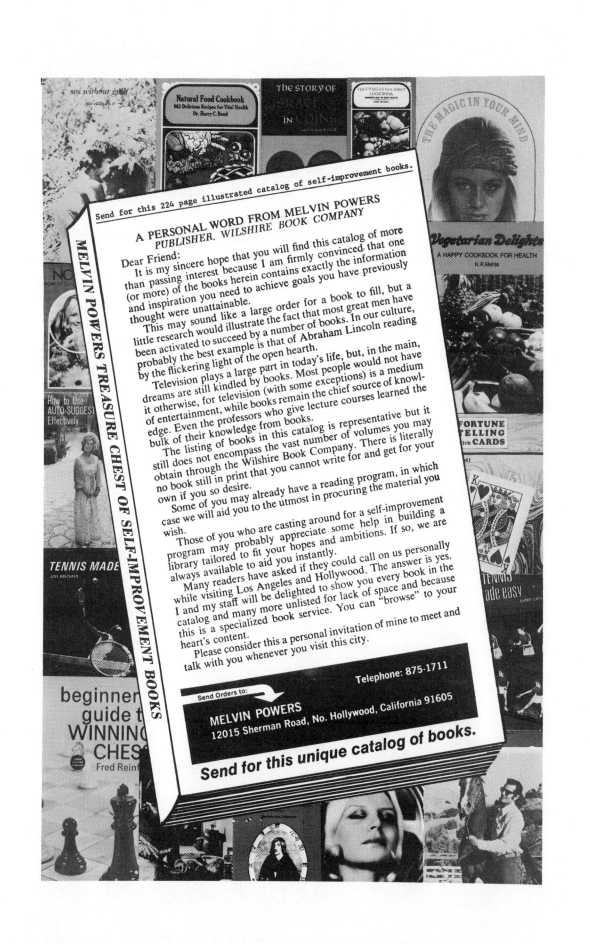

Melvin Powers
SELF-IMPROVEMENT
LIBRARY

ASTROLOGY

ASTROLOGY: A FASCINATING HISTORY *P. Naylor*	2.00
ASTROLOGY: HOW TO CHART YOUR HOROSCOPE *Max Heindel*	2.00
ASTROLOGY: YOUR PERSONAL SUN-SIGN GUIDE *Beatrice Ryder*	2.00
ASTROLOGY FOR EVERYDAY LIVING *Janet Harris*	2.00
ASTROLOGY GUIDE TO GOOD HEALTH *Alexandra Kayhle*	2.00
ASTROLOGY MADE EASY *Astarte*	2.00
ASTROLOGY MADE PRACTICAL *Alexandra Kayhle*	2.00
ASTROLOGY, ROMANCE, YOU AND THE STARS *Anthony Norvell*	2.00
MY WORLD OF ASTROLOGY *Sydney Omarr*	3.00
THOUGHT DIAL *Sydney Omarr*	2.00
ZODIAC REVEALED *Rupert Gleadow*	2.00

BRIDGE & POKER

BRIDGE BIDDING MADE EASY *Edwin Kantar*	5.00
BRIDGE CONVENTIONS *Edwin Kantar*	4.00
HOW TO IMPROVE YOUR BRIDGE *Alfred Sheinwold*	2.00
HOW TO WIN AT POKER *Terence Reese & Anthony T. Watkins*	2.00

BUSINESS, STUDY & REFERENCE

CONVERSATION MADE EASY *Elliot Russell*	2.00
EXAM SECRET *Dennis B. Jackson*	2.00
HOW TO BE A COMEDIAN FOR FUN & PROFIT *King & Laufer*	2.00
HOW TO DEVELOP A BETTER SPEAKING VOICE *M. Hellier*	2.00
HOW TO MAKE A FORTUNE IN REAL ESTATE *Albert Winnikoff*	3.00
HOW TO MAKE MONEY IN REAL ESTATE *Stanley L. McMichael*	2.00
INCREASE YOUR LEARNING POWER *Geoffrey A. Dudley*	2.00
MAGIC OF NUMBERS *Robert Tocquet*	2.00
PRACTICAL GUIDE TO BETTER CONCENTRATION *Melvin Powers*	2.00
PRACTICAL GUIDE TO PUBLIC SPEAKING *Maurice Forley*	2.00
7 DAYS TO FASTER READING *William S. Schaill*	2.00
STUDENT'S GUIDE TO BETTER GRADES *J. A. Rickard*	2.00
STUDENT'S GUIDE TO EFFICIENT STUDY *D. E. James*	1.00
TEST YOURSELF — Find Your Hidden Talent *Jack Shafer*	2.00
YOUR WILL & WHAT TO DO ABOUT IT *Attorney Samuel G. Kling*	2.00

CHESS & CHECKERS

BEGINNER'S GUIDE TO WINNING CHESS *Fred Reinfeld*	2.00
BETTER CHESS — How to Play *Fred Reinfeld*	2.00
CHECKERS MADE EASY *Tom Wiswell*	2.00
CHESS IN TEN EASY LESSONS *Larry Evans*	2.00
CHESS MADE EASY *Milton L. Hanauer*	2.00
CHESS MASTERY — A New Approach *Fred Reinfeld*	2.00
CHESS PROBLEMS FOR BEGINNERS *edited by Fred Reinfeld*	2.00
CHESS SECRETS REVEALED *Fred Reinfeld*	2.00
CHESS STRATEGY — An Expert's Guide *Fred Reinfeld*	2.00
CHESS TACTICS FOR BEGINNERS *edited by Fred Reinfeld*	2.00
CHESS THEORY & PRACTICE *Morry & Mitchell*	2.00

_____HOW TO WIN AT CHECKERS *Fred Reinfeld*   2.00
_____1001 BRILLIANT WAYS TO CHECKMATE *Fred Reinfeld*   2.00
_____1001 WINNING CHESS SACRIFICES & COMBINATIONS *Fred Reinfeld*   2.00

COOKERY & HERBS

_____CULPEPER'S HERBAL REMEDIES *Dr. Nicholas Culpeper*   2.00
_____FAST GOURMET COOKBOOK *Poppy Cannon*   2.50
_____HEALING POWER OF HERBS *May Bethel*   2.00
_____HERB HANDBOOK *Dawn MacLeod*   2.00
_____HERBS FOR COOKING AND HEALING *Dr. Donald Law*   2.00
_____HERBS FOR HEALTH How to Grow & Use Them *Louise Evans Doole* 2.00
_____HOME GARDEN COOKBOOK Delicious Natural Food Recipes *Ken Kraft* 3.00
_____NATURAL FOOD COOKBOOK *Dr. Harry C. Bond*   2.00
_____NATURE'S MEDICINES *Richard Lucas*   2.00
_____VEGETABLE GARDENING FOR BEGINNERS *Hugh Wiberg*   2.00
_____VEGETABLES FOR TODAY'S GARDENS *R. Milton Carleton*   2.00
_____VEGETARIAN COOKERY *Janet Walker*   2.00
_____VEGETARIAN COOKING MADE EASY & DELECTABLE *Veronica Vezza*   2.00
_____VEGETARIAN DELIGHTS — A Happy Cookbook for Health *K. R. Mehta* 2.00
_____VEGETARIAN GOURMET COOKBOOK *Joyce McKinnel*   2.00

HEALTH

_____DR. LINDNER'S SPECIAL WEIGHT CONTROL METHOD   1.00
_____GAYELORD HAUSER'S NEW GUIDE TO INTELLIGENT REDUCING   3.00
_____HELP YOURSELF TO BETTER SIGHT *Margaret Darst Corbett*   2.00
_____HOW TO IMPROVE YOUR VISION *Dr. Robert A. Kraskin*   2.00
_____HOW TO SLEEP WITHOUT PILLS *Dr. David F. Tracy*   1.00
_____HOW YOU CAN STOP SMOKING PERMANENTLY *Ernest Caldwell*   2.00
_____LSD — THE AGE OF MIND *Bernard Roseman*   2.00
_____MIND OVER PLATTER *Peter G. Lindner, M.D.*   2.00
_____NEW CARBOHYDRATE DIET COUNTER *Patti Lopez-Pereira*   1.00
_____PEYOTE STORY *Bernard Roseman*   2.00
_____PSYCHEDELIC ECSTASY *William Marshall & Gilbert W. Taylor*   2.00
_____YOU CAN LEARN TO RELAX *Dr. Samuel Gutwirth*   2.00

HOBBIES

_____COIN COLLECTING FOR BEGINNERS *Burton Hobson & Fred Reinfeld* 2.00
_____400 FASCINATING MAGIC TRICKS YOU CAN DO *Howard Thurston*   2.00
_____GOULD'S GOLD & SILVER GUIDE TO COINS *Maurice Gould*   2.00
_____HARMONICA PLAYING FOR FUN & PROFIT *Hal Leighton*   2.00
_____JUGGLING MADE EASY *Rudolf Dittrich*   1.00
_____MAGIC MADE EASY *Byron Wels*   2.00
_____SEW SIMPLY, SEW RIGHT *Mini Rhea & F. Leighton*   2.00
_____STAMP COLLECTING FOR BEGINNERS *Burton Hobson*   2.00
_____STAMP COLLECTING FOR FUN & PROFIT *Frank Cetin*   1.00

HYPNOTISM

_____ADVANCED TECHNIQUES OF HYPNOSIS *Melvin Powers*   1.00
_____ANIMAL HYPNOSIS *Dr. F. A. Völgyesi*   2.00
_____CHILDBIRTH WITH HYPNOSIS *William S. Kroger, M.D.*   2.00
_____HOW TO SOLVE YOUR SEX PROBLEMS
      WITH SELF-HYPNOSIS *Frank S. Caprio, M.D.*   2.00
_____HOW TO STOP SMOKING THRU SELF-HYPNOSIS *Leslie M. LeCron*   2.00
_____HOW TO USE AUTO-SUGGESTION EFFECTIVELY *John Duckworth*   2.00
_____HOW YOU CAN BOWL BETTER USING SELF-HYPNOSIS *Jack Heise*   2.00
_____HOW YOU CAN PLAY BETTER GOLF USING SELF-HYPNOSIS *Heise*   2.00
_____HYPNOSIS AND SELF-HYPNOSIS *Bernard Hollander, M.D.*   2.00
_____HYPNOSIS IN ATHLETICS *Wilfred M. Mitchell, Ph.D.*   2.00
_____HYPNOTISM *(Originally published in 1893) Carl Sextus*   3.00
_____HYPNOTISM & PSYCHIC PHENOMENA *Simeon Edmunds*   2.00
_____HYPNOTISM MADE EASY *Dr. Ralph Winn*   2.00
_____HYPNOTISM MADE PRACTICAL *Louis Orton*   2.00
_____HYPNOTISM REVEALED *Melvin Powers*   1.00
_____HYPNOTISM TODAY *Leslie LeCron & Jean Bordeaux, Ph.D.*   2.00

_____HYPNOTIST'S CASE BOOK *Alex Erskine*   1.00
_____MEDICAL HYPNOSIS HANDBOOK *Drs. Van Pelt, Ambrose, Newbold*   2.00
_____MODERN HYPNOSIS *Lesley Kuhn & Salvatore Russo, Ph.D.*   3.00
_____NEW CONCEPTS OF HYPNOSIS *Bernard C. Gindes, M.D.*   3.00
_____POST-HYPNOTIC INSTRUCTIONS *Arnold Furst*   2.00
    How to give post-hypnotic suggestions for therapeutic purposes.
_____PRACTICAL GUIDE TO SELF-HYPNOSIS *Melvin Powers*   2.00
_____PRACTICAL HYPNOTISM *Philip Magonet, M.D.*   1.00
_____SECRETS OF HYPNOTISM *S. J. Van Pelt, M.D.*   2.00
_____SELF-HYPNOSIS *Paul Adams*   2.00
_____SELF-HYPNOSIS Its Theory, Technique & Application *Melvin Powers*   2.00
_____SELF-HYPNOSIS A Conditioned-Response Technique *Laurance Sparks*   2.00
_____THERAPY THROUGH HYPNOSIS *edited by Raphael H. Rhodes*   3.00

JUDAICA

_____HOW TO LIVE A RICHER & FULLER LIFE *Rabbi Edgar F. Magnin*   2.00
_____MODERN ISRAEL *Lily Edelman*   2.00
_____OUR JEWISH HERITAGE *Rabbi Alfred Wolf & Joseph Gaer*   2.00
_____ROMANCE OF HASSIDISM *Jacob S. Minkin*   2.50
_____SERVICE OF THE HEART *Evelyn Garfield, Ph.D.*   2.50
_____STORY OF ISRAEL IN COINS *Jean & Maurice Gould*   2.00
_____STORY OF ISRAEL IN STAMPS *Maxim & Gabriel Shamir*   1.00
_____TONGUE OF THE PROPHETS *Robert St. John*   3.00
_____TREASURY OF COMFORT *edited by Rabbi Sidney Greenberg*   2.00
_____TREASURY OF THE ART OF LIVING *edited by Rabbi S. Greenberg*   2.00

MARRIAGE, SEX & PARENTHOOD

_____ABILITY TO LOVE *Dr. Allan Fromme*   2.00
_____ENCYCLOPEDIA OF MODERN SEX &
    LOVE TECHNIQUES *R. Macandrew*   2.00
_____GUIDE TO SUCCESSFUL MARRIAGE *Drs. Albert Ellis & Robert Harper*   3.00
_____HOW TO RAISE AN EMOTIONALLY HEALTHY,
    HAPPY CHILD *Albert Ellis, Ph.D.*   2.00
_____IMPOTENCE & FRIGIDITY *Edwin W. Hirsch, M.D.*   2.00
_____NEW APPROACHES TO SEX IN MARRIAGE *John E. Eichelaub, M.D.*   2.00
_____PSYCHOSOMATIC GYNECOLOGY *William S. Kroger, M.D.*   10.00
_____SEX WITHOUT GUILT *Albert Ellis, Ph.D.*   2.00
_____SEXUALLY ADEQUATE FEMALE *Frank S. Caprio, M.D.*   2.00
_____SEXUALLY ADEQUATE MALE *Frank S. Caprio, M.D.*   2.00
_____YOUR FIRST YEAR OF MARRIAGE *Dr. Tom McGinnis*   2.00

OCCULT

_____BOOK OF TALISMANS, AMULETS & ZODIACAL GEMS *William Pavitt*   3.00
_____CONCENTRATION—A Guide to Mental Mastery *Mouni Sadhu*   2.00
_____DREAMS & OMENS REVEALED *Fred Gettings*   2.00
_____EXTRASENSORY PERCEPTION *Simeon Edmunds*   2.00
_____FORTUNE TELLING WITH CARDS *P. Foli*   2.00
_____HANDWRITING ANALYSIS MADE EASY *John Marley*   2.00
_____HANDWRITING TELLS *Nadya Olyanova*   3.00
_____HOW TO UNDERSTAND YOUR DREAMS *Geoffrey A. Dudley*   2.00
_____ILLUSTRATED YOGA *William Zorn*   2.00
_____MAGICIAN — His training and work *W. E. Butler*   2.00
_____MEDITATION *Mouni Sadhu*   3.00
_____MENTAL TELEPATHY EXPLAINED *Hereward Carrington*   .50
_____MODERN NUMEROLOGY *Morris C. Goodman*   2.00
_____NUMEROLOGY—ITS FACTS AND SECRETS *Ariel Yvon Taylor*   2.00
_____PALMISTRY MADE EASY *Fred Gettings*   2.00
_____PALMISTRY MADE PRACTICAL *Elizabeth Daniels Squire*   2.00
_____PALMISTRY SECRETS REVEALED *Henry Frith*   2.00
_____PRACTICAL YOGA *Ernest Wood*   2.00
_____PROPHECY IN OUR TIME *Martin Ebon*   2.50
_____PSYCHOLOGY OF HANDWRITING *Nadya Olyanova*   2.00
_____SEEING INTO THE FUTURE *Harvey Day*   2.00

_____SEX & HUMAN BEHAVIOR BY THE NUMBERS *Alexandra Kayhle*	2.00
_____SUPERSTITION — Are you superstitious? *Eric Maple*	2.00
_____TAROT *Mouni Sadhu*	3.00
_____TAROT OF THE BOHEMIANS *Papus*	3.00
_____TEST YOUR ESP *Martin Ebon*	2.00
_____WAYS TO SELF-REALIZATION *Mounhi Sadhu*	2.00
_____WITCHCRAFT, MAGIC & OCCULTISM—A Fascinating History *W. B. Crow*	3.00
_____WITCHCRAFT—THE SIX SENSE *Justine Glass*	2.00
_____WORLD OF PSYCHIC RESEARCH *Hereward Carrington*	2.00
_____YOU CAN ANALYZE HANDWRITING *Robert Holder*	2.00

SELF-HELP & INSPIRATIONAL

_____ACT YOUR WAY TO SUCCESSFUL LIVING *Neil & Margaret Rau*	2.00
_____CYBERNETICS WITHIN US *Y. Saparina*	3.00
_____DOCTOR PSYCHO-CYBERNETICS *Maxwell Maltz, M.D.*	2.50
_____DYNAMIC THINKING *Melvin Powers*	1.00
_____GREATEST POWER IN THE UNIVERSE *U. S. Andersen*	4.00
_____GROW RICH WHILE YOU SLEEP *Ben Sweetland*	2.00
_____GUIDE TO DEVELOPING YOUR POTENTIAL *Herbert A. Otto, Ph.D.*	3.00
_____GUIDE TO HAPPINESS *Dr. Maxwell S. Cagan*	2.00
_____GUIDE TO LIVING IN BALANCE *Frank S. Caprio, M.D.*	2.00
_____GUIDE TO RATIONAL LIVING *Albert Ellis, Ph.D. & R. Harper, Ph.D.*	2.00
_____HELPING YOURSELF WITH APPLIED PSYCHOLOGY *R. Henderson*	2.00
_____HELPING YOURSELF WITH PSYCHIATRY *Frank S. Caprio, M.D.*	2.00
_____HOW TO ATTRACT GOOD LUCK *A. H. Z. Carr*	2.00
_____HOW TO CONTROL YOUR DESTINY *Norvell*	2.00
_____HOW TO DEVELOP A WINNING PERSONALITY *Martin Panzer*	2.00
_____HOW TO DEVELOP AN EXCEPTIONAL MEMORY *Young and Gibson*	2.00
_____HOW TO OVERCOME YOUR FEARS *M. P. Leahy, M.D.*	2.00
_____HOW YOU CAN HAVE CONFIDENCE AND POWER *Les Giblin*	2.00
_____I WILL *Ben Sweetland*	2.00
_____LEFT-HANDED PEOPLE *Michael Barsley*	3.00
_____MAGIC IN YOUR MIND *U. S. Andersen*	2.00
_____MAGIC OF THINKING BIG *Dr. David J. Schwartz*	2.00
_____MAGIC POWER OF YOUR MIND *Walter M. Germain*	2.00
_____MASTER KEYS TO SUCCESS, POPULARITY & PRESTIGE *C. W. Bailey*	2.00
_____MENTAL POWER THRU SLEEP SUGGESTION *Melvin Powers*	1.00
_____ORIENTAL SECRETS OF GRACEFUL LIVING *Boye De Mente*	1.00
_____PSYCHO-CYBERNETICS *Maxwell Maltz, M.D.*	2.00
_____SECRET OF SECRETS *U. S. Andersen*	3.00
_____SELF-CONFIDENCE THROUGH SELF-ANALYSIS *E. Oakley*	1.00
_____STUTTERING AND WHAT YOU CAN DO ABOUT IT *W. Johnson, Ph.D.*	2.00
_____SUCCESS-CYBERNETICS *U. S. Andersen*	2.00
_____10 DAYS TO A GREAT NEW LIFE *William E. Edwards*	2.00
_____THINK AND GROW RICH *Napoleon Hill*	2.00
_____THREE MAGIC WORDS *U. S. Andersen*	3.00
_____YOU ARE NOT THE TARGET *Laura Huxley*	3.00
_____YOUR SUBCONSCIOUS POWER *Charles M. Simmons*	2.00
_____YOUR THOUGHTS CAN CHANGE YOUR LIFE *Donald Curtis*	2.00

SPORTS

_____ARCHERY — An Expert's Guide *Don Stamp*	2.00
_____BICYCLING FOR FUN AND GOOD HEALTH *Kenneth E. Luther*	2.00
_____COMPLETE GUIDE TO FISHING *Vlad Evanoff*	2.00
_____HOW TO WIN AT POCKET BILLIARDS *Edward D. Knuchell*	2.00
_____HOW TO WIN AT THE RACES *Sam (The Genius) Lewin*	2.00
_____MOTORCYCLING FOR BEGINNERS *I. G. Edmonds*	2.00
_____PRACTICAL BOATING *W. S. Kals*	3.00
_____PSYCH YOURSELF TO BETTER TENNIS *Dr. Walter A. Luszki*	2.00
_____SECRET OF BOWLING STRIKES *Dawson Taylor*	2.00
_____SECRET OF PERFECT PUTTING *Horton Smith & Dawson Taylor*	2.00
_____TABLE TENNIS MADE EASY *Johnny Leach*	2.00
_____TENNIS MADE EASY *Joel Brecheen*	2.00

WILSHIRE HORSE LOVERS' LIBRARY

_____AMATEUR HORSE BREEDER *A. C. Leighton Hardman*	2.00
_____AMERICAN QUARTER HORSE IN PICTURES *Margaret Cabell Self*	2.00
_____APPALOOSA HORSE *Bill & Dona Richardson*	2.00
_____ARABIAN HORSE *Reginald S. Summerhays*	2.00
_____AT THE HORSE SHOW *Margaret Cabell Self*	2.00
_____BACK-YARD FOAL *Peggy Jett Pittinger*	2.00
_____BACK-YARD HORSE *Peggy Jett Pittinger*	2.00
_____BASIC DRESSAGE *Jean Froissard*	2.00
_____BITS—THEIR HISTORY, USE AND MISUSE *Louis Taylor*	2.00
_____CAVALRY MANUAL OF HORSEMANSHIP *Gordon Wright*	2.00
_____COMPLETE TRAINING OF HORSE AND RIDER *Colonel Alois Podhajsky*	3.00
_____DOG TRAINING MADE EASY & FUN *John W. Kellogg*	2.00
_____DRESSAGE—A study of the Finer Points in Riding *Henry Wynmalen*	3.00
_____DRIVING HORSES *Sallie Walrond*	2.00
_____EQUITATION *Jean Froissard*	3.00
_____FIRST AID FOR HORSES *Dr. Charles H. Denning, Jr.*	2.00
_____FUN OF RAISING A COLT *Rubye & Frank Griffith*	2.00
_____FUN ON HORSEBACK *Margaret Cabell Self*	2.00
_____HORSE OWNER'S CONCISE GUIDE *Elsie V. Hanauer*	2.00
_____HORSE SELECTION & CARE FOR BEGINNERS *George H. Conn*	2.00
_____HORSE SENSE—A complete guide to riding and care *Alan Deacon*	4.00
_____HORSEBACK RIDING FOR BEGINNERS *Louis Taylor*	3.00
_____HORSEBACK RIDING MADE EASY & FUN *Sue Henderson Coen*	2.00
_____HORSES—Their Selection, Care & Handling *Margaret Cabell Self*	2.00
_____HOW TO WIN AT THE RACES *Sam (The Genius) Lewin*	2.00
_____HUNTER IN PICTURES *Margaret Cabell Self*	2.00
_____ILLUSTRATED BOOK OF THE HORSE *S. Sidney* (8½″ x 11½″)	10.00
_____ILLUSTRATED HORSE MANAGEMENT—400 Illustrations *Dr. E. Mayhew*	5.00
_____ILLUSTRATED HORSE TRAINING *Captain M. H. Hayes*	5.00
_____ILLUSTRATED HORSEBACK RIDING FOR BEGINNERS *Jeanne Mellin*	2.00
_____JUMPING—Learning and Teaching *Jean Froissard*	2.00
_____LIPIZZANERS & THE SPANISH RIDING SCHOOL *W. Reuter* (4¼″ x 6″)	2.50
_____MORGAN HORSE IN PICTURES *Margaret Cabell Self*	2.00
_____PIGEONS: HOW TO RAISE AND TRAIN THEM *William H. Allen, Jr.*	2.00
_____POLICE HORSES *Judith Campbell*	2.00
_____PRACTICAL GUIDE TO HORSESHOEING	2.00
_____PRACTICAL HORSE PSYCHOLOGY *Moyra Williams*	2.00
_____PROBLEM HORSES *Reginald S. Summerhays*	
Tested Guide for Curing Most Common & Serious Horse Behavior Habits	2.00
_____RESCHOOLING THE THOROUGHBRED *Peggy Jett Pittenger*	2.00
_____RIDE WESTERN *Louis Taylor*	2.00
_____SCHOOLING YOUR YOUNG HORSE *George Wheatley*	2.00
_____TEACHING YOUR HORSE TO JUMP *W. J. Froud*	2.00
_____THE LAW AND YOUR HORSE *Edward H. Greene*	3.00
_____TRAIL HORSES & TRAIL RIDING *Anne & Perry Westbrook*	2.00
_____TREATING COMMON DISEASES OF YOUR HORSE *Dr. George H. Conn*	2.00
_____TREATING HORSE AILMENTS *G. W. Serth*	2.00
_____WONDERFUL WORLD OF PONIES *Peggy Jett Pittenger* (8½″ x 11½″)	4.00
_____YOUR FIRST HORSE *George C. Saunders, M.D.*	2.00
_____YOUR PONY BOOK *Hermann Wiederhold*	2.00
_____YOUR WESTERN HORSE *Nelson C. Nye*	2.00

The books listed above can be obtained from your book dealer or directly from Wilshire Book Company. When ordering, please remit 15c per book postage.
Send for our free 224 page illustrated catalog of self-improvement books.

Wilshire Book Company
12015 Sherman Road, No. Hollywood, California 91605

Notes

Notes

Notes